Frederic Jesup Stimson

# First Harvests

A Satire Without a Moral

Frederic Jesup Stimson

**First Harvests**
*A Satire Without a Moral*

ISBN/EAN: 9783744675697

Printed in Europe, USA, Canada, Australia, Japan

Cover: Foto ©Thomas Meinert / pixelio.de

More available books at **www.hansebooks.com**

# FIRST HARVESTS

*An Episode in the Life of Mrs. Levison Gower*

A Satire Without a Moral

BY

F. J. STIMSON

(J. S. OF DALE)

## TO THE READER.

---

*I have called this book a satire; yet have sought within that key an overtone of hope and faith. Our early generation of writers could be all optimists: for they wrote of virgin soil. But since their day has passed, our country's first-fruits were garnered. With these we have to deal.*

*F. J. S.*

Boston, November 6, 1888.

# CONTENTS.

# FIRST HARVESTS.

## CHAPTER I.

### THE SILAS STARBUCK OIL COMPANY.

N the northeast corner of Fifth Avenue and Thirty-second Street, just where the long rise of the avenue begins, and vanishes in higher perspective like the stage of a theatre, its long slope always dotted with a multitude of yellow carriages, cabs, and dark-green private broughams, there stands a large brown-stone house of irreproachable respectability. The steps in front of the door are also of brown-stone; and the columns on either side terminate in the hollow globes of iron, painted green, common to a thousand other houses in New York. Upon the first floor above the basement are three windows and a door; in the second story are four windows, one above the door; and in the third, four others again. The windows are all of the same size; but those of the second and third stories are plain, while the lowest have above them an oval design with flowery, curved ornaments. What the original designer of these windows sought to express in them is not clear; but subsequent builders, not seeing the need of expressing anything in window-caps, but supposing some adornment proper in that place, have copied them without deviation, much as a lady ties a bow-knot on her lapdog's tail.

Yet, such as it is, this square brown box contains a flower of American civilization. And flowers are gay, conspicuous, noteworthy in themselves; but the more noteworthy as bearing the seeds that shall be multiplied in next year's crop. No one would perhaps think that this house, standing unadorned and unnoteworthy on the corner of Fifth Avenue and Thirty-second Street, was so rare a possession, or contained in itself so much; that this square box, valued solely because of its proximity to other similar square boxes, represented the American social apotheosis—the pure spheres of perfect democratic joy, the acme, in this republic of terrestrial success. Yet of the fact there can be no question. That little vertebral ridge named Fifth Avenue, with its one or two similar ridges, its few timid excursions and venturings in by-streets to the east and west, represents the flower and the crown of things; only those there live who can command at least wealth or power at will; neither blood nor brains nor breeding can maintain themselves upon that vantage-coin unaided and alone. So have we seen some bed of oysters, planted at just the proper level of the shoal, look down with superiority and scorn upon those below, cumbered with the sea-weed, and those above, left awash at low spring tides. Merely to own this house, and not to live in it; to own it only as some miser owns a picture or a rare gem, for the pleasure of possession—would cost, in interest and taxes, the labor of some score of able-bodied men each year. To live in it, with servants trained to feudal manners and address, with the necessary wines and equipage and flowers and feathers that attend so rare a gem, would cost the earnings of an army. Has the fortunate possessor of the house such an army at his call? Surely; else how could he keep it? We shall see them shortly. And what of the inside of the house?—is it suited to the high position of the inmates? Softly, my good madam; a stranger can hardly know how difficult it is to gain access to this mansion, and how exclusive is the set which Mrs. Gower leads.

For the pedestrians on the pavement look up to No. 2002 with an air of respect. Few of them but know the house as Mrs. Levison Gower's. And even the pedestrians on the pavement, in this select spot, are of a picked and chosen class. Many of them are young girls, robed for this winter (it is the fashion) in trailing gowns of deep-blue velvet; many more are young men, carrying their arms bow-leggedly, as it were, as if not satisfied with the natural stiffness of their starch and buckram, but adding the conscious poise of art, to make you note that they are dressed, not clothed alone. And not one of them that passes but knows and values at its due the house in which you take so little interest. This is the respectable quarter; and the great, ugly house stands insolently, as of social position assured.

But our great city is too great, too human, to show us much of this. Like most fecund mothers, like nature herself, her luxuriance is somewhat slatternly, her exuberance has burst its stays. Here and there our manners, our conventions, trim a hedge or two; but everywhere the forests, and even at our feet, the weeds, grow wild. Fifth Avenue, and its short purlieus, is the home of society; but elsewhere in the island of Manhattan humanity lives, unkempt, full of sap—that great humanity which has made Mrs. Gower, and which she so studiously avoids. For she lives *in* society; and perhaps has never thought that it is on humanity she lives. Let us walk from her great house down the side street in search of it.

For a block or two the houses will stand shoulder to shoulder like a well-drilled rank, well kept, well swept, and uniformed in the same non-committal, smug, respectable brown-stone, a very broadcloth of building. Then the houses begin to grow narrower, with thinner walls, though still they keep their facing on the street. Soon you pass stables, city stables; their stale, sour odor, puffing from the rarely opened windows, is very different from the sweet, healthy smells of a country farm-yard. Now the street is lined with long, low, blank-windowed warehouses, built cheaply of brick and studded with star-shaped iron clamps; you wonder what may be their use, for the windows, even when not curtained with blue paper, are impenetrable and do not avow their vocation; nor, usually, is there any sign, though the ugly walls are covered with advertisements of patent medicines, powders for making bread, powders for washing clothes, powders for feeding children, Giant Destroyers of moths, and the like. But soon this limbo is passed, and you come to the populated districts of humanity. Here the windows are no longer blank; the houses overflow with children; stout mothers sit nursing them in the door-ways and gossip with their neighbors in the second story across the way; things in general are used too much, to keep their varnish from the shop. I am afraid Mrs. Gower would call it squalor.

The retail shops do a driving business in the avenue around the corner; on the curb, under a ragged locust-tree, is a canvas shed for horses, too busy to take their feed respectably in a stable; the brick police station is the only building having pretension to respectability. An ice-cream vender sells his wares openly on the street, in front of a hospitable barber's—the processes of human life are open and avowed; great iron gas-retorts are seen above the roofs of the houses. There is a row of huge smelting-furnaces, with straight lines of stunted willow-trees shading them; and the air is full of the crash of hammered iron. The pedestrians on the sidewalks walk with the same bent arms as on Fifth Avenue; but the arms are bent with labor, and the hands are half clenched, with the curl of being but just released from some accustomed tool. Piles of Spanish-cedar logs on the street denote our approach to the wharves; and now the river, fretted with the traffic of a continent, lies before us.

But our business—Mrs. Gower's business—lies not

among the wharves, but across the river and beyond. If the wind lies in the east, you may set your nose toward it and sniff the air—is there not already a faint smell perceptible, a smell other than that of the salt water, a smell artificial and complex? As we cross the river it increases. We thread our way among the tug-boats, the scows, the flat-ended ferry-boats and other land-lubber craft; passing all the great steamers of the lower town, and the lumber-wharves and water-gardens of the upper, and you may see ahead of you a series of long wharves, jutting far out into the stream. Behind them are many acres of long, low buildings, platforms, piles of barrels, and many huge and lofty towers of plated iron; the wharves themselves surrounded with attendant ships—fine ships, three-masted, with the natural beauty and symmetry that comes from adaptation to the free winds of heaven, and not to steam and man's contrivance. There are no steam-boats at the wharves, and you will wonder why; but, by this time, the rich and unctuous smell from the wharves proceeding will demand your whole attention.

You will perhaps read the long sign, painted in letters, as it were, life-size, displayed in long procession athwart the wharf's end, in square, plain, proper characters of black on white—

THE SILAS STARBUCK OIL COMPANY

—but the reading will be superfluous; for the pleasureless, painless perception of the eye but feebly supplements the pungent, will-arousing sensation of the other sense. It is the old battle of the idea and the will; and the will, as always, wins. And all the world is smell.

Many things grow clear to us as the smell grows stronger. While we mildly wonder that a sense so little cultivated in æsthetics can bring so strong a pain, we also perceive the reason for the absence of steamers; for petroleum is a dangerous blessing, fond of fire, and it takes fire to make water do its work—a lazy element, much like the human soul.

Is there a perfume called *mille fleurs?* A thousand odors woo our preference as we land among the great ships; but there is a certain agreeableness in some of them, as we get used to the worst and begin to discriminate. We can even understand the workmen growing fond of them, as they tell us that they do; that they are also conducive to long life seems more doubtful. All over the oil-yards are smells; as many in variety as the colors of aniline dye, from the first rather pleasant smell, like a cellar full of cider, barrels of cider with the bung-holes open, to the more fetid varieties. Many places have the sickening, capitive odor of ether, from the volatile surface-naphtha; this, being dangerous, has a peculiar fascination of its own. For naphtha is light, volatile, inflammable, impulsive, the aristocrat of oils; and its odor intoxicates.

But come—we must not dally with this naphtha, this *crême de la crême* of the upper crust—come to the receiving-tanks upon the hill. There is a lesson in the making of oil, as in most things. I make no doubt Mr. Tyndall would find the process quite of a piece with the evolution of the soul. Here you see the crude oil as it came from its native earth, in the pipe-lines from the wells; it looks like greenish molasses, and smells of the devil. Natural depravity, we must suppose. But see it in the tail-house; or, rather, let us first look at the stills, those broad, black towers, under which the fire rages, like those in the city of Dis. Here is the burning and the broiling that throws off the grosser atoms from the pure oil of light; first, alas! first of all, our pleasant naphtha, our cream of oils; a short hour or two is enough for that, and it is gone. Here you see it, through the glass cover to the iron trough in the tail-house, the first "run" of all. What a strange liquid, as it breaks and dances in its flow—light, shining, mobile, broken into sharp facets and flashes like cut glass; a spirit, not an oil.

Flossie Starbuck used to fancy this was the water of the streams of hell. A great poet had had the same idea before, which is surely to the credit of Flossie's imagination; for she knew nothing of great poets, as a child.

This tail-house, or receiving-house, was a favorite haunt of hers, on half-holidays when her father would take her to the works, for a treat. It was pleasant, on a warm day, to stand at the window of the iron blower-house and watch the great fan whirl its four hundred revolutions in a minute, and feel the rush of cool air in through the open windows; but it was more interesting to sit in the tail-house and admire the "runs" of oil—the quick naphtha, dry and shining, with its etherous, heady fragrance, and then the duller, yellower oils, under which the flow of mixed water went in globules of a dirty blue. Florence could have told you as well as any workman when the naphtha-run had passed and it was time to turn the oil into the tanks, and whether it were Standard, Regular, or Water-White—the same discrimination that now she exercises upon humanity. Then, when the black, pitchy residuum began to show, she would get the superintendent to talk to her of the aniline, and of the lovely colors which the nasty, black stuff would make; and how the foul-smelling paraffine was made into chewing-gum "for young misses." Flossie never used chewing-gum; but later in life, when standing before Transatlantic Titians, it had come over her with a pang that she had once admired aniline dyes; cards of which, magentas, sea-greens, mauves, the superintendent used to give to her, and she to place upon her bureau.

Have you had enough of oil? There is no beauty, you say, not much of truth, and many bad smells. One moment; before we turn away let us glance into the spraying-house. This was always Flossie's *bonne-bouche*, and it shall be ours.

The spraying-tank is another great, round iron tower, rusted and dingy like the rest; but inside—have you seen the Alhambra? When Flossie first went into the Court of the Lions, passing in through the low gate in the ugly brick tower, to the green pool and the plashing fountain, and the sunlight streaming in from above upon the snowy columns of rosy marble and the rainbow-hued arabesques of those fairy vistas, the grouped columns changing, as she walked, like clusters of fair women holding converse in a garden—her first thought was of this. A fathom deep the oil lies in the central pool; and as we come in from the dark passage the spraying-fountain bursts upon us like a vision of glory. The great room would be dark, for there are no windows, but that an iron slide, high up above, is drawn back a quadrant of the circle of the wall; and through this a mighty shaft of sunlight pours downward into the whirl of golden spray. Here is the fountain of gold of the Arabian Nights.

Cool and still lies the oil in the amber pool, clear as some golden air; while above, the fountain whirls it in a million golden beads, spraying into spray as fine as water, falling a golden rain, but silent, without a splash, into the liquid rest of the basin, where it, fine as water, foams. Thence it is ever drawn back again, and forced through the fountain in the sun, until all commoner atoms are lost and the pure oil is sprayed to test. And the yellow drops run in steady curves and arches light as any lintel of the Moorish palace, and chase each other with a merry music till they fall in the amber pool; and there the full sun shines fair upon its surface in a gorgeous purple, green, and iridescent sheen. And so pure and beautiful the oil lies when the fountain is still, so clear, with the steam-pipes in the bottom keeping it warm lest it should grow cloudy! Here Flossie would sit and dream for hours, before she waked to the world and its real joys, watching the oil as it was sprayed to test.

And how do they know when it is pure enough to stand the test? The process is simple. An electric spark is applied, at the various degrees of heat, until the oil takes fire and flashes in the pan. Temptation is the test of all things in this world.

Yet many a fortune has been made in this place; and chief among them was, and still is, the fortune of Mr. Silas Starbuck, late of New York City, now of parts unknown, refiner of whale and sperm oils, deceased in 1872; half the income of which fortune, the corpus being vested in three testamentary trustees of prominence in the Presbyterian Church, and immense wealth of their own, is annually paid by said trustees (after deducting all necessary expenses of repairs, insurance, taxes, care and management of the property, their own commissions, and an annuity of $1,000 each to the American Bible Society and the Board of Foreign Missions) to the only daughter of the said testator—Florence, now wife of T. Levison Gower, Esq., whose "elegant residence" at No. 2002 Fifth Avenue we have already admired.

The question, how a man made his fortune, has in our days not only a commercial but a psychological interest. Society has never had any objection to the sale by gentlefolk of themselves; but it is only of late years that it has permitted them the sale of anything else. You could formerly predicate with much certainty that a gentleman who had money had either inherited it or married it; now the problem has become more complex. Society to-day graciously permits a man to make money; it is even not over-critical as to the means; and we may almost look forward to the time when a man who has gone down-town to make it will be able to go up-town and spend it himself, and not vicariously, by his grandchildren. This was not quite the case, however, when Silas Starbuck was alive; and this fact had a very important bearing on Mrs. Gower's life. Old Starbuck, as you know, made his money, not only by the refinement of oil, but also by selling his oil when refined—a fact society could hardly overlook.

Si Starbuck was generally thought the weakest, as he was the youngest, of the four sons of old Captain Starbuck, who commanded for many years the brig *Loan*, and then the ship *Fair Helen*, both clearing from Old Town in the island of Martha's Vineyard. Thaddeus, Obed, and Seth were all older brothers, who lived and grew to be captains in their day. Si was a lazy fellow in his youth, and unadventurous; he usually kept snug to the ship, and if he ever went aloft willingly, it was to get the five-dollar reward that the owners paid the man who first discovered a blow. Si was quick enough at seeing things, and was much cuffed by his brothers—perhaps more for this one excellence than for his many shortcomings. Silas commonly had to act as cook and general swabber-out; all the same, he managed to keep a sound skin to his body, and had more time for reading than the rest. At home, when the Starbuck family got together about the fire with the older men, *emeriti*, who stayed at home and swapped stories, Silas was the cynical listener to their yarns of risk of life and capital. Even when they told the history of the great three-thousand-barrel sperm take of '38, from Fairhaven, his eyes glistened more over the balance-sheet than at the stories of their doings in the Pacific when the whales were killed. So, naturally enough, when Silas got his time, he left the ship and drifted over to the continent, going first to New Bedford, where he began refining the materials which his brothers found.

The event justified his sagacity. None of his brothers made fortunes; Thaddeus was killed by a black-fish in the Northern Pacific, and Seth died of the scurvy in Hudson's Bay. When Silas began to be really successful in New York, he kept up little intercourse with his brothers. Mrs. Gower does not remember them at all; so, at all events, she tries to think, though she had one grèat scare. In '64, just as she was beginning to think of her coming out in society, her uncle Obed, then a hale, grizzled old fellow of sixty winters (most of which were Arctic ones), made himself very prominent by resisting a Confederate cruiser with harpoons and a couple of bomb-lance guns. This was a terrible event for pretty Miss Flossie, as it got into all the papers, making quite a hero of poor old uncle Obed; and several of her father's friends had no more *savoir faire* than to speak of the old whaleman as her father's brother at a dinner-party. However, uncle Obed never troubled them in New York; and shortly after her marriage (to which he had been invited by cards accidentally mailed only two days before the wedding) he died, to her inexpressible relief; whether childless or not, she never troubled herself to inquire. Now, however, Mrs. Gower speaks with much pride of her brave old seafaring ancestors.

Thus it came about that all the virtue of the race, as well as all their wealth, is now vested in Mrs. Gower and her brother, Howland Starbuck. The wealth has but gilded the wings on which she soared; her virtues were her own.

## CHAPTER II.

### FLOSSIE STARBUCK ASPIRES.

THERE was a time when Mrs. Gower was not fashionable. It is necessary, for our purpose, to go back to these dark ages. Her maidenhood was passed in unobtrusive splendor behind a frowning brown-stone front on a cross street only two doors from Fifth Avenue. This house was one of a thousand: nine hundred and ninety-nine other New York houses were just like it. Here old Silas Starbuck for his twenty last years, led an even life, torpid in his undigested gold. Here Miss Florence pressed her girlish nose against the window-pane to stare at the opposite houses and wonder who the inmates were, and whether their lives were like to hers; or she strained her large eyes sideways to reach the perspective of morning ash-barrels, reaching in either direction to the avenue beyond. She did not then even know that brown-stone fronts were expensive, when she looked and speculated so wearily upon them.

A little later she began to speculate upon the people in them, and wonder more particularly about them, as she saw them, when coming from church, meet each other on the avenue and bow. No one ever bowed to them; though sometimes an oldish man would stop and speak to her father. It was at this time that it occurred to her to read books; and she became romantic, and would dream, after the manner of democratic maidens, of some courtly suitor, some young prince, who would fall in love with her, and give her rare old family jewels and take her to court balls.

This era lasted but a short time with Florence Starbuck, for she was very clever and sensible, even as a girl. She soon learned to fix her ambitions on possible things. And, indeed, she had no envy for the impossible. She soon learned to covet only those goods which her neighbors possessed, according to our practical version of the commandment, that "thou shalt not hanker after the ideal." There was a certain clumsy accord of motive between old Starbuck and his daughter, but he was far from appreciating her refinement of desire, or fancying what high things went on in his daughter's pretty head when the weekly "Home" paper dropped from her idle hands, and she sat knitting her virginal white brow for longing of the world. He had really only known himself to be rich a short time; and the brown façade which kept him from the fashionable street still seemed to him the acme of earthly ambition, as the printed list of charitable benefactors did of heavenly. Wealth had come very suddenly when it did come; and he felt it hard that his wife, of whom he had been fond in a certain way, had not lived to enjoy it. He had married her in old New Bedford days; and she had died, shortly after Florence's birth, in the New York house. Mrs.

Gower often thought, with something like a shudder, of what she might have been, had her mother lived. Mrs. Gower, like most of us, had thoughts that she admitted to others, thoughts she admitted to herself, and thoughts she admitted to no one, not even herself; and this was one of the last.—Do not think her hard-hearted; she is, with all her faults, one of the best-hearted people in the world, for one so clever. Satisfy her ambition, and she is good-nature itself; and she hates to do an ill-natured thing, even to her enemies. Florence, by the way, was a name she owed to the mercy of her mother; old Starbuck would have called her Nancy, as he had called her brother, Silas. Fortunately, in his case, Mrs. Starbuck got in the Howland from a maternal grandfather; and he is now S. Howland Starbuck, Esq., in the advertisements of companies—Mr. Howland Starbuck on his card.

Of course Flossie went to a fashionable school on Fifth Avenue, where she chose her friends judiciously, and it was at this time that she began to read books. She derived much profit from books, and has always owed much to them; even now she reads a little, as an old habit not quite outgrown. I don't know what it was fired her maidenly ambition; "Lucille" had not been written then, nor Ouida's works, but I doubt there was something similar. And it was certainly books that gave her her first inkling of a *beau monde*. She used to be very generous among the girls, her schoolmates, but never sought to take the lead among them, and was only known as a rather nice little thing from Eighteenth Street. She never even tried to make their brothers' acquaintance, which was duly ascribed on their part to her proper sense of the fitness of things. The brothers were more interested in her. Once she was asked to spend a week's vacation with Miss Brevier; but she never invited any of her school friends to her own house. If she had not been so clever, she might almost have become popular. As you see, Flossie learned much at school; but she took away more, and most of all she had carried thither with her.

In her maiden meditation, Miss Starbuck gave much and serious thought to what could be done with her father and brother. Silas, Jr., was a big, large-boned fellow with a heavy jaw; thick as to legs and head; in whom the family traits came out with peculiar coarseness, much as when you raise a mullein in a garden. The effect of wealth had been to produce him with greater luxuriance and less pruning, in more size and even coarser fibre. However false may be this analogy, there is no doubt that his brave old uncle, who had struggled with famine and the setting ice in Arctic seas, belonged to a much finer type of manhood. Fortunately, as Miss Flossie reflected, there were no ethics in the question. Fashion asks no awkward questions. Style, in the year 1868, in New York, of all the cardinal virtues, was perhaps the easiest to attain. They had the money—if she could screw it out of Mr. Starbuck.

There, however, came the first difficulty. Not that Mr. Starbuck did not fully sympathize with her aims, so far as he understood them; but it was difficult to make him understand them all. She soared in higher circles. For, remember, Flossie, like most New England girls, had a natural refinement of her own. And she was very pretty—*petite* in figure, then, with a most delicious little face, a face with a thousand lights and no definite expression. Her eyes though—her eyes were expressive; there was an archness, a directness, and a certain dewy softness.—Flossie soon learned that she must be careful of her eyes, and only use them on great occasions. It was one of her many studies, out of school, how to make them look demure; particularly before older women—older women, stout in figure, who would set their heads back on their comfortable shoulders and gaze at her, through double eye-glasses, with the liberty of age.—At such times Flossie used to drop a sort of curtain over those eyes of hers and look straight before her. She was secretly afraid of these older ladies; and this helped her, for she really became embarrassed.

But to return to Mr. Starbuck. He was willing to live in an expensive street, and even to keep a costly carriage, in an expensive stable, with a cobble-stone court-yard, at eight dollars the cobble-stone, and put his name in three figures on subscription-papers; but there his liberality stopped. This was all very well; and Flossie used the carriage to go to Stewart's and shop, and, on rainy "Sabbaths," for the church. But old Starbuck, who spent the income of a hundred thousand in façade, would have thought himself a Sardanapalus if seventy-five cents a day had gone for a pint of claret. Frequently they even dined without soup; and all wines, in old Starbuck's mind, were grouped under the generic name of Rum. Mr. Starbuck had no æsthetic objection to rum—rather the contrary—but he thought it not respectable, and kept his tastes in that direction as a private sin. On days when the minister dined with them a decanter of pale sherry was brought out—a species of rum sanctified, as it were, by church use, and not expensive. Mr. Starbuck's evenings were devoted to slippers and snores. Certainly, no poor girl had ever more unpromising material to work on. Flossie felt that, at best, her father could be little more than a base of supplies; she could never use him for attack.

Improbable as it might seem, Miss Starbuck decided that her social salvation rested with her unlikely brother Silas. The discovery of the possible use of so clumsy an instrument, at her age, must be reckoned a master-stroke. An awkward schoolboy, he had met certain other youths whom Flossie felt she would like to know; with some of them had gone skating or played games in the streets. Flossie encouraged her father to give him plenty of pocket-money; he was only a year older than she, and she might be expected partially to fill her mother's place. It was to her that he owed his horse and buggy; this was before the days of dog-carts. Sometimes he would bring his friends home in the evening; she would discourage their coming to dinner, but would throw her influence with his to favor anything that could be reasonably accorded at other times; and Flossie would excuse it to her father when they stayed a little late, or would shut the doors between Si's upper-floor room and the library when they made too much noise. Sometimes, when Si lost too much at vingt-et-un, he borrowed of his sister; and she was not so much shocked as old Starbuck would have been. She knew that young men would be young men, and that Si must make friends, if at all, by his pleasant social vices rather than his father's business virtues. This sounds cynical; but she did not reason it out in such bald, unpleasant analysis—it all came from delicate feminine intuition, of which she had more than her share. She was a quick-witted girl, living in a great city, with nothing at home to attract her. What else could she think about? Her vision went no farther than her brown-stone horizon. She was not romantic; her intellect quite over-balanced her emotional nature. And she had no Browning societies, and had never read Emerson nor Ruskin.

At nineteen she had been out of school a year, but had no definite launching in society. She looked much younger, being as immature in person as she was the contrary in mind. She saw hardly anyone except her school-girl friends, with two or three of whom she still remained intimate; they were kind to her, in a patronizing way, and invited her to their own parties; sometimes they would even send for her, at the last moment, to fill a vacant place at a dinner. A few of her friends' brothers, and all of her brother's friends, had been attracted by her; none of them knew her well, but they were in the habit of joking about her when alone. Most of her friends' brothers took little interest in her, and thought her slow. But then (said their sisters) she has seen so little of the world, poor thing! Flossie felt this, too; but, as her friends said, she was an unselfish little creature, and her mind was chiefly occupied with a sisterly solicitude for brother's future. She would have liked him to go to college; but he did not share his sister's wishes, and the father utterly disapproved of it. He considered the college-bred man, when successfully perfected, as a pretty poor article; and college itself as a place where young men learned to drink and smoke, and spent their money in buggy-hire and billiards, unbeknown to their fathers. He insisted on Si's going into the office; and Si, having finished school, did in fact spend a portion of his mornings in that nursery of millions, his afternoons in the park or elsewhere, and his evenings over cards or at Academy balls, or elsewhere again, all unbeknown to his father. It was at this time that Si picked up that fine knowledge of life which fitted him, as a man of the world, to take, afterward, so prominent a position in society.

There is no unlucky accident which an adroit person may not turn to happy advantage. Si might never have been a success in literary circles; but he began to develop quite a popularity among young men of a very good set. At this time it was by no means necessary for a New York fashionable to be liberally educated. And young Starbuck had several valuable accomplishments—he was a good whip, and soon became a tolerable 'vet and knew every jockey on the road; he played a capital hand at poker, and told stories and talked slang with a certain pungent humor of his own; and he could even thrum an accompaniment on a banjo. He was blessed with perfect health, large appetites, plenty of money; sparred well; was both stupid and good-natured, and had all the other elements of greatness. Fortunately, Flossie had no very clear idea of what Si did with his friends; and, secretly, her respect for him rose when he came home late at night and the next morning talked familiarly of the Duvals, and Lucie Gower, and "Van." ("Van" was Mr. Killian van Kull, of the Columbian and Piccadilly clubs.) It was at this period that Si, thanks partly to the intercession of his sister attained to the ownership of a latch-key, and began to come home very late indeed, and talk mysteriously of French balls. Flossie had a very vague notion what these might be; and old Starbuck was not over-strict on that score. He would have thought wine-bibbing infinitely worse, and cards a shade more heinous than either. And, in fact, he was not insensible to Si's social successes. True, old Starbuck was on the same board of directors with T. L. Gower, Sr., and one of his co-trustees in a charity; but he secretly felt—all democrat in a democracy that he was—he secretly felt it a much greater triumph in his career that young Gower and his son should get drunk together. This is a coarse way of putting it; let us hasten through the beginnings of things and get out where we may see the stars once more.

## CHAPTER III.

### FLOSSIE STARBUCK ATTAINS.

LEVISON GOWER, Jr., the Perseus to our Andromeda, that angel who was to take Flossie's hand and lift her with him to a higher sphere, was a pallid young man with a long nose, a short forehead, a thin neck, and a prominent Adam's apple. Large noses are aristocratic; and Gower valued his as typical of his pure Dutch blood. It was disappointing, though, after so fine a beginning, to find his brow retreat in a rapid little slope; and then, taking a quick round curve, to find your eye resting on the nape of his neck almost before you knew it. Horizontally lying across his forehead was a deep crease, perhaps three inches long, running half an inch below the line of the hair and half an inch above the abutment of his nose; this line did duty for determination and thought. The mouth and chin were large again. With this kind of face, Gower at twenty-two looked virile and worldly, and at five-and-thirty he looked twenty-two. What more can be said of him? His trousers never showed the impression of his knees, though his legs were long and thin; and there was more definite expression in the pattern of his colored shirt than of his face. This was before the fashion of scarf-pins; but he now wears—and would then have worn—a glass head of a bull-dog in a light-checked satin scarf. Gower's ideas hardly ever change, which is fortunate for his peace of mind, and his tastes never, which is fortunate for his wife. Yet, were you to introduce young Gower anywhere (in American society, of course), the answer would be wreathed in smiles—Mr. Gower, of New York, I suppose? And in Flossie Starbuck's mind these three words would have been fit climax for anything, from the caption of a tomb to a Newport hotel-register—*Levison Gower, of New York.* It was as Randolph of Roanoke. Crude as Flossie Starbuck's notions were, she was fortunate enough to aim high the first time.

Gower first knew her brother in Eighteenth Street, where they used to play games together Saturday afternoons. Si was physically stronger than young Gower, and, from the first, inspired him with respect. Gower had not at this time learned his own advantages, and Starbuck used to treat him quite cavalierly. This rough patronage produced a respectful affection which years could not efface; and when they next were thrown together, owing to a similarity of tastes in roads and equipages, Si was still fortunate enough to remain the passive member in the friendship. This intimacy was further cemented in ways before indicated; and very soon, Gower, finding Starbuck a pleasant companion at wine-suppers and popular at public balls, bethought himself of bringing him home to dinner and introducing him to his sisters. Si was too stolid to show embarrassment, and his physical presence carried him through anything. The Misses Gower rather liked him; here was a man who was rich and manly, and yet made them feel their own superiority. Even the great Killian van Kull, Gower's popular and accomplished cousin, took a fancy for Si. "Buck" Starbuck, as he dubbed him, began to be popular. Here was a man who could gamble and fight, who was ready for anything at night, and never ill-natured nor headachy the day after. Both Kill van Kull and Si had health, animal spirits, and a taste for dissipation; and little Lucie, as they were accustomed to call Levison in the intimacy of the trio, soon became their very admiring and submissive dependent. Thus Si had the luck to start in life with two of the most valuable friends a young man could have had; for Kill van Kull represented fashion and popularity, and Gower position and wealth. So he passed his first five years after leaving school, when he was supposed to be in business, and not wasting his time and money in college. Old Starbuck would have winced, had he known Si's true courses, had he even known as much as Flossie did; but, after all, young Starbuck was building better (in this world's way) than even his sister knew.

For it often became necessary to send someone home to bring Si's clothes, or bear his excuses—he had gone up the Hudson to spend Sunday with the Duvals, or on a yachting-trip with Kill van Kull; and it was often inconvenient for him to leave Kill himself. No one was so convenient in these times as Lucie Gower; and he was good-natured, and could easily run back for an hour or two. Besides, if Si had gone, he might sometimes have met his father, and have been detained peremptorily. Thus Gower became a sort of male Iris, a messenger between pleasure and duty; and he was soon familiar with the high, empty house on Eighteenth Street. He usually saw Flossie at these times. There grew to be a sort of understanding between the two. She was so much cleverer than Gower was; and she knew exactly how to face old Mr. Starbuck. And Gower learned to have confidence in her, and often told "Buck" that his sister was a brick.

"Starbuck's pretty sister" was getting to be a little better known among the young men now, though not unpleasantly talked of. She kept very quiet; and the one or two girls that knew anything about her—Miss Brevier, for instance—spoke well of her. Meantime, Si was getting on with the fast set, that set which the Duvals and old Jake Einstein were timidly forming before they dared dominate—the set which carried the tastes of the French shopkeeper into society. They spent much money, and a few fashionable hangers-on, like Van Kull, found it pleasant to stand under the golden shower.

Now came a great event in Si's life. Van Kull and Gower found it tiresome to always go to a bar-room and sit on hard chairs with Si, when they wanted to drink and smoke after a theatre or a dance. It was proposed that Si should become a member of their club—the Piccadilly, of Madison Square. And in a few months or so Si had the pleasure of seeing his name, S. Howland Starbuck, printed in the blue book of that fashionable refuge for would-be solitary males.

It was a great event for Si, and possibly, also, for his father. Old Starbuck knew very well that, although old Mr. Gower was a member and colleague of his in church matters—affairs of the other world—he never would have gone sponsor for him, as he had for his son Silas, in a club election in this. Yet this knowledge did not offend him; he was glad to see his son Silas rise in the world, and bore no malice. Perhaps he was even pleased that his son could go where he could not. It was right that Si should make friends, and perhaps just as well that he had not gone much into the business, after all. For about this time the oil from Oil Creek began to attract attention in the markets. Long before—centuries before—the Indians had been used to dip their blankets along the creek's still surface until they were thoroughly saturated, and then to obtain the oil by the simple process of squeezing; for the oil was known to be "great medicine" and good for rheumatism, sores, and troubled souls. In the salt-wells near Pittsburg, on Saturday nights, when the brine was well pumped away, the miners were annoyed by the increasing flow of the green, bad-smelling stuff, which by Monday would have disappeared, pressed back by the new flow of brine into its deep crevices in the subterranean rock. But no one had thought of value for the stuff—except the few quack doctors or credulous ones who, trusting to the old Indian legend, skimmed a little oil from wooden cribs about the creek and sold it as a medicine of nature's patent, in the Philadelphia drug-stores, for one dollar the ounce. At this price the fluid was not a dangerous competitor with Mr. Starbuck's product; and even when one of these same Philadelphia druggists analyzed the oil, found its value, and made a contract for the output of one of the salt-wells, the only effect of his enterprise was to ruin its value as a medicine by making it free to anyone (like those other medicines of water, air, and out-doors), without rendering it as cheap as the coal-oil already made from cannel-coal. Still, the flow, once begun, did not cease; wells were sunk whose daily flow exceeded the capacity of many a whale; already, refining whale and sperm was not what it had been; and there was more competition in petroleum, and he was not so well situated for the raw material. Old Starbuck began to think it was time he sold out; the works had been very profitable, and the expense and hazard of changing machinery and *clientèle* made the future risky. Few of his competitors had the energy to make the change, the process of refining being so different, but went on filtering the diminished catch of whale and sperm, until the divine law of the survival of the fittest put a quietus to their struggles. By all this Starbuck profited, as was to be expected. The S. Starbuck Oil Company was formed; capital, Two Millions; Starbuck himself remaining one of the directors. The business and works were then supposed to be worth about $800,000. One-half the capital was paid up, and $800,000 of it paid to S. Starbuck, Esq., for the works, machinery, business, and good-will; besides this cash, Starbuck received $800,000 in stock of the new company at its face value. The stock was then considered worth par, and he was shrewd enough to keep it always well above eighty; in fact, he continued to manage the concern for a year or two, and was even so clever as to get it back to a healthy basis, although he had first watered and then milked it to the tune of a million and a quarter. When he had succeeded in this, he sold half of his remaining stock, all he could safely get rid of, and retired absolutely from business. Eight months after this, his work being satisfactorily finished, to himself, in this world, he left it, in October, 1872. In April, 1873, the engagement of Miss Starbuck and Mr. T. Levison Gower, Jr., was formally announced.

People were much surprised, but less so than if Lucie Gower had married someone of whom they knew something. Now they commonly knew nothing of Flossie, except that she was "Buck" Starbuck's sister. Things have changed since; and Si is Mrs. Levison Gower's brother now. Miss Brevier was delighted, and went about telling her friends that Flossie was a perfectly sweet girl. Silas Starbuck's friends commonly said "*By Jove!*" among themselves, and nothing when Si was present. Flossie was already twenty-four, and had been generally supposed, as much on account of this as of her retired life, not to be about to marry. Still, there were few ill-natured comments about it. Her modesty did her a good turn here. And no one much envied her young Gower, except for his wealth; and she had plenty of that.

The Gowers themselves looked more askance at the match. After all, it was their family that she was going to marry into. And she might have many relations. Only old Gower, seeing that she had the essentials, had the sense to accept the thing from the first. He knew that his social position was a rock on which a fair structure might be built with her money. Old Gower had come to New York about 1830 from one of the hill-towns in Northwestern Connecticut; and had first been known as engaged in the banking business, with one of the Lydams as his partner. It was a Miss Lydam whom he married. He was very rich, or had that reputation; and was a prominent magnate in one of the largest evangelical denominations. There he had met and known and appreciated old Starbuck. He was not sorry, however, that that gentleman was dead. Mr. Gower felt toward him much as a *ci-devant* marquis might have felt toward the rich farmer-general father of his daughter-in-law. Mr. Gower lived in the most democratic city of a democracy; but a democracy lends itself to sudden and extreme social distinctions. The imaginary line, drawn hap-hazard, must be drawn all the deeper to endure a decade. A society which has no Pyrenees must give an extra attention to the artificial forts of its boundaries. Old Mrs. Gower felt deeply these truths. She knew that Mr. Starbuck had been in oil; but she also said to herself that her son would raise Flossie to his own level. What that level was we have seen.

Meanwhile, the two lovers were very happy.

Flossie allowed herself, by anticipation, a little more style in dress. She appeared with young Gower in his buggy in the park, radiant, and really very pretty. Lucie Gower's friends congratulated him boisterously, and called her Flower-de-Luce—a name which persisted ten years or so, until some savage wit changed the Flower to Fruit. She was then still slight; and, for the first time, dared to show how pretty she was. "How she has come out since her engagement!" was the common remark. Indeed she had; she was very happy; she felt as if she had been born anew, into a world of which previously she had only seen the brown-stone front. Gower went to see her every day; and though these *tête-à-têtes* were rather long, she consoled herself with the idea that the marriage would soon be over. He, too, was impatient; and very proud of her. He secretly liked to have his friends dig him in the ribs—as they would do, with Gower. He had never possessed any girl, before, who had loved him solely for himself; for surely there was nothing else to attract Miss Starbuck?—he had little money. Lucie felt a flattering sense of ownership in this fair creature that was going to link her life with his. The simple fellow was touched by it; and he never really ceased to be in love with her, though too weak to resist temptation in any simple and attractive form. Si, too, was immensely delighted. He thought Lucie little better than a fool; but then, he was just the man to make a capital husband. And, on the whole, he would not be a disagreeable brother-in-law. However, after the first relief and contentment of the thing were over, and Flossie fairly disposed of, it no longer concerned Si very much.

Never was a marriage so happy, or the course of true love so smooth. There was a delicious excitement about it all to Gower; he felt as if he had multiplied himself by four. And Flossie—Flossie's feelings were more complex. She obtained Miss Brevier's services as a bridesmaid; and it was arranged that the newly-married couple should live on Fifth Avenue at the corner of Thirty-second Street. The old Starbuck house in Eighteenth Street was sold, and Si went into lodgings—as he had long desired.

The wedding-presents, though few in number, were very handsome; Flossie had the satisfaction of seeing her wedding under the head of "Fashionable Weddings" in the *New York Herald;* two clergymen performed the ceremony; and in the evening the bride and groom went to Boston. After a fortnight they returned and installed themselves in the Fifth Avenue house, which had been elaborately decorated and extravagantly furnished for their coming. Old Mrs. Gower gave a grand reception in their honor. And about the same time, young Gower began to find himself in his club-window, sucking his cane, and wondering what he should do with his afternoon, very much as usual. He puzzled much over a certain feeling he had, but was not clever enough at self-analysis to make it out. But it was as if the theatre had ended too early, and there were nothing to do with the rest of the evening.

Not so Mrs. Gower.

## CHAPTER IV.

### ARTHUR HOLYOKE'S DREAMS.

HEN the living poet and the dead came out to see the stars once more, the Florentine found himself upon a grassy slope, alone in the early morning, with his silent guide. So, when Tannhäuser, after his ten years' sojourn in the Venusberg, broke through the walls of the mountain in a rift made by a prayer, he too found himself on the brow of a green and sunny mountain valley, filled with the long-forgotten breath of morning; and, in place of the devil's music, a shepherd piping to his sheep. So, reader, you in flesh and blood, as I hope, may follow me, in the story, to the time of dates and daylight, and a place—the time, September, 1883; the place, the village of Great Barrington, far down in Berkshire in old Massachusetts. The early morning shadows still reached long across the green carpet of meadow in the intervale; the shadows of the houses, and of the great masses of elm foliage, and of the tall spire of the meeting-house up on the hill; the undulating masses of greenery that robed the lower hills were striped here and there with autumn scarlet, like a blackbird's wing; and the silver lace in the meadow grass, and the long silken cobwebs in the air, and the rich violet-blue sky, shading off to pink like an onyx near the horizon, were precursors of the coming glory of the day.

No one was stirring in the village. In the ploughed uplands a few farmers were idly walking, hither and thither like generals on the battlefield of their success, tightening a sheaf of fodder or replacing a yellow squash or two that had rolled off from a summit of the great golden pyramids standing, piled like cannon-balls, in the cornfields. But the day of sowing was over, and the day of reaping was over, and little remained but to sit and look at the crops and grow fat. Up on the hill, the roads were empty—who should travel when there was no need? Even the plodding oxen-teams were idle in their stalls, being fattened and coddled, perhaps, for the annual cattle show. So that Gracie Holyoke and Arthur had the beautiful Stockbridge road, and the morning look of the mountains, all to themselves. They rode at a sharp canter, but with little conversation; at least, so a groom might have thought riding behind them; as the two heads never seemed to turn inward. But there was no groom, and the chestnut horses had a way of riding so closely side by side (being in this constantly drilled) that to turn one's head was hardly necessary.

Were these two in love? A city groom, used to ride behind many a preening pair in their smart T-cart, seasoned and wearied with his master's catechism of flirtation, which he had so often overheard; being there in theory to play propriety, but in fact, as he well knew, only as a license to flirt, much as a policeman is stationed in the Park for the skating when the ice is thin—such a groom would have said No. For they hardly ever look at one another. But perhaps an older groom, good dan Cupid himself, the blind passenger who perches like dark care on so many a horse's back, and drives dark care away—he might answer Yea: for they are not flirting.

Now, there are several legitimate states of being in love, as videlicet, to be in love and know it, to be in love and not know it, to know that she loves you and to think that you love her, to be in love, but with another person than the one you think:—but to know it and not be in love is but a modern and puerile intellectual trifling; this we call flirtation. And in that these two were surely not. Were they then simply indifferent to one another? Unlikely—so early in the morning. And surely, the cosmic chances are all in our favor: is it not the normal relation, to be in love? Given, a young man of twenty-one and a lovely girl some few months younger—and the uplands, and the forest, and the sun, moon, stars, storm and springtime—and show me one such younker not in love and you will show me a wretched fellow you had best avoid.

No such selfish saint or sordid sinner can this slender Arthur be, who turns in his saddle and shows the clear-cut New English profile with the delicate but winning smile. But see, the smile has faded into earnestness; leaning yet farther from the saddle, he is looking up into his companion's face, and seeming to be searching for something there. Does he find it? Ah, Cupid, good dan Cupid, were you right once more? or were we both too hasty—for she has not blushed, but the one rounded cheek we see, as we press after them, grows quickly pale, and we can just make out the dark eye-lashes that droop quickly down, breaking the contour; and now they do not speak again, but ride at the run in mutual silence—oh, a silence that is surely mutual, if ever silence was—and we have much to do, being old and no longer in love, to keep behind these two, who do not dally. This was all that happened in the ride. Only, coming home, and both dismounting (she without waiting for his aid) and he taking her hand to say good morning (as he had done a hundred times before, that very summer) the color mounted in the young girl's face (as it had never done before) so that she turned the face aside which was too near her heart, and ran indoors in haste and left him there.

This was all that happened on that ride—it was all that had ever happened—but in it, Arthur Holyoke had made bold to ask his cousin to become his wife; and she had bade him wait till evening for his answer; and then they both had ridden home. A city groom would have seen nothing of it all; yet these things had been done. A short probation, you will say, until the evening only; and Arthur hardly thought of it as such, but walked home briskly, hat in hand, castle-building; his dark gray eyes turned inward, and the wind making free with his curly, undecided-colored hair. For what probation was there more, after all their lives had so far been together, than living on together, man and wife? Not that she loved him then so much as he loved her—but that was to be expected. She loved him more than he deserved, he knew; but then, that is true of most pairs, and the men must needs not waste their pity, but resign themselves, as it is the way of women. And Arthur walked along the straight garden path that led from door to highway in Judge Holyoke's old place, switching off the prim asters with his riding-cane. For his uncle's house was built in the days of gardens, not of lawns—can we not imagine the large contempt with which the dwellers of a prairie would regard a barbered rood or two of grass?—and the flowers were part of Gracie's presence there, and she of them.

Arthur was not too stout, but strong and graceful, almost Greek in figure as in face; a strange, strong scion of that narrow-chested clergyman-father, so stout in spirit, but so fragile in this world, who had died and left him to his uncle's care, the Judge. There are many such: it seems our people (like some mute, inglorious poet) have had their period of pale and interesting youth, and now are comfortably stout and genial, in their easy-going middle age, the wasting spiritual fires quelled: like a sometime tractarian clergyman, now optimistic in a fat living. Arthur, however (not to carry the analogy too far), was spiritual enough in his way, though not the orthodox; delicately balanced, mobile, imaginative, Celtic more than Saxon, and rather Greek than either. Nor could you truly say that his way wanted depth, unless depth means sluggishness or stillness. Arthur was a

New Englander, and New England is in reality the essence of all things American, in germ and future; and the people, the crowds, are already rather Greek than English. Irreverent, fond of novelty and quick —in politics, if not in art, they are Athenian. The public of Aristophanes is the public of the American burlesque; of lions, fair ladies, lecturers; of advertised politics, priests and prophets, of the mind-cure and of the secular Sunday newspaper.

Arthur Holyoke had been brought up by the Judge, chiefly on the simple plan of keeping him in the country and giving him plenty of books; a most admirable plan, never to be enough recommended. The Judge spent his winters in the city; then Arthur was kept at boarding-school; one of those quiet little boarding-schools of the wooden Doric variety, now disappearing. The Judge travelled abroad, or went to England or to the West, every summer; Arthur was left at Great Barrington. One winter Arthur had passed in Boston with his uncle, and had attended lectures at the Institute of Technology; it was the winter that Gracie had been away with her aunt in New York. This happened in one of these years when the whim of Hellenism seemed, in Boston, to be permanently eclipsing the Hebraism which has really made that city; and Arthur was intoxicated by the new atmosphere, as a hardy wind-flower might be in the rich sweet air and tempered light of a grapery. You do not make grapes of blackberries by putting them under glass; but you modify them considerably. If you had asked Arthur what was to be his profession, he would have answered engineering; but his inward consciousness was that he should be a great poet. But he knew the pitying contempt with which the world regards its contemporary failures—and its contemporaries are always failures—in that line; and in spite of his assurance that he had it in him (whilst others had not) he did not mean that it should be known until it was known only to his glory. These dreams had blended with his dreams of life with Gracie, until it was hard to say which was more the cause and which the effect; they grew apace together. To-day his dreams of love had the ascendant; and he wandered about the country many hours, rapt in his love and her. They would live where? in the city, of course; in New York, where was the largest focus for his genius. That, too, was the place where the most rapid fortune was to be made; for, of course, they must have money, and the money must be made quickly, that he might get his leisure and return to his poetry again. For this was to be the ultimate, the crown of his life. Engineering would not do; some quicker way than this must be found; banking, or railroads. The years of business would be irksome, no doubt; but then, with Gracie with him!

So the boy wandered, through the afternoon, working many a gorgeous variegation on the themes of love and fame; with but the least substratum of gold among them, as if to give strength to the pigments of his fancy. Meantime, Gracie, on her part, had been thinking, now happily, now in shades of sadness, oftener still in prayer. Yet she went about the household on her usual duties, passing silently like the daylight through the long library, where the old Judge sat over his briefs and closely-wrought opinions, nor ever noticed so slight a thing as a young girl's mood.

Arthur found her in the garden, when he came, in a favorite place of hers, sitting on an old stone seat by the little brook, where it was most densely overshadowed by the flowering shrubs. She had that serious look in her dark eyes which he loved best in them, and she neither blushed nor smiled when he took her hand and sat him down beside her. Arthur had often fancied that at this time a flow of speech worthy of a Petrarch would be his; but as it was, the simplest words alone seemed strong to him. "The day has seemed so long to me!" Perhaps he thought it true; but it was not. The day had seemed short, and full of dreams. She made no answer; but, in a moment, turned her head and looked at him, gravely, as it seemed to Arthur, fondly, as it might have seemed to an older man. "I do not think we ought to be engaged," she said; and this he could not make her unsay in all the afternoon.

But the old tragicomedy was re-enacted, which is so old, and will seem so new to our great-grandchildren; and Arthur knew, at the first, that she loved no one else; and at the last, he knew, or might have known, that she loved him. But the *yes* she would not say, but only, *wait;* and when he urged, But you may care for some one else? she only said, "I shall care for no one else, Arthur"—and at the last it grew to be but a pleasant play, so sure he was of her. It was settled between them that he was to go to New York and make his fortune and hers; and that then he was to come back and ask her father's consent; or sooner perhaps, if the fortune was too slow in coming. She would not write to him, she said,—but she would answer a letter now and then—and he kissed her once for the first time, under the old lilac bush, before they left. And more, a thousand times more, he felt in love with her than he had even been that morning; and so they came out of the greenery into the broad sward with the long slanting shadows of the sunset, he still holding to her hand.

They were close on the Lenox road; and he had to drop her hand in haste, as an open carriage came swinging by, bearing an old acquaintance of ours—Mrs. Levison Gower and a guest of hers from Lenox. The guest must have made some quick remark to Mrs. Gower about them; for they both turned and looked at the young people, and she bowed to Gracie; and then the light wheels whisked by, leaving but the dust, and the crisp sound of the horses' trot. Arthur had noticed the glance, but did not speak of it; he saw that Gracie was blushing again. He forgot even to ask who Mrs. Gower was, as he took Gracie's hand again in his; and together, slowly, they went down the broad garden-walk.

## CHAPTER V.

### OF GRACIE HOLYOKE AND OF HER HEART.

MAN'S grand life, says some one, is a dream of his youth realized in and by his later years; what then shall we say of a woman's? Think not on this; but let your soul answer. The answer should be there, in the hearts of all; but whether it comes from memory, from things now half forgotten, or from within, or from some birth-dream had in childhood, who shall say? Yet is it there; like a child's dream of a star; happy he whose manhood sees the star, its dream not yet departed. And all of us have fancied women so, at some time in our lives; have we never known one such? For but one such is enough, mother, bride, or daughter. Some slight girl whose maidenhood was a sweet bloom, like Mary's lily in the Temple; and then we may have lost sight or knowledge of her, for a time. And then perhaps we have met some other woman, some old woman, with white hairs; not the same, of course, and yet it seems as if we could have pieced together their two lives and make them like one brook, that we have known in places only, which brings soft fields and flowers. And be sure that there was in between some womanhood, some mother's life, not known save to her sons and God, not preached in meetings and conventions; deep hidden in some human fireside, like the brook that makes so green a summer wood—Such lives are white and shining, like a dream of God's made real on the earth.

And all the world seems thirst, and lust, and envy, and desire; the fires of heaven are put out, and all men struggling, trampling, for the colored stones of earth; and yet such blooms do come upon it. But they blossom stilly, like silent lilies born above the meadow-mire. White and pure they shine, and breathe in heaven's sunlight, and give out heaven's fragrance, borne each upon its slender stem above the blind, black bog.

The day after this, Gracie had an errand, up in a little town beyond the hills. Arthur asked that he might go there with her; then they both might ride instead of driving. So they started, after luncheon; the new brown leaves lay crisp beneath their feet, and the light that flooded the valley was like yellow wine. Their way lay up over the hills to the eastward, and then, cresting their summits, along a rambling grass-grown road, between the crumbling stone walls and old unpainted farmhouses. What paint the farmers had to spare, they put upon the barns; a poor powdery stuff, weak in oil, and leaving but a brushing as of red earth upon the seasoned boards; the windows of the farmhouses looked out forlornly upon the fields already lonely, grim and unrelieved by any curtain. The places where gardens had been used to be, were common for the hens; along the fences for a hundred yards on either side of every house was a littering of chips where the wood-piles had been, but the piles were scant this year, and of half-grown birch; the reason was easy to see, for the great hills rolled off around them denuded of timber, save here and there a new growth of scrub oak. Beside each house the old well stood, its sweep pointing to the sky, but now disused and replaced by a patent log-pump, painted a garish blue.

Arthur rode very close to Gracie to-day; there was an exhilarating space and sweep to the free wind that brought bright color to their cheeks, and their clear eyes sparkled as their glances soared far over the brown downs and rested with delight upon the distant sky-line. There is something about our New England uplands like the barren worn-out plains of Old Castile; yet these two might have stood for a youth and future that one cannot hope from Spain.

They came out from the table-land down into a combe that had been worn for itself by a little stream now dry; as they ambled down the winding grass-grown way, the trees began again about them, oak and pines, then firs; a house or two was passed, and then a little school-house, the houses boarded up, and the school-house closed. They came down upon the turnpike, which had come by the longer way, around the hills; here was a bit of a village, a blacksmith's house, a country store and an old hotel. The weather-worn wood of these seemed older than any thatched and plastered cottage in old England.

Gracie's pensioners lived in a little house close by,

the blacksmith's wife and her six children; she had some medicine for them, and Arthur a few newspapers. While Gracie went to see them, Arthur led the horses to the inn; there was a swinging sign of George Washington over the door, which the pride of each successive owner had kept well varnished ever since the memorable night when he had stopped there,—though nothing else about the place was in repair. No one came to the door as Arthur walked up, and he tied his horses to a well-nibbled rail, and went in. There was a long bare entry leading from the front door, with a row of doors; each with a tin sign above it, "office," "dining-room," "ball-room" (now half obliterated), and "bar." Arthur opened the last one, and went in.

There was a high black stove with a hard-coal fire, in the centre of the room; around it on the floor a square wooden tray, filled with sand. The walls were covered with gay posters, a cattle show, an advertisement of melodeons, of a horse stolen, of an auction sale of a farm, farming utensils, a horse and cow, many sleighs and wagons and some household furniture. An old man sat in one corner, in carpet slippers, with a newspaper, and a look upon him as if he had not been out-doors that day.

"Well, Lem?" said Arthur, "business quiet, eh?"

"There ain't much business, Mr. Holyoke," said the hotel-keeper, without changing his position, "'xcept what's in here." And he pointed to the bar, and the pitcher of water, and the row of tumblers behind it.

"I want you to give my horses a feed," said Arthur, "we came over from Great Barrington."

"Came over from Barrington, did ye?" said he. "And what's the news in town?" And without waiting for an answer, the old man rose and hobbled to the side door. "Mike!" he cried, "Mike!" There was no answer. "I guess the feller must ha' gone to Lee," he added, grumbling. "There's a cattle show there, to-day."

"Let me go," said Arthur; "I'll look after them."

"You'll find the feed in the bin," said the inn-keeper, relapsing into his stuffed chair, with a sigh of relief.

"And what's the news from your son, Mr. Hitchcock?" said Arthur, when he came back.

"Lem's still out in Ioway," said Mr. Hitchcock. "There ain't much call for a young feller of sperit to be loafin' around here. I brought him up for the business; but I guess the old place'll have to keep itself after I am gone."

"Still at your old books, Mr. Hitchcock, I see," said Arthur, taking up a well-worn copy of Tom Paine. "Why, I didn't know you read French!" And Arthur turned over with interest the leaves of a book the other had just laid down; it was a volume of Voltaire.

"I l'arned it when I was a b'y in college. Perhaps ye didn't know as I was a college-bred man?"

"I might have known it," said Arthur. "But you didn't send Lem there?"

"No," said the other, shortly. And then, with a

chuckle, "They've pretty much all come to my way of thinking, now. D'ye notice the old meetin'-house as ye came along? They've had to shut it up, ye know. Have a cigar?" And Mr. Hitchcock brought two suspicious looking weeds out of a gayly pictured box, and extended one to Arthur. The latter took one, knowing the old man would be mortally offended if this rite of hospitality were passed by.

"Whose house was that I saw boarded up?" said Arthur, for the sake of something to say.

"What!" said the old man, "ain't ye heard? That's Uncle Sam Wolcott's. The old man was livin' there with his daughter and her little b'y." And Hitchcock took a comfortable pull at his cigar.

"Yes," said Arthur, "I remember now."

"The child's dead," said he.

"What?" said Arthur. "Dead?"

Hitchcock nodded assent. "Killed him, ye know."

"Killed him? who—"

"The grandfather—Samuel Wolcott. Killed him with an axe, Sunday week. Them air gospel folks got him crazy."

The old man spoke with a sort of grim satisfaction, and Arthur looked at him in amazement. "Great heavens! you don't mean to say he murdered him? Where's the mother?"

"Lucky for her she warn't there at the time, I guess. Fust time I ever knew o' church doing a critter any good."

"But where is she now?"

Hitchcock waved his hand in the direction of the

biggest poster, "*Farm for Sale.*" "Gone back to her husband's folks, I guess. And when she come back, she found old Wolcott a-hangin' to a rafter in his barn."

"But what possible motive—" began Arthur aghast. "Had he no other family?"

"He had a sister—I never heard what became o' her. She married a feller by the name of Starbuck, from New London way, an' I mistrust he turned out bad. I guess the old man got kinder disperited. An' then the gospel folks—But he was the last of the old Wolcott family, an' they was gret folks in their day. So they put him an' the infant in the family tomb, and sealed it up."

Arthur looked at the old hotel-keeper, and then out at the empty street. Gracie was coming along under the elm-trees, the yellow leaves falling about her in the autumn wind. "I must be going," said he.

"Have a little something hot, before ye go?"

"No," said Arthur, "thanks, I guess not." And he made haste to get away, feeling the spirit of the place come over him like a pall.

"Well, good-bye?" said the other. "Always glad to see ye. But we've all got to come to it. Some day, ye'll find me hanging to the beam up there, I expect." Heedless of which gloomy prognostication, Arthur made haste to get to the stable and brought out the horses. They mounted, and rode some time in silence.

"Did Mr. Hitchcock tell you?" said Gracie with a shudder.

Arthur nodded. Something in the terror of the place brought out his love the stronger, as he looked at her, the tears in her deep gray eyes. "I wonder that we had not heard of it," said he; "but these places are so out of the world."

"Poor man, I have so often wondered if we could do nothing for him," said she. "I went there once; but he almost ordered me out of the house."

"Hitchcock says it was some religious mania," said Arthur.

"He never went to church when I knew him," said Gracie. "He cared most for his sister; and I think her husband turned out ill. Poor people, does it not seem cruel they cannot be taught to live? They could be so happy here, in this lovely country, if they only knew."

"We are happy, are we not, dear?" said Arthur.

"Yes, Arthur. It almost seems wrong—" and Gracie looked out over the hills ahead of them, where the sun was already low in the sky.

"Are we going home, now?"

"I want to stop a moment at the Kellys—that Irish family, you know."

Instinctively, they had taken another road back, leaving the old meeting-house and the now ended homestead on the right; and as they came up on the brow of the first hill, they passed a large wooden cross, painted freshly, with a gilt circle and the mystic letters I. N. R. I. in the centre. A short distance beyond this was a square old-fashioned farmhouse, with a fine old doorway, needing paint like all the other houses. But the yard was full of pigs and hens and chickens; and about the door a half-score tow-headed children were playing. These ran up to Gracie as they rode up. "Mother's in the kitchen," said the biggest of the girls, putting a finger in her mouth. The boys stood still, and stared at them, abashed.

Gracie went in; and Arthur stood and looked about him. The fields were already stubble; but lit up with yellow piles of squashes; a noise of cattle came from the rambling old stable; and behind the house was a low peat-meadow, fresh-ditched and being drained. The healthy Irish stock had grown luxuriantly, where the older line was dying out. Gracie came out, smiling. "She is a nice old body, Mrs. Kelly," said she. "And now, for home!" and they put their horses at the gallop, and were soon up on the bare downs again. And Arthur, like a man, began to plead his suit once more.

## CHAPTER VI.

### THE JUDGE SUMS UP HIS CASE.

JUDGE HOLYOKE sat in his library, trying to reconcile good law with good conscience by distinguishing the present case, in which the plaintiff was clearly in the right, from a former one in which he had been as clearly in the wrong. The opinion was a hard one; and the Judge had got no farther than the summing up, when there was a knock at the door. The Judge always wrote his opinions with ease and clearness when law and right coincided; but when they did not, he would lie awake of nights to produce an opinion which would remain a marvel of learning and obscurity. His high brow wrinkled a little when he heard the knock at the door; he hated to be disturbed while in the agonies of judicial creation; and as Arthur came tentatively in, he looked at him sternly, as upon a counsel who ventured upon an unexpected motion, with a curtly short-cutting *well?*

(He has come for a larger allowance, thought the Judge; he knows that he is of full age, and wants his full income.)

(How shall I ask him for his daughter, thought Arthur. Well—at all events, he must know that she is mine.)

Arthur sat down, still hesitating. The Judge waited impatiently, though he thought he knew what was in his mind; for it was part of his legal training never to give his own ideas until he had fully extracted those of the other side. Thus, mutual misunderstanding like that of a scene in a comedy was averted; for when Arthur did begin, it was to the point.

"Uncle John," said he, "I am engaged to Gracie."

Uncle John was in fact more staggered than if he had moved him for a non-suit; but his judicial calm was as unruffled as if it were but a *similiter* in pleading. "And is Gracie engaged to you?" he answered, illogically, but to the point, in his turn. And Arthur's hesitation in replying gave him time to hastily adapt himself to the issue and make up his judicial mind; which was, as usual, that the court would reserve its decision. Arthur, however, hesitated but for a moment; and then with a faint blush mantling his ingenuous face, "I think, sir, she might be, if you would consent."

"But, dear me," said the Judge, "I don't consent! Don't understand me for one moment as consenting! Where's Gracie? Did you tell her of this—of this surprising motion of yours?"

"No, sir," said Arthur, "I thought—that——"

"That you wanted an *ex parte* hearing? Now I can't pronounce a decision, sir, in the absence of the parties; and Gracie has not made her appearance in this suit as yet!"

"I'll go get her," said Arthur, promptly.

"No, sir, you'll do nothing of the sort," said the Judge, appalled at this evidence of collusion between the parties. "You'll go away from here for some years before you get her; and then——"

"And then?" said Arthur, eagerly.

The Judge looked at him curiously over his round spectacles. "What do you propose to live upon?"

"I am coming to that," said Arthur. "I have fifteen hundred a year——"

"Two thousand," said the Judge, absently.

"Two thousand?" said Arthur, "I did not think it was so much." And he began rapidly to calculate how much farther the extra five hundred would carry them.

"Well," said the Judge, "you don't propose to marry my daughter and live in Boston on two thousand a year, do you?" But, secretly, it seemed to him the proper thing to do.

"No, sir," said Arthur; ("Oh," interpolated the Judge, rather disappointed.) "I—I have decided to go to New York and enter a banking-house. And, in that, sir, I want to ask your help—and your advice."

The Judge was silent a minute. "In order that you may use the one and decline the other, I suppose, with thanks. Well;—and granting this point (for the sake of argument)—What next?"

"Then," said Arthur, "I shall try to make some money; and then, if I succeed—will you give your consent to our engagem—to our marriage?"

"Dear, dear," thought the Judge, "how persistent he is! I haven't given my consent to your engagement as yet," he answered. "Why do you wish to go to New York?"

"I don't know, sir," said Arthur, taken by surprise. "At least, it is a larger field—one may get on in the world more rapidly—and I thought, with my engineering training, as agent of a banking house I should be sooner able to support a wife."

"Do you think Gracie would be happier there than in Boston?"

"I don't know—we had not got to that yet, sir," said Arthur, cleverly enough. True, they had not; and the Judge smiled a little.

"I mean, in case we should consider this most preposterous scheme?" he added. "Do you mean to be a banker all your life?" he asked, suddenly.

"Oh, no, sir—at least, that is—I should like——"

"Suppose I should ask you to take some practical position on a railroad in the far West?"

"I think I should rather be in New York, sir.—But, of course, I should want to follow your advice."

"Would you give up the New York plan entirely, if I asked you to?"

"Yes, sir," said Arthur. "If you gave me Gracie."

The Judge paused. Arthur sat, twirling his light straw hat in his hand, but looking earnestly at his uncle. "Shall I send her here to you, sir?" he said, finally, finding the suspense intolerable.

The Judge looked at him gravely, over his spectacles.

"On the whole, I think New York will be the best place for you. I will write to Mrs. Livingstone about it to-night. But not a word of this to Gracie, mind. And now, good-night."

Arthur got up; but he hesitated nervously at the door, before turning the handle.

"And suppose—suppose she asks me, sir?"

"You will tell her I unqualifiedly disapprove of the whole project," thundered the Judge in his most court-like manner; and Arthur must fain go content with that answer. But he met Gracie in the parlor, and told her that her father would not give his consent as yet; but that he had written to New York, and would find him, Arthur, a place in some banking-house.

And so, these two went on to talk of more important matters; or rather, Arthur did; as, how long he had loved her, and how much, and how he had come to speak upon just that day; until Gracie, hearing nothing from her father, feared that he might be ill or worried, and gave Arthur his dismissal, and with more formality than usual. A certain constraint was between these two now, most new and delightful, to Arthur, at least; but quite different from the old cousinly ease.

Meantime, the Judge had dropped his papers from him and set to considering this last case, that was so much nearer home. He had no objections—of course, he had no serious objection to his daughter's marrying Arthur—if Arthur was good enough for her; for cousinship is but a slight objection in New England. The Judge had always looked up to his elder brother, the clergyman, as being far his own superior; but somehow, with his son and his own daughter, it seemed otherwise. The Judge strenuously kept out of his mind any consideration of Gracie's leaving him, lest it should bias his decision; he felt an odd desire to submit the case to some one else, as one in which he was too much interested to sit.

Perhaps in every middle-aged or elderly mind, there is a slight impatience with the matrimonial doings of the younger, as being always somewhat premature and ill-considered. When one's own life is neatly rounded off, when one has duly weighed its emptiness, and properly resigned one's self to it; when that resignation, which once seemed so unlike content, has become a habit; there must be a certain impertinence, —you being so ready to say *enfin!*—in any one's starting up and crying *recommençons!* Of course, Judge Holyoke knew that Gracie would some day wed—of course, he wished her to be well, *i.e.*, happily married—but not exactly here—not now—not to this one nor to that one. Not that he doubted that Arthur was in earnest—or that he spoke the truth in saying Gracie loved him—nor did he think that they were both too young to know their own minds. It is the fashion to scoff at first loves, but the Judge believed in them; whether rightly or wrongly, we cannot say; but this was part of that which made him trusted, even by the prisoner upon whom he was passing sentence; and yet, a just judge, too.

But somehow, things had changed so much since the Judge was young, that he did not see how any one could soberly contract to see them change much further, or take the risk of any new beginning. He himself had been a Rousseau, a Robespierre, a Lovelace with a dash of folly and Tom Paine, to the worthy people of the town where he then sat, the people who were then sleeping in the hillside yonder; and yet, how fine a town these same good folk had made, in the days when he was a young law-student under old Judge Sewall! But in middle life, the world and its movement had passed him; and now, the gay folk and the band were almost out of sight ahead of him, and he behind with the feeble and the stragglers, the old and the obstructive, and no longer any hankering to be drum-major.

For it seemed as if the old prizes had lost their lustre; and there were no longer any public for a man; an honest one getting so little applause, in this world's stage, and the general taste being vitiated, and too coarse to relish the finer flavors of the human soul. He believed Arthur to be an honest man, with the education and breeding of a gentleman; more he did not ask, his smartness, or his faculty for getting on. The old Judge had little of the avarice miscalled of age; he thought too little of the worth of money for one who grieved so much that it alone had worth; perhaps Arthur, in his way, thought as much of this. With Gracie married, he at least might well go off the stage. Many creatures live but to their time of reproduction; this is all that nature seems to care; and the time which is given to live with and cherish his children to nature would seem but surplusage. He had lived and married; he had found all that even his youthful ambitions had dared to formulate or hope; but was he quite content? Somehow, the sky, so blue in the morning, had grown troubled and overcast toward the twilight. There was no one thing he could say was wanting; he had done what he had sought to do; he had been honored more than he had hoped; he would leave—what? A few well-wrought opinions, valuable until the next statute; a reputation as a nice old-fogy; a few poor dollars, some books, and—

The door opened softly, but the Judge did not hear it; and his daughter entered and placed her soft hand on his. He started, as if he had been dreaming. Gracie was troubled by his absence of mind, and feared she might be the cause; she looked at him, not timidly, nor inquiringly, and yet so that the old man's eyes grew softer as he looked at hers. "No, dear, you did not disturb me,—neither you nor Arthur," he added, at her half-spoken word. "Tell me, do you care for him very much?"

"No more than I do for you, dear," said the girl; but in her manner the Judge could read her silent strength of love. And more was said between them; but come, we are not fit for such scenes, you and I; let us go out gently and leave these two alone.

Meantime, Arthur, the cause of all this, was sleeping quietly, with the sleep of a hunter of any manner of wild-fowl, and the dreamlessness of insouciant youth. For Gracie loved him—that was clear, both to happy Arthur and the wakeful Judge.

. . . . . . . . . . .

There is a curious timeliness in our modern ailments; a timeliness which would be still more striking if we could know the elements of each man's life. In older times, men wore out slowly, by labor or by rust; they set about dying deliberately, as they worked their land or managed their daily concernments. But in these days of steam and dynamite, our mode of death is sudden, quick and certain, like an explosion or a railway catastrophe; less like the processes of nature than those of man. Paralysis, like nihilism, has developed in the nineteenth century, and chooses, as if by some secret intelligence, its moment with a terrible skill.

So, one such night as this, and not long after—of the exact date I am not sure—death came upon the Judge, as he was sitting with his papers, working late at night and lonely, striving to fashion human statutes to fit diviner laws, that justice might be seen of men.

# CHAPTER VII.

## ARTHUR SEES THE WORLD.

T was near the end of the first hour in the New York Stock Exchange. The floor was crowded. A few of the young brokers, who had less business and more time, having executed their orders, were now ready for skylarking and horse-play. But it had been a great "bull" morning, and the greater number, many of whom were older brokers, and had only been attracted personally to the scene as the news of the great battle spread abroad about the Street, were still madly pressing around the painted signs which were set, like standards, to mark the stations of the stocks. The high roof of the hall seemed too close to make the noise endurable; the air itself seemed torn and tired with the cries of the combatants. The rays of light which came down from the high windows were full of shreds and the dust of battle; the worn floor was littered with bits of paper, telegrams and orders, the exploded cartridges of that paper warfare. To the contemplative stranger in the gallery—if any contemplating stranger there had presence of mind and spirit calm enough to remain so—it seemed as if the actors in the scene, rushing madly from one skirmish

to another, crying their orders, now unheeded, now to a crazy crowd, were the orators or leaders of a vast mob, trying each to work his will upon the multitude. Or he may have thought it a parliament, a congress that had overleapt all rules of decorum, where each member forgot all save the open rush for private gain. But one who understood might still have seen the battle wax and wane; might have seen here the attack and there the repulse, here the concentration of forces and the charge, there the support brought up to the post that showed signs of wavering. And it *was* a battle, of a sort more common now than that of arms; and who shall say, less real than it? Surely, they were fighting for their hearths and for their altars; such altars and such firesides as they had. And many a city palace, and many a country cottage, were hanging with their owners on the outcome of the day. Each magnate of the market, each leader in the fray, stood surrounded by his staff and subaltern officers; while the telegraph boys and camp-followers rushed hither and thither, and nimble clerks hastened from the room with messages and returned with new supplies.

Near the end of the great arena where the chief point of onslaught seemed to be, stood the standard of the Allegheny Central—Allegheny Central, the great railroad that made their houses and their yachts and carriages for hundreds of the rich, and to which some ten thousand of the poor looked for their daily bread. No great corporation had a better name than this: none was surer, none more favored by widows with their mites, by shrewd lawyers, by banks, and by trustees. A greater power, almost, than the people, in the States through which it ran, it was well and honestly managed, and little in favor with speculators and those who like best of all to win by other people's losses; perhaps the easiest way. This stock had therefore been chosen by the flower of the "bull" army, and was the very wedge of their attack. A great crop had been sown upon its line that year; and about the sign of Allegheny the maddest fight of all was fought. A dense crowd encircled it, a small sea of high hats—some already crushed in the conflict—and a babel of hoarse voices; and even on its outskirts were others madly pushing, pressing to get in. The figures cried went up by leaps at a time—Ninety! Ninety-one! a half! three-quarters! Ninety-two for any part of ten thousand! And the smaller men, who had no thought of purchase at such a time, were drawn in as by a whirlpool, such was the excitement of seeing others get what all were there to make, such was the resistless attraction of success.

Among the men who took no part, but stood curiously, on the outskirts of the fight, were two whose faces and figures would attract you even in that crowd. They were apparently friends; at least, they had come in together. The older was a young man of twenty-four or five, very handsome in his way; that is, he was lithe, graceful, tall, with dark hair neatly cut, a small black moustache, shaped like a gentleman's—it was not the moustache of a gambler, nor yet of an elegant of the dry-goods counter—and, above all, with an indescribable air of high finish and high living. His clothes were beautifully cut; his hands white, his cheeks red, his nervous system evidently in perfect order, and his digestion unimpaired. He came in sauntering, carelessly pointing out the people of interest to his friend; his manner was perfectly indifferent, as he drifted from one sign-post to another, chewing between his lips the green stem of some flower,—as a countryman puts a straw in his mouth when making a horse-trade. He passed by the Allegheny Central and stopped in front of the Louisville and Nashville sign; and no one suspected that he, Charlie Townley, of Townley & Tamms, had just sent brokers into the heat of the fight, by order of headquarters, to sell twenty thousand shares of the Allegheny Central itself. He cast no glance behind him, but was engaged in pointing out to his friend three well-known brokers—one famed for his wit, the other for his wife, and the third, to continue the alliteration, for his wiles. The companion was of different build; but we need not describe him. Arthur Holyoke had arrived in New York the very night before. He had come on from the country with his cousin and her aunt, Mrs. Livingstone, with whom in future Gracie was to live. He had been with Gracie all those weeks since her father's death; but his quick perception had prevented him from speaking to her again of their engagement. Gracie was a girl whose standard of conduct was placed above the plain and obvious right; who would go out of her way to seek duties that were almost romantic, justice more than poetical, motives ethereal, and benefits to others that their better angels might have overlooked. And Arthur was enough of a poet himself to feel that he would not wisely mention love to her for many months at least; not because her father had not approved it, but because he was no longer there to approve.

When Judge Holyoke had written to his sister-in-law about Arthur, Mrs. Livingstone had spoken at once to Mr. Townley, who was an old friend of hers; and he had promptly offered to let Arthur serve an apprenticeship in his own business. Mr. Townley, the old gentleman, that is; for Charlie, despite all his finish and importance, was but a line-officer, representing them actively in the field. He was only a far-off orphan cousin of Mr. Townley's, and a clerk in the firm of Townley & Tamms, on a salary of $2500 a year. But his alertness and his wide awake air had gained for him the pleasanter duty of representing the firm in its seat in the Stock Exchange; said seat being, as we have seen, a privilege to get standing-room therein if possible.

No one knew all this of Townley. Most of his merely society acquaintances supposed him to be the senior partner's son; even his intimate friends thought of him as the probable heir, in a fair way to be a partner, an impression which Charlie artfully heightened by his extravagant mode of life when away from his boarding-place, his late hours, and his general inattention to all but the showy work of the firm. It was evident that he took far more interest in keeping his dress correct than in the books of the firm; and, the Stock Exchange once closed, no young man of fashion could be more safely relied upon for an afternoon of sport, or a ride and dinner at the Hill-and-Dale Club.

But all this Arthur had yet to learn; for the present, he was interested in the battle around him, the conflict of the two spirits, hope and despair, affirmation and negation, enterprise and nihilism, in this safety-valve of traffic, where alone the two forces meet directly, each at touch and test with the other. For the Stock Exchange is a kind of gauge, testing the force of the national store and the national need of money; and the bears, too, have their healthy function, keeping down the fever in the body politic.

In the shriek and roar of all the crowd about them, the young men could hardly converse intelligibly; but that might come after; meantime, Arthur was fully employed in seeing. Few of the men showed evidence of much mental anxiety; opposite them, to be sure, a pale-faced little Jew stood in a corner, nervously biting his lips; but most of the crowd were red-faced, and panting with the physical excitement alone, as if it were a foot-ball match. As they looked on, a fat, good-natured-looking broker with an impudent face and a white hat cocked on one side of his head, came out of the Lake Shore crowd, and with the slightest perceptible wink to Townley as he passed, joined the madder fight about Allegheny Central.

"Ninety-one," said he, "a thousand!"

"Come out of the floor," said Townley to Arthur;

"come up-stairs; there's going to be some fun." At first, no one paid any attention to the new-comer; and when our friends got to the gallery, the fat broker was still offering his stock at ninety-one to an unheeding world, and the state of affairs was much the same as before. Only, that at this distance the noise had something in it less human; it was inarticulate, monstrous, and the sight of half a thousand men, struggling, every eye fixed on his neighbor's, made a something awful in the experience, as if they two on-lookers were unseen Valkyrs, looking down upon some battle of the Huns.

"Ninety-one," they heard the newcomer say again; and this time he was answered; for there was a howl of derision, and then a sudden sway in the crowd, and a rush to where he stood. "Ninety and three quarters," said he; "a half," and there was another howl; but by this time the leaders of the inner defence had heard of this flank movement, and their tactics changed. "Ninety!" "Nine and a half!" "Eighty-nine!" "Eight and three quarters!" "A half!"

"Seven, for ten thousand," said the solitary broker, coolly; and the roar doubled in volume, if such a thing were possible; and the rush to sell began, at rapidly dropping figures. The fat, good-natured broker turned away, and started to go, having sold the stock down five points in hardly fifty seconds; when crash! a small soft orange went through the centre of the impudent white hat. With a yell of derision, the crowd· turned their fury upon this;

whack! crack! flew the unlucky hat, from one fist to another, amid the cheers of the multitude, until a well-directed kick landed it beside Arthur in the gallery. This gave a new object to their humor; and with one accord the assemblage began singing in regular well-tempered cadence, evidently referring to Arthur:

> 'Lambs! Lambs!
> One shorn lamb!"

Arthur, blushing, hurried from the gallery; and Charlie Townley followed him, laughing inordinately.

"They'll get used to you in a day or two, my dear fellow," said he. "They wouldn't have done it if they hadn't seen you with me."

When they got into the corridor below, they met the broker of the ravaged hat. He had got another by this time, and winked, this time with a broad smile, at Townley as they came out. "I did that pretty well, I think?" said he.

"First-rate," said Townley. "How much did it cost?"

"Not over twenty thousand shares, I guess, and twelve at least went to your friends. The boys didn't like it, though, did they?" And the man's mouth grinned wider, as he thought of the scene we have described.

"Charge the hat to the pool," laughed Townley. "Who's selling,—not the Old Man?"

"Tammy, I guess," said the other. "Doubt if the Old Man even knows it."

"Ta-ta," said Townley; and they sallied forth, Arthur much wondering at these metropolitan methods of doing business; and Townley completed his duties as host and cicerone by giving him a very elaborate lunch at a down-town club and putting his name down among the candidates for membership. "You needn't feed here unless you like," said he; "but it's so convenient to bring a fellow to." Indeed, Townley had been very friendly to the young countryman; and this was no less than the third club at which he had "put him up" that day. "You can try 'em all, and then make up your mind which ones you'd like to join," said he. At a word of remonstrance from Arthur, he had glibly anticipated all objection. "Now don't talk about extravagance," said he; "I tell you, no fellow ever made money in New York who didn't spend it first." And Arthur had been silenced by this paradoxical philosophy.

Townley's friendship had even extended to providing him with a boarding-place, a room in the house where he himself lodged; and toward this the young fellows took their way, early in the afternoon. Arthur was already tired, with his short and idle day; he was overcome by the rush and the whirl and the magnitude of things. He had heard talked of, had handled, had seen the management of, huge sums of money; he had seen millions in the process of their making; but how to divert a rivulet of the Pactolean stream to himself seemed a greater mystery than ever. It took so much to make so little! Such huge heaps of bullion had to be sweated to yield to the manipulator the clippings of one gold dollar! Truly, on the other hand, Townley talked to him of millions made and lost as if they had been blackberries. It was, "There's old Prime—he made a million in that Panhandle deal," or "There goes poor old Howard—the shorts in Erie used him up," until Arthur saw that he was seeing here a most instructive process: nothing less than the creation and founding of American families. Here were the people, the progenitors of future castes; the sources of inherited estate, of culture, of consideration; this old man with the battered hat, that sharp-faced young Israelite, were the ancestors, the probable fathers and grandfathers of the men and maidens who were to be "society" in the future Republic; the first acquirers of—not the broad acres, but the city lots—the rich houses, the stocks and bonds, the whole equipment of life, that was (if our laws are maintained) to make sleek the *jeunesse dorée* of the twentieth century. A million! It is not much, in many ways, in most ways that we read about in books and bibles; it is not a factor of the Crusades, nor of the War of the Roses, nor yet (as we are informed) of the kingdom of heaven. But most things that Townley saw were multiples of it; and now Townley carefully avoided reading books; for even General Gordon, you remember, writing from Khartoum to posterity, records the reflection that mankind and his works are governed by his ventral tube. Now of ventral tubes, a million is the deity; books should, as they used to, speak to souls. And Arthur, thinking of all this, who had marvelled first at all their eagerness, now wondered rather at their carelessness; of these men, taking and losing such things so lightly.

Arthur could not have had a better cicerone than Charlie Townley. He knew his New York like the inside of his pocket; its streets, its ways, its women, its wiles, its heroes and its favorites; its eating places, drinking places, breathing places; its getting up and its lying down. When they passed Fourteenth Street, his manner changed very apparently; the æsthetic overcame the practical; the hard shine of millions was displaced by the softer radiance of women's eyes. Many of these same eyes were, in their turn, riveted by the display of women's wares in the shop-windows about Union Square, which gave Townley the opportunity of gazing at his ease; although, it must be owned, if any of these eyes looked up and met his own, he seemed little disconcerted.

They stopped and made a call at the Columbian Club, which was crowded with men, breaking the long journey homeward to their firesides, domestic or otherwise. And as, in some country hamlet of the Middle Ages, we can fancy the little ale-house, standing on the heath, midway; Jock and Dickon are plodding home tired from the long day's plowing; behind this one smoking chimney the cold November sky lowers drearily, the last pale tints of the tired day are fading, and the common is bare, and the naked moorland left to the wolves; and the two men stop in a moment at the Cat-and-Fiddle to have a bite and a sup, a cup around the tavern-fire, and a bit of human companionship, to talk about the price of corn, and of Hodge the tinker's son and Joan his sweetheart, and the doings of the new squire, whose round brown towers peep from the coppice of the distant park—so, too, here in our New York, the jaded men drop in, and chat about the price of stocks, their neighbor's horses and his wife, and have a glass of bitters round the fire. Townley took vermouth, lamenting bitterly that his health permitted nothing stronger; but other paler men than he administered brandy-cocktails unto themselves, or pick-me-ups of gin. Here Charlie brushed himself, and took his silver-headed cane; and again the pair sallied forth upon their journey, crossing Madison Square and striking up the Avenue. Many damsels, richly robed, now lit up the long way; there is usually a received type at any period for the outdoor gorgeousness of womankind, and this year it was blue—a walking-suit of blue, from neck to heel, close-fitting, and all of velvet. Dozens and scores of velvet gowns they passed, and Arthur noticed that his guide, philosopher, and friend looked at many of them as if they were familiar sights, but bowed to few. Now there had been many, in Union Square, to whom he had nodded, at the least. He seemed to read Arthur's thoughts, for he said:

"These are all off-side girls. You don't see the others out at this time."

"What do you mean?" said Arthur.

"Why, they're not in society, you know." And he lifted his hat to one of them, who had given him a most *empressé* bow, including in it Arthur. "There's one of the prettiest girls in town," said he, meditatively; "Kitty Farnum. They're awfully rich, too; old Farnum's got no end of money." This thought seemed to depress Charlie for a minute, and they walked on in silence. Now Arthur had met Miss Farnum at a New Haven ball, where she had been a very proud belle indeed.

"There," said Townley, at last, as they crossed a side-street, "is Mrs. Levison Gower's." There was a certain reverence in his tone, as he said this, that his voice had not yet shown in all that day, and Arthur looked with a proper admiration, though not clearly understanding why, at the house we have already described.

Their lodgings were near by (so Townley always spoke of the boarding-house where he lived), and the young men separated to dress for dinner. Arthur had been rather surprised that so elegant a person lived in a boarding-house at all; but the fact was, Townley preferred to use his money elsewhere than at home. But he never dined with the other inhabitants; in fact, his acquaintance with them was extremely slight, as he always breakfasted in his room; and to-night he put a finishing touch upon his hospitality by inviting Arthur to a very pretty little dinner at the Piccadilly Club. But after this, Townley had an engagement, and Arthur was left to his own devices. He smoked his cigar and read the evening paper; then he began an article in the *Edinburgh Review*, took up the *Spectator*, and ended with *Punch;* after which he became unoccupied, and his spirits dropped visibly.

By this time several men had strolled in; there was

much laughing and gay spirits; around him were all the luxuries of mind and body that the inventive bachelor mind has yet devised for the comfort of either such part of himself. But as Arthur leaned back in the deep, throne-like leather chair and sipped (if one may so say) his *reina victoria*, his consciousness went back to a certain sunny hillside, with the light of the rich autumn morning, and the joyous beat of the hoofs upon the dewy grass.

He had been to see Gracie only the day before; but he drew on his overcoat and walked around to the Livingstones. A light was in the second-story window of the high house; and he rang the bell hopefully.

"Mrs. Livingstone?"

"Not at home," said the man, gravely.

"Is—is Miss Holyoke in?"

"The ladies are out, sir," said the man, decidedly.

"I will not leave a card," said Arthur, answering the man's gesture; and he walked sadly back to the club-house.

Surely, Arthur felt, the forms of life and the trammels of the great city were coming home to him.

## CHAPTER VIII.

### ARTHUR SEES MORE OF THE WORLD.

HE firm of Townley & Tamms were of the oldest and best-known bankers and brokers in the Street. Mr. Townley had been known in New York over fifty years; he had a taste for art, and was a director in the Allegheny Central Railroad. Tamms was a newer man; a younger man with a square head, stiff red beard, broad stubby fingers, and great business ability. Arthur was expected to be there a little after nine in the morning, which made it necessary for him to breakfast at the boarding-house on Fifth Avenue at sharp eight. Most of the other men did the same, except Townley, who had his coffee in his room.

These men were not interesting; in fact, they seemed to Arthur singularly unattractive. Their faces were all chopped or rough-hewn into one prevailing expression, as rows of trees by the sea-shore are bent the same way by the wind. It would be best described as a look of eagerness; their eyes were sharp and piercing, and they even ate their breakfast eagerly. They all seemed common to Arthur; and he one of them, reduced to his lowest terms of expression, a unit of population, nothing more. They were all hurrying through breakfast, folding their napkins, putting on their great-coats, and going down town for money, and for nothing else; so was he. To be sure, he had a woman he loved at the end of it; but so, perhaps, had they.

Arthur rose impatiently, leaving his second egg, and passed out, receiving a clipped or half-audible "good-morning" from most of his fellow-boarders; the sort of salutation that hurried men may give who must still dimly remember or recognize, while they may regret, the necessity for small social courtesies. He put on his overcoat, and started walking down the Avenue.

There was no reasoning himself out of it, his spirits drooped; not with the sentimental and romantic melancholy of a young man (which is a sort of pleasant sadness, and results in nothing worse than pessimistic poems, nocturnal rambles, and a slightly increased consumption of narcotics and stimulants), but with that more practical, less tolerable, discontent which the grown man has in moments when the conviction is irresistibly borne in upon him that his position in the world is not a brilliant one, and his worth, to make the best of it, is unappreciated. For those who choose to be sad over these things there is no remedy. And in New York, he felt himself—number one million three hundred and fifty-six thousand two hundred and two.

Arthur had, too, a strong desire to go and see Gracie, much as a child wants to go to its mother's lap and cry. But how much farther off she seemed than if they had stayed at Great Barrington! It was impossible, of course, for him to see her; she had insisted that there should be no announced engagement between them. He doubted even if Mrs. Livingstone knew of it. But how long it would be before they could be married, before they could live in a house—in a house like that one there, for instance! And Arthur waved his cane unconsciously at a house on the corner of Thirty-second Street, in which, though ugly enough outside, it seemed to him it might be reasonably possible for him to maintain his own identity and their dignity of life. Then he remembered that Townley had pointed it out to him the day before as Mrs. Levison Gower's house, and that he had been introduced to her at Lenox. Probably she would not remember him now.

Going to the office, he sought that corner of a desk which was in the future to be his station in the world. Townley arrived late, and gave him a hasty nod; it was a busy day, and he had been up late in the night at the first ball of the season. Arthur's work that day consisted in writing letters for the firm, following Mr. Tamms's hastily pencilled instructions; but the first letter he wrote of all was not signed by the firm signature, and it bore the address "Miss Holyoke, care of Mrs. Richard Livingstone, 6 W. ——th Street, City." Such letters as these it is that make the world go on; and truly they are more important than even the foreign mail of Messrs. Townley & Tamms. This relieved his mind, and the daily labor for his daily bread coming happily in to sweeten his meditations, he got fairly through to four o'clock, when Townley proposed that they should go to drive.

Arthur protested his duty to his employers.

"Nonsense," said Charlie; "the governor knows you've got to get into harness by degrees. Besides, he doesn't pay you anything for your services—and they arn't worth anything, yet," he added. The last argument was unanswerable.

Charlie's cart (it is quite impossible for us, who have known him nearly two days, to call him Townley any more) was very high, very thick, and very heavy, and was purchased in Long Acre; the horses, which answered the same description, were also imported; and the harness, which corresponded to the cart in thickness and heaviness, came from Cheapside. Townley's coat, clothes, top-hat, whip, and gloves were all native of Bond Street or Piccadilly; and in fact, the only thing about him which was produced fairly beyond the London bills of mortality was the very undoubted case of green Havana cigars that he offered to Arthur the moment they had left the Park. They drove up Fifth Avenue, past the same procession of pedestrians they had seen the day before, and Arthur could not but note how much more interesting they seemed to their fellow-creatures from the summit of their dog-cart, and how the interest had become mutual as they entered the Park and joined the procession of T-carts, phaetons, and victorias. He admired the dexterity with which Charlie kept the tandem-reins and the whip properly assorted in his left hand, while the right was continually occupied in raising his hat to pretty women who had bowed.

The Hill-and-Dale Club, the newly established country institution, a sort of shrine or sacred grove whither city folk betook themselves to commune with nature, was in Westchester County, not far from the historic banks of the Bronx. An old country mansion, former quarters of Continental generals, rendezvous of Skinners and Cowboys, had been bought, adorned, developed, provided with numerous easy chairs and sporting prints; and lo! it was a club. The wide lawn in front was turned into a half-mile track for running races; a shooting range and tennis-grounds were made behind; and you had a small Arcadia for mundane pleasures. Here could tired mortals loaf, chat, eat, drink, smoke, bet, gamble, race, take exercise, and see their fellow-creatures and their wives and cattle. Expatriated Britons found here a blessed spot of rest, a simulacrum of home, where trotting races were tabooed, where you were waited on by stunted grooms, and could ride after your hounds, and always turned to the left in passing. Before this Elysium did Charlie pull up, and throwing the reins to a stable-boy, led Arthur to the inner Penetralia. After inscribing his name in the club-book (making the fourth, thought Arthur) they went to the smoke-room, where they met a dozen of the fellows (some of whose faces seemed already familiar to him) and executed the customary libation. Here Charlie stood boldly up to a composite ambrosia of which the base was brandy, saying that he thought a fellow deserved it after that drive. Some conversation followed; but I sadly fear 'twould not be worth the trouble of reporting in cold print. Then Charlie proposed they should go look at the stables; and they did.

"That is the beast for you," he said, pointing to a gaunt, fiery-eyed creature with a close-cropped tail. "Vincent Duval is going abroad, and you can have him for four hundred."

"But, my dear fellow, I can't——"

"Nonsense, Holy," said Charlie familiarly falling into the nickname that then and there sprang full-grown like Minerva from his inventive brain. "Look here, young fellow, I want to give you some advice. Let's go in and smoke on the piazza." They found easy seats above the broad green lawn, half across which reached already the shadows of a belt of huge bare forest trees that rimmed in the western end; and there, inspired by tobacco and the beauty of the scene, did Charles Townley deliver himself as follows:

"My dear boy, we live in a great country; and in a free country a man can make himself just what he likes. You can pick out just the class in life that suits you best. This is the critical moment; and you must decide whether to be a two-thousand-dollar clerk all your life, a ten-thousand bachelor, or a millionaire. If you rate yourself at the two-thousand gauge, the world will treat you accordingly; if you spend twenty thousand, the world, sooner or later, will give it to you. There's Jimmy De Witt, for instance; after the old man busted, he hadn't a sous markee—what was the result? He had an excellent taste in cigars and wine, knew everybody, told a good story—you know what a handsome fellow he is?—no end of style, and the best judge of a canvas-back duck I ever saw. Everybody said such a fellow couldn't be left to starve. So old Duval found him a place as treasurer of one of his leased railroads down in Pennsylvania, where all he has to do is to sign the lessee's accounts; he did this submissively, and it gave him ten thousand a year. Then we made him manager of the Manhattan Jockey Club—that gave him six thousand more; then he makes a little at whist, and never pays his bills, and somehow or other manages to make both ends meet. And now they say he's going to marry Pussie Duval. Do you suppose he'd ever have been more than a poor devil of a clerk, like me, if he'd tried economy?" And Charlie leaned back and puffed his cigar triumphantly.

"But I mean to pay my bills," said Arthur.

"Well, he will, too, in time," said Charlie.

Arthur smiled to himself, and reflected that the corruptions of New York were rather clumsy, after all, and its snares and temptations a trifle worn-out and crude; but he said nothing, and by this time their tandem was brought around and they whirled off to the city. When they got home, he found a note:

"Mr. and Mrs. William H. Farnum request the pleasure — Mr. Holyoke's company — small party, Thursday the twenty-eighth," etc., etc.

He tossed it over to Charlie. "Since you're such a social mentor, what must I do to that?" said he.

"Decline it, of course," said the other; "I've got one myself; you see they saw us together. You mustn't show up, the first time, at the Farnums."

Arthur was nettled. "I shall do nothing of the kind," said he. "I shall accept it."

"As you like," laughed the other, good-naturedly. "I shall accept, too, as far as that goes; but you needn't go. They can put it in the newspaper that I was there, if they like." Arthur opened his eyes; what sort of young nobleman, then, was his friend, disguised as a clerk upon a salary?

"Perhaps you object to my calling on the Livingstones?" said he, with biting sarcasm.

"Not at all—the Livingstones are all right," said unconscious Charlie. "But don't go to-night; come to the opera with me. In fact, you can't make calls in the evening any more, you know."

"What opera is it?"

"I don't know," said Charlie, serenely. "What does it matter?"

Arthur had nothing to reply to this; and the opera turned out to be "Linda." But Charlie was right; the audience proved more interesting. Here was a dress parade of all that was most fashionable in New York; for it was a great night, the first of the season, and every one was anxious to put herself *en évidence.* Townley was out of his seat three quarters of the time; and Arthur paid little attention to what was going on on the stage. The wicked marquis came, saw, and sought to conquer; the sentimental young heroine sighed and suffered, repelled both the marquis and his diamonds, and fled from the wilds of Chamounix to the seclusion and safety of Paris; and the jewelled ladies in the boxes (familiar with this tale) gave it now and then their perfunctory attention, recognizing that all this drama was being well and properly done, the correct thing, according to the conventions of the stage. Directly opposite him, in one of the grand-tier boxes, were three women who attracted his eyes unwittingly. Two of them were young, and both were beautiful; one, with heavy black hair and fair young shoulders sitting quietly; the other not quite so pretty, but with an indescribable air of complete fashion, a blonde with the bust of a Hebe, talking with animation to quite a little group of male figures, dimly visible in the back of the box; and the third a woman of almost middle age, with the figure of a Titian Venus and hair of an indescribable ashen yellow. Surely he knew that face?

"Who is that in the box opposite—the middle one, I mean, with the two beauties?"

Charlie lifted his opera glass, and then as quickly dropped it. "She would thank you," he said, "for your two beauties. She is the only married woman of her set who isn't afraid to have pretty young girls about her. That's Mrs. Gower, and she's looking at you, too."

Arthur looked up and met her eye; she made a

very slight but unmistakable inclination of her head, and Arthur bowed.

" You're in luck, young 'un," said Townley. " Now you've got to go and speak to her."

" Have I ? " said Arthur. " I know her very slightly."

" She doesn't seem to think so, and you needn't remind her of it," said Charlie, the worldling ; and Arthur, having noted the number of the box from the end of the row, started on his quest. He came to the door that seemed to be the seventh in number from the stage, and paused a minute with his hand upon the knob. What young man's heart, however much its pulsations may be dedicated to another, does not beat awkwardly when he is on the point of addressing three lovely women, two of them quite unknown, the other nearly so ? Then again, suppose he had counted wrong, and not got into the right box ?

His hesitation was cut short by the sudden opening of the door and the exit of a gentleman from within. Before it closed, Arthur had plunged boldly into the dark anteroom, and was blinking earnestly out from it, somewhat dazzled by the blaze of light and the gleam of the three pairs of white shoulders in front.

" Ah, Mr. Holyoke, I hoped you would come—Mr. Wemyss, Mr. Holyoke—Miss Duval, Mrs. Malgam, Mr. Holyoke, of——"

" Of New York, I believe," said Arthur, bowing, and accepting the chair which the gentleman addressed as Wemyss had given up, at a look from Mrs.

Gower. Certainly, Mrs. Gower had charming manners, he thought; and it was very pleasant of her to be pleasant to him.

"Of New York? I am so glad—I knew that Great Barrington was only your summer home, but I had feared that you were wedded to Boston. Where is Miss Holyoke?" Mrs. Gower added, without apparent malice; and Arthur cursed himself inwardly as he felt that he was blushing.

"She is living with her aunt, Mrs. Livingstone," said he. And then, with a wild attempt at changing the subject, "Do you like 'Linda,' Miss Duval?"

(Crash! went the big drums; whizz, whizz, in cadence came the fiddles. The wicked marquis, who had also turned up in Paris, was at his old tricks again.)

"I think it is perfectly sweet," said Miss Duval. "Patti does it so well!"

"It must be very pleasant for her to have you here," said Mrs. Gower, innocently. "I was so sorry to hear of poor Judge Holyoke's death. And so you have come to settle in New York? How delightful! Let me see—I have not seen you since last summer, at Lenox, have I?"

"It is very kind of you to remember me," said Arthur.

"Or was it Lenox?" Mrs. Gower went on. "I remember seeing Miss Holyoke one day as I drove by, in Great Barrington," she added naïvely.

Arthur felt that she was watching him, and was seeking for a reply, when fortunately Linda came forward, almost under the box, and told in a long aria, with many trills and quavers, with what scorn she repelled the marquis's advances; the marquis, in the meantime, waiting discreetly at the back of the stage until she had had her *encore* and had flung madly out of his ancestral mansion. This being the musical moment of the evening, all paid rapt attention; and when the last *roulade* was over Mrs. Gower rose and they all proceeded to help with opera cloaks and shawls. "Mr. Holyoke, you must come and dine with me—are you engaged—let me see—a week from Friday?"

"You are very kind," said Arthur. "No, I think not."

"Then I shall expect you—at half-past seven, mind,"—and our hero had the felicity of walking with Mrs. Gower to her carriage, the others coming after them, with the two young ladies. The carriage-door closed with a snap, leaving Arthur with Wemyss and the other man, whom he did not know. Wemyss seemed to feel that their acquaintance had come to an end; so there was nothing left for Arthur but to return to Charlie Townley.

"What the deuce is Mrs. Lucie up to now?" thought he, when Arthur had recounted to him his adventures; but he said nothing; and Arthur was left for the last act to give his entire attention to the stage. Virtue triumphed, and Vice (who, as represented in the person of the lively marquis, seemed to be a pretty good sort of fellow after all—an amiable rascal, the kind of chap of whom you would feel inclined to ask, What would he like to drink?) was duly forgiven; and he showered his diamonds as wedding-gifts upon the bride. So that Linda, thrice fortunate Linda, not only followed the paths of virtue, but got her lover and the diamonds into the bargain; and with this moral and a Welsh rarebit Arthur and his friend sought home and pleasant dreams.

## CHAPTER IX.

### ARTHUR GETS ON IN THE WORLD.

THERE should never be more than six at a dinner, unless there are fourteen. You can have your dinner either a parlor comedy or a spectacular play: but you must choose which you will have. Mrs. Gower was well aware of this; and hers consisted of a leading lady, a first young lady, a *soubrette*, a virtuous hero, a heavy villain, and a lover. With these ingredients, you may have a very pleasant dinner; but you must be a sufficiently skilful observer of humanity to detect the *rôle*. For people say that there are not such *rôles* any more, and that we are all indifferent and good-natured, and none of us heavy villains.

Arthur was too inexperienced for this; for, like all young men, he also supposed that all these characters were conventional fictions of the stage. He did not believe in villains. Perhaps it would repay us to formulate Arthur's views, as those of a respectable young New Englander of good education and bringing-up, with whose fortunes in life our book is largely concerned. Roughly expressed, they might be put in canons, much as follows:

I. The world is in the main desirous of realizing the greatest good of the greatest number.

II. Unfortunate necessities—the primal curse of labor, or what not—occupy the greater part of the time of the greater number with sustaining life; so the leisure of the fortunate few is doubly pledged to the discovery and attainment of the object before mentioned.

III. Money is a regrettable necessity; but its acquirement, even from the selfish point of view, is but a means to an end. That end, where personal, is the enjoyment of the pleasures of life—*i.e.*, literature, art, refined society, travel, and health. The larger end is intelligent charity, or public work.

IV. Vice exists, like vermin, as a repulsive vulgarity.

V. Crime exists pathologically—*i.e.*, it is either an abnormal disease, or the consequence of a pitiable weakness.

VI. Honesty is the first virtue of the greater number; honor, which is honesty with a flower added, is the peculiar virtue of a gentleman.

VII. Gentlemen are honorable and brave; ladies are like Shelley's heroines, or the ladies in the Idylls of the King.

VIII. The chiefest quality of humanity is love; and the object of all human endeavor is to observe and avail itself of the love of that being which is not humanity.

So much for his ethics; and, as we have said Arthur was a poet, it may not come amiss to add an approximation of his theory of æsthetics. This was, in brief:

IX. All beauty is the visible evidence of the love of God ; nature is a divine manifestation ; and literature, art, and music are the language in which humanity may reply. Thus, in particular, all highest poetry is but this—the discovery of the love of God.

Such were his tenets, the standard of Arthur's exalted moments, as he supposed them then to be of others. In trying to live by them, he knew that he was weak, as all men are. Of all the people whom he knew, Gracie Holyoke alone seemed always to observe them.

So it may well be that Arthur did not, on that night, justly estimate the worth of those about him. He had, simply, a very enjoyable dinner ; he was innocently pleased with the glitter of the glass, the sparkle of the diamonds, the richness of the china, the beauty of the women, the finish of their talk ; it was a venial sin for him to like the food and wines,—but there was perhaps one other ingredient in his pleasure, the subtilest of all, which escaped him. Leaving this, for his account, let us speak of the others.

And here we may save space and the wearied reader's attention, for they had no ethics and no æsthetics ; and their philosophy of life was simple. Probably their sensual sin was not so great as Arthur's—for terrapin and duck were a weariness to most of them —but in the *summum bonum* they all agreed. To be not as others are, and have those others know it—such was their simple creed. Jimmy De Witt was on the whole the most innocent ; his being yearned for horses and yachts, even if they were not all the fastest; and he was not a bad fellow, a great friend of Lucie Gower himself, and so sitting *in loco conjugis*, for the husband of the hostess was absent. To him came next Mrs. Malgam, who was—but all the world, yea, even to the uttermost bounds thereof where the society newspapers do permeate, knows all about Mrs. Malgam. Upon De Witt's other side, convenient, Miss Duval—"Pussie" Duval, grand-daughter of Antoine of that ilk who had kept the little barber shop down on Chambers Street; then Arthur, on Mrs. Gower's right; and on her left Caryl Wemyss again, a modern Boston Faust, son of the great poet who was afterwards minister to Austria; his son, thus born to the purple of diplomacy, had lived in Paris, London, and Vienna, executed plays, poems, criticisms, music, and painting, and, at thirty-five, had discovered the hollowness of things, having himself become perfect in all of them. So he became a critic of civilization—and this is how he was not as other men—for it was the era of the decadence, and he the Cassandra who foresaw it. Mrs. Gower, our leading lady, made the sixth.

From being the lonely Cinderella of an unexplored fireside, Flossie had grown to be one of the most famed and accomplished hostesses in all New York. She had the tact of knowing what topics would touch the souls of the men and move the women's hearts, and of leading the conversation up to these without apparent effort or insolent dictation. She could make Strephon talk to Chloe, or Marguerite to Faust, without taking the awkward pair by the elbows and knocking their heads together. And all this sweetly, simply, while reserving the preferred *rôle* to herself, as a carver justly sets aside for his own use his favorite bit of venison. Ordinarily, these six people—four of them, surely—would have talked about other people and their possessions; but Mrs. Flossie rightly fancied that Arthur, knowing little of the world, could only talk about books, or at most, about the world in the abstract. Taking up the talk where it was left at the opera, an early speech from Arthur to the effect that he did not mean to go much into society gave her the necessary opening.

"You must not do so," said she. "Society is as important to a young man as work. Is it not, Mr. Wemyss?" (One of the charms of this woman's cleverness was that indefinable quality of humor which consists in the relish of incongruities; her reference to Wemyss for the uses of work, for instance.)

"Society is sour grapes to those beyond its pale," said Wemyss, "but those who can value it press from it the wine of life." (Wemyss gave a little laugh, to indicate that he did not mean to be taken as a prig.) "Seriously," he added, "no person of wide intelligence can afford to ignore the best society of a nation, whatever it be, for it represents its essence and its tendency. It is the liquid glass of champagne left in the frozen bottle, and has more flavor than all the rest, it is the flower, which is at once the present's culmination and the future's seed."

"Oh, that is so true!" cried Pussie Duval. Miss Duval would have made the same remark had Mr.

Wemyss asserted that abuse of stimulants was the secret of Hegel. The others stared rather blankly. Arthur had never considered it quite so seriously; and to Mrs. Malgam and Jimmy De Witt, interpreting it esoterically, society needed no more explanation than the Ding an Sich.

"Then again," said Wemyss, "did you ever go to a party of the people? I don't mean at Washington—there they get a little rubbed off—but at home. Well, I went to one, once—some people who had lived for many years in the house next to mine on Beacon Street—and I do assure you, it was *triste à faire peur;* they thought you were flippant if you even smiled, and took offence, like awkward boys and girls, at the least informality. One longed for a Lovelace, *si ce n'était que pour les chiffonner.* Now, in the world, one's manners are simple, easy; you have some liberty; people don't take offence—*il n'y a jamais de mal en bonne compagnie.* But the trouble with society in this country is," he continued, "that it has no meaning. Now it must have a meaning to be interesting; it must mean either love or politics. In France, if not in England, it has both. But here, all the meaning of it stops when one is married."

"Thank you," said Flossie.

"Madame," said Wemyss, "you are one of the three sirens, singing in the twilight of the world. But in this dark night about you, society exists only to make all young men get married. In the old time, it had a more serious reason for being. In courts where there was a more social element in politics, intrigues were always quasi-political; parties were made at evening parties; and ministries were entered from boudoirs; you met the Opposition in his salon, and embraced the minister's principles with—"

"Look out, Mr. Wemyss," said Mrs. Gower, playfully.

—"when you paid a compliment to his wife. But here, society and politics are worlds mutually exclusive; how would the Governor of the State appear at a dinner-party? Politically, the best people are laid on the shelf, like rare china. Society's only recognized function is to bring young people together; when brought together, they are supposed to join hands and step aside; it is a marriage-brokerage board, and its aim is merely matrimony."

"What a social failure you must be, Mr. Wemyss," said Flossie.

"In America," retorted Wemyss. "But even a man who has not married has some social rights. I like a society of men and women—not of Jacks and Gills. But if I tell Mrs. Grundy her gown is becoming, likely as not she'll call for the police, in this country."

"I think she'll take a bit more than that without bolting," laughed Jimmy De Witt.

"The fact is," said Wemyss, who felt that he was becoming epigrammatic, "all worldly pleasures, from the original apple, rest on the taste of the forbidden fruit. The joys of war, the delights of business, the pleasures of gossip, the satisfaction of swearing,—they're all the fun of breaking some commandment.

Voltaire never would have put pen to paper but for the first; the pleasure of art is to worship graven images; the spice of newspapers is the false witness that they bear against your neighbor. And what becomes of fashionable life without the tenth, or a faint and ever-present memory of the seventh? Now all Americans covet their neighbor's bank-account; but they are far too practical to covet their neighbor's wife. Positively, we are too virtuous to be happy: for this Arcadian state of things makes society necessarily dull. Like most of the devil's institutions, it requires considerable red pepper."

Arthur stared at Wemyss, much astonished; but all three ladies seemed to take it as very excellent fooling indeed. Even Jimmy looked as if he didn't wholly understand it, but knew it must be very good.

"But it's the paradise of girls. It offers every opportunity to ardent youth. It shows its prizes in a glamour of light and dress-making, just as a Parisian shopkeeper puts gas-reflectors before his window. Bright eyes and white shoulders are garnished in extraordinary silks and satins; a blare of fiddles and trumpets fills up vacancies in their intellect; and thus, with all their charms enhanced, they are dangled before the masculine eye when his discernment has been previously befuddled with champagne?"

"Positively," laughed Mrs. Gower, "we must leave you to your cigars. There's no knowing what you'll be saying next—and before an unmarried lady, too. Pussie, my dear, go out first, and deliver Mr. Wemyss from temptation."

The three ladies rose, and the men drew back their chairs.

"You must really look out, Mr. Wemyss," said Mrs. Malgam; "in one of your lyric moments you'll forget that some girl isn't married, and be engaged before you know it."

Wemyss shuddered. "Ah, my dear lady, I wish I could forget that you were married——"

"Hush, hush," cried Mrs. Gower, rapping Wemyss's knuckles with her fan, "and *soyez sage*, when we are gone."

But when left to themselves, Mr. Wemyss said little besides a word or two about literature and art. His conversation might have been a model to a governess fresh from boarding-school. Jimmy De Witt told a few stories, and Arthur had great difficulty in talking at all. Mr. Wemyss snubbed them both, as was his habit with intellectual inferiors; and after a very short cigar, they all repaired to the drawing-room, where little happened that Arthur saw; for, as all the company save Mrs. Gower seemed to regard him as an interloping hobbledehoy, to be tolerated only as a fantasy of Mrs. Gower's, he shortly and not over-gracefully took his leave.

He walked to the club, and smoked, somewhat nettled with things in general, and full of much desire to punch Mr. Caryl Wemyss's elegant head. Others had had that mood before Arthur; but you see our hero is by no means an exceptional personage. Being, however, the best we have got, we feel bound to see him through. Still, no Loyola would have chosen that dinner to be the time and place to reply to Wemyss with the propositions we have stated for Arthur at the beginning of this chapter; and the young idealist had wisely held his peace.

# CHAPTER X.

## IN WHICH ARTHUR MEETS A WEARIED SOUL.

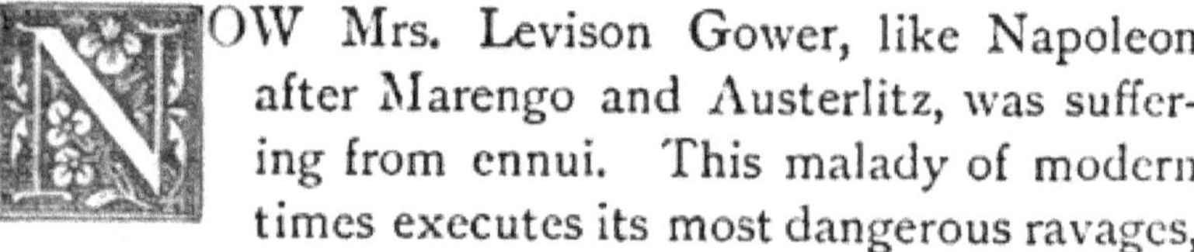

NOW Mrs. Levison Gower, like Napoleon after Marengo and Austerlitz, was suffering from ennui. This malady of modern times executes its most dangerous ravages, like the gout, only among those who can afford it. It is a sort of king's evil, privileged to the nobility and gentry; and that Flossie Starbuck's healthy constitution ever succumbed to it is testimony—is it not?—to her extraordinary natural refinement: for born to it she certainly was not. She was a woman of some five-and-thirty summers—let us rather say, of some fifteen seasons, as being both politer and more closely descriptive—but with her thick blonde hair and her youthful figure, round and lithe as any girl's, she was divine still in a riding-habit or a ball-dress, and could face the daylight of a north window without flinching. But the fact was, this Marguerite in appearance had been out fifteen seasons; if not so erudite as Faust, she was even more *blasée* with the world; kermesses had become stupid, interesting young men with rapiers and mysterious attendants in red had lost their interest, even jewels had ceased to make her heart beat as of yore: Mephistopheles alone remained eternal.

All the joys of her girl's ambition she had tasted to the full. Every social eminence that she had seen, she had in turn attained. Each one of the diversions of a woman of fashion, she had pushed to its ultimate—gayety pure and simple, haughty and costly exclusiveness, travel and adventure, the patronage of literature and art, even religion and charity. But Mrs. Gower had been so unfortunate as to take her greatest pleasure at the beginning of her young life. Compared with that triumphal moment when first, surrounded by ladies with names she had hitherto known only in the newspapers, she had taken her place among the patronesses of the F. F. V. Ball as "Mrs. Levison Gower, Jr."—what were all the second-hand joys of the imagination, of looking at books and pictures, even the more solid satisfactions of houses, opera-boxes, horses and liveries, or of social power? The life of the world was Mrs. Gower's book; she made her own drama; any starveling in a garret could have the other kind. But that earliest pleasure was indeed divine. She had met the enemy, and made them hers. And how the dowagers had scowled at her, at first! The haughty Vans, the poor and lofty matrons of the old manorial families of New York, exemplary, unapproachable, Presbyterian. She had routed them with a flirt of her fan; she had dared their feudal armor with her bared fair breast. Their dowdy daughters had been snuffed out of fashion like candles in electric light; a spark of wit had made them laughable, a glance of her soft eyes had brought their brothers to her feet. Her *chic* had won the day, and soon they all began to copy her. Her phaeton and her ponies replaced the antiquated family rockaways; her style made up for breeding, and largely it was Flossie's work that money in New York became the all-in-all, and blood an antiquated prejudice to jest at. And all the Einsteins and the Malgams and Duvals made haste to cluster under Flossie's standard, wanting such a leader; and we Americans throw up our hats and cry how nice and democratic is the change—do we not? How proud was simple Lucie Gower to find him husband to a goddess! How natural for Caryl Wemyss to worship her, the spirit of his favorite decadence!

But still, that early and delightful triumph had been the climax of her life, as it now seemed; all other pleasures had proved silly or insipid. What gratification was it to her to move in the best society? The whole pleasure lay in getting there. She cared nothing for the best society, except in so far as she could humble it, and make it hers. Secretly, Flossie found more sympathy in her new friends of the Duval set than in the old-fashioned Van Kulls and Breviers of her husband's family. The best people bored her. But the Duvals were nothing if not amusing, and had a truly French horror of the *ennuyeux*.

But she was a leader of it; there was still some satisfaction left in that. Her leadership was unquestioned; through whatever will-of-the-wisp of folly she chose to lead the dance, the many (and these the richest, newest, and most prominent) would follow. Mrs. Malgam alone could for a moment contest her prominence—"Baby" Malgam, whose fashionable inanity and lazy beauty had proved almost as good cards as Flossie's cleverness. And the further she went, the faster would her people follow; for the Duvals and Einsteins were wild to *écraser*, by ostentation of their wealth, all those whose position rested on the slightest shadow of superiority that money could not buy. All these people, Flossie knew, would hail her as a leader and grovel at her feet; she, who represented, for her husband's family, an older style than theirs, if she would be with them and of them. And the old style of things, which had satisfied her for fifteen years, was just now, certainly, beginning to bore her. The drama of her life lacked action.

Well: whither should she lead? What next? Charity, intellect, art, and dancing had been worn to the last thread; hounds and horses were in, just now; and society, in pink coats and silk jockey-caps, was making nature's acquaintance on Long Island and in Westchester County. But what on earth or in the waters under the earth was to come after this, Mrs. Gower did not yet know. Still, it was comforting to feel that when she *did* know, it would be done; this was certainly a pleasure; perhaps the only real one left to poor Flossie in her years of disillusion. As a *parvenue*, she was never tired of having her will over those who had been born her superiors; and it is a delightful novelty that in these days of no prejudices a *parvenue* need no longer climb to the level of society, but will find it both less troublesome and more tickling to the vanity to pull society down to her.

The free fancy of Mrs. Gower's matron meditation was interrupted by the entrance of a *deus* with a *machina*—in other words, by a footman with Mr. Caryl Wemyss's visiting-card.

"Is Mrs. Gower at home?" said the footman; and he commanded larger wages for the subtle infusion of "her ladyship" he was able to give a plain American patronymic if used in the third person. He also had calves; and made no other than a financial objection to silk stockings, if required.

"Let him come in," said Flossie; and she drew a footstool to her and disposed herself more at ease, before the wide wood-fire.

Wemyss entered perfectly. There were two manners of meeting ladies most in vogue at this time, which may perhaps be described as the *horsey* and the *cavalier*. Of the former, which was perhaps the more fashionable, Jimmy De Witt was an excellent example; he would have come in with boisterous *bonhomie*, a stable-boy's story, or a blunt approval of Flossie's pretty ankle, which was being warmed before the fire; but Wemyss affected the old-fashioned, and was pleased to be conscious that his manners were, as he would have said, *de vieille roche.* He took her hand and bowed deeply over it, as if he wanted to kiss it, but did not dare; then, drawing a low ottoman in front of the fire, he sat down, as it were, at her feet.

"Well, Mr. Wemyss, how did you find Boston?" said Mrs. Gower, by way of beginning.

"Boston, my dear Mrs. Gower, is impossible.

There used to be some originals, but now there are only left their country acquaintances, or their self-imposed biographers, who feebly seek to shine by their reflected light. Emerson might do, for the provinces; but Emerson's country neighbors! Their society is one of *ganaches* and *femmes précieuses*—oh, such precious women!—of circles, coteries, and clubs, with every knowledge but the *savoir faire* and every science but the *savoir vivre!*"

"But," said Mrs. Gower, "surely I have seen some very civilized Bostonians, at Newport, in the summer?"

"You have—like a stage procession," said Wemyss with a smile. "And so, if you stand long enough in the window of the club there, and are fortunate, you may, of an afternoon, see Mrs. Weston's carriage and footmen go down the hill; and perhaps, if you smoke another cigar and wait, you may be so happy as to see Mrs. Weston's carriage and footmen going up the hill again. The rest of Boston drive in carryalls."

Mrs. Gower laughed. "Now I always thought it would be such a charming place to live in—so many celebrated people have been there—so many associations——"

"My dear lady, it is consecrated ground if you like," said Wemyss, interrupting. "And a very proper place to be buried in. But I tried living there for three months."

"And so, now, you are going back to Paris?"

"I came on with that intention."

"Why don't you go then?"

"I am afraid it's too late," said Wemyss, looking at his watch. "My steamer sails at four."

Mrs. Gower made a little ejaculation of surprise; and then laughed a trill or two. "Mr. Wemyss, you are a great humbug," said she, throwing her head back upon the pink satin cushion, and looking at him from the corners of her half-closed eyes.

"We have to be," said Wemyss, with a sigh. "Now there's the trouble of Boston; they can't understand that. And the six or eight of us who do, grow rusty for want of practice."

"But you have one another?"

"We know one another down to the ground. There is no excitement in that; it is playing double-dummy without stakes."

"And so you are going to Paris?"

"And so I was going to Paris?"

"But your steamer leaves at four, you say? What are you tarrying here for?"

"*Mais, pour vos beaux yeux*——"

"Mr. 'Olyoke," said the footman from behind the heavy curtains. Wemyss struck his two hands together in mock desperation; but as a matter of fact, the interruption was opportune, for he did not in the least know what to do next. There is a certain point in talk beyond which anything not final is an anti-climax.

"Say you are not at home," said he, eagerly.

But Mrs. Gower chose to be very gracious to Arthur. She gave him her hand with the simple cordiality of a schoolgirl. "I am so glad you have not forgotten our drive," said she.

Arthur had quite forgotten it; so he filled up the time by bowing to Mr. Wemyss; a salute which that gentleman received with some stiffness. Mrs. Gower made a very suggestion of a tinkle in a bell that stood at her elbow.

"Horridge, are the ponies ready?"

"Mrs. Gower's carriage his hin waiting," said Horridge, with a respectful gasp or two before the vowels.

"You see, Mr. Wemyss," said Flossie. "I hope you have not missed your steamer. I must not keep you for one moment longer."

"I see I shall have to postpone my trip," said Wemyss. "*Madame!*" (this with much formality.)

"*Monsieur!*" (Mrs. Gower quite outdid Mr. Wemyss in her exaggeration of a long curtesy.)

"Now, Mr. Holyoke," said Flossie, when the cosmopolitan had departed, "I am sure you will give me your company for a drive in the park?"

If there is no Englishman who would not enjoy walking down Pall Mall on the arm of two dukes, there is surely no American who would not like to be whirled through the world at the side of Mrs. Levison Gower. They drove for an hour in the park; and Arthur had the pleasure of raising his hat to Jimmy De Witt, Miss Pussie Duval, Mrs. Jack Malgam and Antoine Duval, Jr., Killian Van Kull, Charlie Townley, and many others unknown to him who bowed to her. She talked to him of books and poetry; of Heine,' Rossetti and of Shelley; and the tender tones of her voice would have moved an older man than Arthur to sympathy with her. "I had thought that she was worldly," said Arthur to himself. "There must be some secret in her life I have not yet discovered," (this was very possible, seeing he had only been with her three hours)—"some great suffering or repression which makes her wear this fashionable garb as an armor to veil her wounded heart. It is despair that makes her plunge so wildly into this whirl of company and show; the loss forever of something she once longed for, that drives her to distraction and diversion. Love of pleasure it is surely not."

Ah, poor Arthur, no doctor ever yet of soul or body but gave a biassed diagnosis of a pretty woman's soul. How easy it is to weave romances over soft gold hair! How natural to read poetry and lost loves in the light of lovely eyes that look so sweetly now in yours! So good Bishop Berkeley showed us that we mortals see but an image of external things, an inference from the sensation of our own retina; and we silly men, like idolaters, worship but the image we ourselves create. The lily of the field still draws us, not the potato-flower, worthy vegetable. And we fondly assume that the lily cares nothing for its vestment; that it toils not, nor spins, and has its eye upon the stars alone.

Arthur now really felt that he was a friend of Flossie Gower's. His favorite poems were all hers, and she quoted from many of them, with sighs. She had shown to him what the cynic world had never seen, the regrets and longings that lay beneath the pearls and laces that clothed her heart's casement; the true woman, not the fashionable figure known to others. How pleasant it was, to have a friend like her; one whose own life was over, and had all the more sympathy, for that, with lives of others. She asked him to come and see her whenever he liked; and Arthur thought how comforting it would be, to go to this woman for sympathy and advice, so much older than he, and yet so young at heart!

So seriously did Arthur think all this, that it quite jarred upon him when Charlie met him on his return and boisterously complimented him. "Well, old man, you are going it, and no mistake!" (Mrs. Gower's name was pronounced *Go-er*, which gave opportunity for endless puns.) "I say, old fellow, you come down fresh from the pastures like what-d'ye-callem—Endymion—Adonis, or the other masher—and sail to windward of the whole squadron!"

Arthur shook Townley off a little impatiently, and refused to dine at the club, as he requested. But, taking dinner alone, with the other boarders, he could not but say to himself that they were not pleasing to him; their minds seemed narrow and their ways uncouth. They were more affable than on the first day, perhaps because it was the evening, not the morning; there was even a certain clumsy attention in the manner of one or two of the younger men, as if they would laugh at his stories, were he to tell any. After dinner, he read a novel in his study with a cigar, feeling comparatively comfortable in the rooms, which already seemed less strange to him; and at eleven o'clock he went to Miss Farnum's party. (One always spoke of Miss Farnum, Miss Farnum's house, Miss Farnum's dinners—not her mother's.) Townley, true to his intention previously expressed, was not there; the dressing-room was full of very young men, pulling on gloves and chattering; one older gentleman with a fine pair of shoulders and an honest face was in the corner next Arthur, and attracted the latter by his looks. "I wonder where they keep their brushes," was all he said; but he said it pleasantly; and Arthur and he walked down together.

Miss Farnum, who was a marvellously beautiful young woman, met them almost at the door. "Ah, I see you know one another already," said she.

"But we don't," said the stranger, smiling; and Arthur was introduced to him as Mr. Haviland. Then Miss Farnum turned to present Arthur to her mother; which formality over, our hero found himself very much alone; and he naturally drifted away into a corner, where he found Mr. Haviland awaiting him. It was pleasant enough to stand there and watch the influx of young beauties; girl after girl came in, in clouds of pink or white, bowed and curtesied at the door, and drifted into the comparative quiet of the main dancing-room, where they eddied around by twos and threes, waiting to be accosted by simpering youth. Haviland was very civil to him, and introduced him to many of them; so that Arthur found himself walking and dancing first with a blonde in blue or white, next with a *brune* in pink or yellow; they were all lovely, but it was difficult to permanently differentiate their natures in one's mind.

The ball was a very brilliant one, and the rooms were full; many of the ladies were pretty, and all seemed rich and well educated. But there was an indefinable spirit of unrest, of effort at shining, of social anxiety, which struck Arthur as a new note in his New York social experiences; and Charlie Townley's patronising remarks recurred again to him. When he went back to Miss Farnum, her reception duties were over; they had a waltz together, and then wandered into a conservatory for cool and rest.

"How different it all seems from New Haven," was Arthur's first remark; and she said yes, it did; and asked him if he were really living in New York, and if it was not Mr. Townley with whom she had seen him walking the other day.

"Mr. Townley is a great friend of mine, you must know; and I think it is too bad of him not to come to-night. And, by the way—whom were you with in the park this afternoon?"

"With Mrs. Gower," said Arthur.

"Mrs. Gower? Mrs. Levison Gower? Was it? I didn't see—" and no one would have guessed that the acquaintance of the lady mentioned was yet an unrealised dream to Miss Farnum. She led Arthur off soon after, and presented him to some of her most particular friends; Arthur was so fortunate as to secure one of these young ladies—Miss Marie Vanderpool—for the german; and they had seats very near the head. Altogether, Arthur was in the high tide of social favor; and nearly every one whom he met talked to him of Mrs. Gower, and he marvelled a little that that lady—who had spoken almost tragically to him of her loneliness—should have so many dear and admiring friends. When he went home, it was with three or four tinsel orders at his buttonhole; and Haviland, whose coat-collar was yet undecorated, met him in the hall.

"Are you going the same way?" said he to Arthur; and when it turned out that they were, he asked him to drop in and have a cigar. Haviland knew that Arthur was a stranger in the city; and it soon turned out that they had one or two acquaintances in common. Then, as is the way of men, their conversation drifted to the last pretty face they had seen—Kitty Farnum. "She is a great friend of mine, and I stayed until the end on her account," said Haviland; though I don't dance." They stopped at Haviland's house; and entering, Arthur was inducted into the most delightful bachelor rooms, down stairs, filled with books, weapons, and implements for smoking.

"Yes," said Haviland, speaking of Miss Farnum; "and it's a great pity to see her going as she is now. Why" (he went on, in answer to an inquiring look from Arthur) "she is wild upon getting into society, as she calls it, or her mother is for her. There is a girl, rich, beautiful, refined, well educated, and she positively looks up to a set of people the whole of whom aren't worth her little finger, as if they were divinities."

"It certainly seems very funny, if it's true," said Arthur.

"Funny?" fumed Haviland, "I assure you they are as much her inferiors as they would have her theirs. Fashion is a vulgar word, and fashionable people are a fast, vulgar set; fast, because they are too empty-headed and uncultivated to enjoy any pleasure of taste or intellect, and vulgar because they are too stupid to understand any other superiority than that of mere display."

Haviland spoke almost savagely, intemperately, as it seemed to Arthur, about such a trivial thing. "Can he be in love with her?" thought he; and he wondered why he told him all this.

"It's her mother," Haviland went on, "she has brought her up to marry some fine Englishman, and wants to get New York at her feet first."

And Arthur, who had noticed how intimate Haviland had seemed with Kitty Farnum that evening thought that he had discovered his secret. Their conversation then took a serious turn, to their mutual profit and pleasure; and when Arthur finally went home, the night was going away, and the business of the day beginning. He liked Haviland better than any man he had met, thus far, in New York. But still, his ideas were changing.

## CHAPTER XI.

### THE STORY OF A QUIET SUNDAY EVENING.

SUNDAY was a long-looked-for day to Arthur. It was only the second Sunday after his arrival in New York; but it was as if he had been many months in the city already; and on the evening thereof he was to take tea at the Livingstones'.

Tea is not a formal meal; and surely it could do no harm if he went there early? It was almost six o'clock, and well on in the twilight when he arrived at the house; Miss Holyoke was in the parlor, the servant said; the other ladies were up-stairs. The low tones of a piano reached his ear as the man was speaking; and Arthur recognized a soft and serious Bach prelude, very quiet, very tender, very old in melody and simple chords. It was a favorite piece of Gracie's; and Arthur stood at the door, unseen, and watched her play. Her black dress and slender figure was just visible in the faint light that came in from some other room; but her face, sweet and pale, was clearly outlined against the long window and the last light of the November day; it touched her chin and brow and her parted lips; and the look of these was like the music she was playing. The prelude died away, in minor modulations, like a low amen; and Gracie sat playing idly with the ivory notes, her head drooping, and a dim shining from the firelight in her dark hair.

When the others came down, they found these two sitting together, like brother and sister, and talking in low voices to each other. Arthur knew Mrs. Livingstone; but the others of the family were still strangers to him. Mr. Livingstone was an old man, much bent, with older manners and appearance than his years warranted; then there was an only daughter, Mamie, and a favorite cousin of Mr. Livingstone's, Miss Brevier. Mamie Livingstone was a pretty young girl, with slightly petulant manners, as if she had been a little spoiled; she had a wonderfully mobile face, and quick intelligent eyes, and was evidently warm-hearted and impulsive, and very fond already of her cousin Grace. She regarded Arthur critically, and with some disapproval; in fact, she snubbed him more completely than that young gentleman had yet been snubbed—thanks to Mrs. Gower—in New York.

"Where is Mr. Townley, mamma?" said she, imperiously. "I want to see Mr. Townley."

"Hush, Mamie," said Mrs. Livingstone, slightly shocked; and the old gentleman looked at his daughter with a meek astonishment, as is so often the way with contemporary parents. Charlie had been invited in acknowledgment of his kindness to Arthur.

"Mr. Townley," said Mr. Livingstone in a quavering voice, "is a very old friend of mine, in whom I have always had the greatest confidence. I have yet to make the acquaintance of his young—connection."

"They say he waltzes like an angel," said Mamie the irrepressible; and just then the door-bell rang, and the subject of their conversation appeared, with his usual irreproachable exterior. Arthur had never seen him so subdued; he sat next to Miss Mamie, but treated her quite *du haut en bas,* talking much to Mr. Livingstone. Arthur could see that he was on his best behavior; and his best behavior was extremely unobjectionable, though he came very near being caught in the middle of some airy personality when Mr. Livingstone inaugurated the meal by saying grace.

After tea was over, Miss Mamie manœuvred Charlie into a remote corner, where he seemed to find her more worthy his attention. The evening was very quiet; Mr. Livingstone gravely reading some review, and addressing from time to time a solitary remark to his wife, who sat with her hands folded, placidly. Gracie talked to Arthur of himself, and our hero told her of all that had happened since he came to New York. Her life had, of course, been a quiet one, divided between books, her music, and charitable occupations. In all these Miss Brevier had encouraged and assisted her; Gracie spoke very warmly of her, her intelligence and character. This was after Miss Brevier, in the other room, had begun reading aloud to the old couple, in a low and sweet, but very clearly modulated voice.

"When can I come next?" said Arthur to Gracie as they rose to go. There was a sweetness in her presence that had won his heart a thousand times again; she seemed a rarer being, in this peopled city; he adored her.

"You must not come often, dear Arthur—my aunt thinks it better for us both. She thinks that we are both too young, and that you must try a year or two in society to make sure that you really care for me—and I for you," she added, in a tone hardly audible. Arthur's only answer was to press her hand; and so they parted.

When they got into the street, Townley lit a large cigar, with a slight sigh of relief. "Lively little girl, that Miss Livingstone," said he; "but I say, old man, what an evening! No wonder she wants to come out."

"I am sorry you found it slow," said Arthur, testily.

"Oh, well, I know it's devilish respectable and all that sort of thing," said Charlie. "Good middle-class domestic life; they're just like our grandfathers, and our grandfathers were nothing but *bourgeois* after all; that little girl will sink all that, or I'm mistaken. Come round by Sixth Avenue a minute, will you?"

There was a certain incongruity in Charlie's words, as it seemed to Arthur; it might have been Wemyss who was speaking, instead of this careless young Epicurean, who usually troubled himself little with abstractions and general categories, but occupied his understanding with perceiving the most practical sort of causes and effects. The fact was that Townley had used the current slang of his set, word-counters for thought, and his mind was already far from the subject, and his lips framed to the whistle of an air from "Iolanthe." They turned into Sixth Avenue (which is a strange, conglomerate street—insolently disreputable at times, elsewhere commercially prosperous, or even given to small tradesmen and other healthy citizenship, but always, in its earlier days, at least, rakishly indifferent to brown-stone-front respectability) and stopped at a little shop in a tiny two-story brick block. On the left was a little glass door, with the simple legend *Rose Marie* upon the panel; and in front of them a toy staircase, leading to the imminent upper regions. Through the glass of the door Arthur could see one or two bonnets on pegs in the window, and he divined that the shop was a milliner's. "Is Miss Starbuck in?" said Charlie to a child who appeared with a candle. The child (who was either deformed or very old-looking for her age) looked keenly at Arthur, whose eyes fell helplessly before her searching gaze.

"She has gone to a concert at the Garden," said the child. As they spoke, there was a murmur of men's voices from an adjoining room, and a rough clatter of applause, with knocking of heels and sticks.

"All right," said Townley. "Good-night." And after this somewhat inexplicable call the two young men went back to their Fifth Avenue lodgings. Here they found John Haviland, largely reposing himself on two chairs before Arthur's hospitable hearth.

Haviland and Arthur had met many times since the Farnum ball; and Arthur was more pleased than surprised at finding him in his rooms to-night. "I'm so glad you waited—I've just come from the Livingstones," said he. "Charlie, let me introduce my friend Mr. Haviland—Mr. Townley. Have a cigar—oh, you've got a pipe, have you?"

The others already had cigars; and disposing themselves in attitudes of permanent equilibrium, all plunged into the divine cloud of vapor until such times as the genius of the place should move them to speech.

"Is the Miss Holyoke who is staying at the Livingstones' your cousin?" asked Haviland, finally.

"Yes," said Arthur. "Don't you know her?"

"What a queer old thing that Miss Brevier is," said Charlie. "Can you believe it, she used to be a bosom-friend of Mrs. Levison G.!"

"Pity Miss Brevier dropped her," said Haviland, dryly.

"Miss Brevier drop her?" said Charlie, whose sense of humor was sometimes, at a critical moment. deficient. "You are chaffing."

"Mrs. Gower," said Haviland, gravely, "does more harm than any woman in New York."

"She is a person of European reputation," suggested Townley.

"She is unquestionably proficient in the latest and silliest vices of the aristocracies we came over here to escape from," retorted John.

Townley laughed a little, while Haviland puffed vigorously at his pipe.

"I say, Arthur?" said the former, "speaking of

Mrs. G., have they asked you to join the Four-in-Hand Club?"

"What's that?"

"It's a club organized for the purpose of driving twice a year up to Yonkers with string teams and liveries, and showing your most esteemed young ladies in flaring light-colored dresses to all the sidewalk population of New York," broke in Haviland, "and paying four thousand a year for the privilege!"

"What rot," laughed Charlie. "In the first place, it needn't cost you one thousand a year, for one wheel apiece. Four fellows can own a drag together, you know. And it's great fun. Mrs. Gower got it up, and all the boys belong. Why, old Mosenthal came to me the other day with tears in his eyes, and offered to keep two full-rigged drags, if we'd only let him come in—and lend me one of 'em, he meant," added Charlie with a grin.

"How cheap for him," growled the other, "if he could buy the envy and consideration of the society of this great republic for the price of a few horses!"

Townley's good-nature never forsook him; but he looked at Haviland as if puzzled; and the latter rose to go. "I called on the Livingstones last week," said he to Arthur, "and met your cousin. Good-night, Mr. Townley."

"What a prig he is," said Charlie, with a sigh of relief when Haviland had gone. "I always supposed it, from his looks. I knew that he refused to join the Four-in-Hand Club; and you hardly ever meet him in society—except at some queer place like the Farnums' for instance. He mugs down town at his office all the day, and improves his mind in the evening, I suppose, or reads goody-goody stories to little Italian children, down on Baxter Street! He's good as gold, you know."

"Don't you ever mean to work yourself?" asked Arthur.

"Not that way," laughed Charlie. "It's not in my line. Books and things are played out, I tell you." But the full account of his plans of life Charlie was too canny to impart, perhaps even to admit to himself.

For Charlie had not always been thus. There was a time when he was fresh from Princeton College, and he used to fill his table with English and foreign reviews, and could talk intelligently of their contents. He had begun his business life with enthusiasm, and was only known as a promising athlete outside of it. He showed great industry at the office, and some ability, and had been referred to by his elders as a well-informed young man.

But Charlie was a smart fellow, wide awake, and it did not take him long to get, as he fancied, *désorienté*. Suddenly, the second or third autumn of his business career, he had given up his reading, dropped his industry and early hours, and, for reasons well known to himself, he became the Charlie Townley known to us and the world. He had almost abandoned Wall Street for the Piccadilly Club and the Park; he dropped out of sight, on 'Change, and reappeared smiling in "society." And so well did he play his cards, that he, a poor and almost friendless stranger, without money or influence, with but one solitary advantage, that of a name not unknown in New York, had become—it would be premature to say what he had become, or why he did it; like all great generals, he had his strategy, not to be fathomed by the enemy, still less by emulous friends. Let us stick to the what, nor pry into the why or wherefore.

What he did, then, was to become the most ineffable dandy in all New York. With perfect clothing and fine linen, the exactly new thing in sticks and hats, and a single eyeglass decorously veiling his intellect and dangerously wide-awake eye, Charlie had become that thing of which the name may change from dandy to *lion*, from buck to swell, from blood to dude, but the nature endureth forever. But this was but dressing the part, it was merely the transformation of the exterior, the *travesti;* it was here that Charlie's career began. He only spoke to those whom others spoke to, and said only those things that others thought; he preferred married women to the society of maidens, even to the charm of blushing buds; though he selected one or two virgin beauties every season to whom he royally threw an occasional sunbeam of his society. These were always faultless either in family, or in beauty, or in fashion—for Charlie was catholic in his recognition of merit—and they appreciated the word or look he grudgingly accorded them and were duly grateful. Soon, his approval would give a *cachet* to almost any girl; but careless Charlie was all unconscious; girls were slow, he said. Mrs. Gower, Mrs. Malgam, Mrs. Jacob Einstein, formed his court. With these he reigned; by them he was taken up and formed, and later, by them adored, as the heathen worship the brass or wooden idol they themselves have made. This was at the time when Mrs. G. had gone in for *belles-lettres;* she and Townley read de Musset and Balzac together, and Theophile Gautier's poems. Who would have supposed that Charlie had ever read de Musset! It was at the same period that Levison Gower, Senior, died, and Mrs. G. adopted the hyphen; there was an English titled family of that name, and she fancied the difference of one vowel would only lend a *vraisemblance* to the descent; but society saw the joke and called her Lady Levison for all one season. There never had been any Levison in the Gower family; Gower senior's father had come from Connecticut, and his first name was John Lewis. The family estate consisted of an old farm-house and a few acres near Windsor Locks; the house is now burned down, and upon the ancestral acres grows rank tobacco.

What precious humbug is all this! Well, well, let us not despise humbug; *nihil humani alienum.* Let us rather see this humbug; let us put it on a pin, and examine this insect. You may be sure Charlie found his account therein. Frivolity is a word for dullards; I wish the ministers could enforce their precepts half as well as the dressmakers. Fashion is a marvellous potency, the public opinion of small things; in a democracy who can despise it? As I write, fashion tells our womankind, Put birds upon thy bonnet; and lo! four hundred thousand women in New York alone wear fowls. How many years ago was it, now, that some one said, Sell all that thou hast and give it to the poor? And four hundred thousand in the world have done it, not yet.

As for Charlie—in Mrs. Edgeworth, or in "Sandford and Merton," or other book of our childhood I once read a fable: how Honesty, Industry, and Ability formed a partnership for the acquirement of ambergris from whales. And Ability caught a hundred whales in the first year, and Industry carefully separated from all these whales a few ounces of ambergris, and Honesty sold this ambergris for a large sum of money. And Rapacity, who had been lying by, laughing, all this time, signed the check and took the ambergris; and lo! the check was worthless. And Society looked on and laughed, and said Rapacity was a smart fellow; and in the next year there were many worthless checks, but no ambergris.

Now Charlie was not Rapacity; but he was a clever fellow and could see this and other fables as they were enacted before his eyes. And he would not steal; nor would he go to the North Pole and search for whales. But he was in search of *les moyens de parvenir.*

## CHAPTER XII.

### A COMMUNIST AND HIS SISTER.

EANTIME a discussion upon society in general and other things in particular, something like that of Haviland and Townley, was going on in the back shop of the little brick store upon Sixth Avenue. A certain James Starbuck had lodgings there with his sister; that is, he was usually there when he was in New York. But this his occupation seldom permitted; for he was employed as a sort of small paymaster or inspector of the great Allegheny Central Company, a corporation which owned coal-mines, oil-wells, pipe-lines, factories, bonds, stocks, and other contracts so complex that the mind of even its owner grew confused at thinking of it. Starbuck was a slender, pale, narrow-chested American mechanic, whose bright eyes contrasted strikingly with his feeble frame and stooping shoulders, and whose sharp look betokened an unhealthy intelligence. His work was one which did not, however, require manual exertion, and he did it faithfully. His sister Jenny was very different in appearance; handsome, fond of pleasure, high spirited, they had only their cleverness in common.—But with Jenny's case we have nothing to do.

Of course, the reader, on the alert for coincidences and dovetailings of plot (as one always is in a novel, however veracious) has noticed that the name of Starbuck is not strange to this story; and has smiled to himself, superior, as his sagacity foresaw a link of connection in this fact. But was James Starbuck a cousin of clever, fashionable, refined Flossie? Starbuck did not know it. What, in active, progressive America, in the migrating America of the last fifty years, need a man know of his antecedents? They go for little in his life. Starbuck remembered his father well enough; and how he had struggled from pillar to post, from one frowzy city street to another, with the jaded, tawdry woman who was his wife; until one day, from a new and prosperous little city in the oil regions of Pennsylvania, he had gone, never to be seen or heard of after, by wife or child. And there they had lived, as they had been left there; and his mother took to dress-making and a boarding-house for miners, and his pretty sister had been sent to the public schools, and he had found work with the Company. His sister went through the High School, and then came home discontented; she could not bear their mode of life, nor like her mother's boarders—great hulking fellows who came home at night grimy from the wells and mines, and were, at best, but laboring-men, though they had money enough. Then her mother had died; and her brother had proved unequal to the actual labor of the business; but his quickness, his Yankee intelligence, had not gone unobserved, and he had been given this sort of clerkship or travelling agency, which made it possible for him to live at either end of the line. But he could not support her yet, though she persuaded him to move to New York; and she quickly found a place with Rose Marie, who was a little, beady-eyed old Frenchwoman, and slept in the remotest attic-chamber, so that she grew to be rather a myth, and Jenny's friends used to disbelieve in her existence, and called Jenny Rose Marie, in joke.

But we, who know everything, will not attempt to escape the reader's perspicacity. Yes (though it has nothing to do with the story), James Starbuck was in fact the grandson of that old whaling-captain Obed, Flossie's father's elder brother—he would have been her second cousin, then—quite too far for city kin to be counted, even had Mrs. Gower known anything about it. His father, by some curious chance, atavism, or some other influence, had taken after the uncle, and ceased to follow the sea; but, not like his uncle, he had not prospered, and had lived upon the world when he could; when he could not, he brought his wife back to her home in the small country town in Connecticut. The father was one of those curious fellows who turn their hand to anything, and of whom the best you can say is that they are hardly respectable, and the worst that they don't quite deserve to be hanged. Their lives are one long misdemeanor, but (unless we count fraudulent bankruptcy, and except an occasional bigamy) they rarely commit a crime. This Horace Starbuck had his ups and his downs, his ins and his outs; but the friends and the places of his prosperity knew him not in his adversity, and *vice versa*. There was no more continuity to his career than there is to a string of cheap assorted beads; and I doubt if even the devil took any serious interest in him. He was clever, too, in a way, with that common-school education no person born in New England can be without; he had made an invention, and owned a patent or two in the course of his life, and formed several corporations, in Connecticut and elsewhere, for their exploitation. It chanced that in one of these (it was upon a patent for machine-made shirts) some stockholder had actually paid up his stock; this lucky chance was the means of bringing seven thousand dollars into Horace Starbuck's pocket, the largest sum he ever possessed at any one time of his life. He promptly got himself married to a girl in his own town, which was probably, on the whole, the most defensible action of his career. They went on a wedding-trip to New York, where Starbuck went into six new corporations; and in a few months they were as poor as ever, and these twin children were born to them. Mrs. Starbuck's health gave out after this; and she never had any more children. Her husband's business made it necessary for him to travel a great deal; and she sometimes went with him, sometimes not. Hardly a commercial hotel in the United States but Starbuck had stopped there; he made his nest in hotels, as a spider does in dark places by the sea. His travels led him all over the northern part of America and to Australia; his assets consisted of a diamond-pin, a gold watch and chain, and four collars and a shirt, besides the clothes he wore; and he subsisted mysteriously. At one time he had considerable reputation in Ohio and Indiana as Dr. Westminster, the cancer doctor; he wore his hair long, and had his portrait so taken printed in the newspapers; his treatment consisted in an application of leaves of bracken or fern, steeped in hot water, and business prospered, until he foolishly used cabbage-leaves instead, and a patient died of the blister. He made some money by curing stammering, at one hundred dollars the cure; if the patients did not pay him, he threatened suit, and they were glad to get rid of him at any price. At times he gave temperance lectures (drinking never was one of his vices); and if worst came to worst he could play three-card-monte, though he hated to resort to this, as being fairly beyond the liberal moral line he drew for himself. He never had any permanent occupation; when luck ran strong against him, he would return to the little Connecticut town, where his wife had a bit of real estate and a home with her brother, old Sam Wolcott, and there vegetate. He honestly and in good faith considered himself a gentleman; he always wore a black coat, and once came near getting a Labor nomination for Congress. But the workmen, when it came to the point, would none of him; though he did occupy a seat for a year as a Prohibitionist in the Connecticut Legislature. He was given to long disappearances; and at the time of his Australian tour it really seemed to his wife as if he were never coming back. However, he walked in home, one day, with the gold watch and chain, and quite a little sum of money; and did not finally disappear until that time in the Pennsylvania mining-town, whither he had gone to buy oil-land, having at last persuaded his wife to sell her little bit of real estate in Connecticut, against her brother Sam's advice. All this James Starbuck did not know, of course; but in a general way he did not accord much respect to his father's memory. He considered pride of ancestry a most disagreeable form of aristocracy; and whereas his father would speak of himself as a gentleman, James Starbuck boasted openly that he was nothing but a plain laboring-man. James was perfectly honest in financial affairs, and he tried to look after his twin-sister. Much of his childhood had been spent with his uncle Sam; and his earliest recollections were of that little district-school the reader may remember. For uncle Sam belonged to the salt of the earth, good old Puritan stock, and lived to be the last of it, the day he hanged himself, and the Wolcott family tomb was sealed.

They had had a scene to-night, apropos of her visit to the garden-concert. She had gone with an ornate and expensive person, a sporting gentleman, whose ostentatious affluence had won her fancy; and whom James detested. She called him one of her "gentleman-friends;" and they had angry words about him, for I suspect, after all, James was a better judge of a gentleman than his father had been. But she had his own cleverness and strength of will; and it was difficult for James, who despised all authority himself, to exercise it upon another. Both brother and aister were, and had always been, absolutely and utterly devoid of any semblance or savor of religion; how absolutely, only those who have lived in certain classes of society in modern American manufacturing towns can know; and there was a large range of motive upon which it was perfectly hopeless for the brother to call. He knew it, and he was too bluntly honest not to recognize it; so he ended merely by hoping that his sister would not make a d——d fool of herself; which as they both had common-sense and practical minds, was perhaps the best argument he could use. But Jenny, perfectly conscious of her ability to take care of herself, was quite well aware of all that could be said on both sides; and replied that if Jim chose to smoke pipes in his shirt-sleeves with common laborers, there was no reason why his sister should not accept a gentleman's invitation to go to a concert. An English navvy might have stopped her going with a knock-down argument; but no pure-blooded American ever strikes a woman, and James could only swallow his wrath, admitting that his sister was a free human being in a free country, and if she preferred pleasure and he power, why it was the way of humanity. He was conscious that his own aims were selfish enough, and though he dimly felt that jewellery and fashionable hats and shawls were vanities, it was hard to put that idea into their language. For he believed in labor and commodities; and these, at least, were commodities. What fault he found was in their distribution alone; and his sister was but taking her way to get them unto herself. But to see her aping aristocracy added a drop to the hate he bore that *bête noire* of his class; though surely Dave St. Clair was no aristocrat, as he had to admit. Dave St. Clair was the gentleman who had taken his sister to the garden.

What was it, then, that made him hate the world? It was money, accumulation, capital, as he had learned to call the word. And he went back to the little coterie in the back room, and fervidly resumed his speech where his sister's departure had interrupted it.

"I tell you," said he, "we must change it all. A man is only worth what he makes. They tell us society would be a chaos without private property; I tell them it is private property that makes a chaos of society. They talk about the law! the law! I tell them the world would be better without law. It is a bogey, invented to scare off us ignorant fellows from the plunder the rich have appropriated, just such a bogey as religion was, only religion has been exploded. It is the law's turn to go next. All property is robbery; and it is only because land-owners are the worst thieves of all, that we feel differently about other things. The earth belongs to the human race; and no man can rightly own its surface, whether he got his title from a feudal baron or a Spanish general, any more than he can own the air of heaven. But property in other things is just as bad; and Jay Gould is a worse man than the Duke of Westminster, though he has ten million acres and Gould only a few hundred. How much of his wealth represents the honest labor of himself or his forefathers?"

There was a murmur of applause at this. There

were some half dozen men in the room, all sober and apparently intelligent, and all natural-born Americans.

"But somebody must own things," one of them remarked. "Somebody must own the mills, and the railroads, and the machinery. Why up to our works we've got a single engine that cost nigh unto eighty thousand dollars."

"We can all own them," Starbuck went on earnestly, "just as we all made them. Who do you suppose made that eighty-thousand dollar machine—the banks with their money and so-called capital, or the men as put it together? A man is worth just what he makes, I tell you. Can Jay Gould make an engine? But because we've all got to have a little land, and a little plant and money, are those as have got it to take away from us ninety-nine per cent. of all we make? Yes—if we're fools enough to stand it. A man can have what he can keep and use, what he can eat and what he can wear. If he chooses to store up his day's labor, to set aside the bread and meat he earns, he can do so, and keep it till it spoils. But this dog-in-the-manger business ain't to be carried no further; and if a feller squats down on land, and don't use it, an' another feller without no land comes along and wants it, that first feller has got to get up and git—that's all. A man's a man for what he is, for what he can do—not for what he owns."

"But who's going to support the Government?"

"Government," said Starbuck, with a snort of disgust, to the speaker, who was something of a ward politician. "Government! We don't want no government, Bill. What's the use of a government, except to scrouge out taxes, and make wars, and support standing armies and lazy politicians?—To protect life, liberty, and property, they say; property may go to h—l for all I care; and I guess life and liberty can take care of themselves; they aren't much helped by government, anyhow. And don't you suppose we fellers can look after them? And our own schools, and our roads and things, too, each town and city for itself?"

The man addressed as Bill paid little attention to these last remarks, but was talking politics with his neighbor. "Vote for F—— this year," he was saying; and Starbuck caught the end of his sentence as he finished his own remarks.

"Vote!" he interrupted, with infinite contempt. "Vote, vote again! I tell you, you're only doing yourselves harm. It ain't no sort of use. The ballot-box is just the last toy the bosses have got up, to keep you fellows quiet. Why, all this machinery keeps up the Government, and the laws, and the property, and the very things we've got to fight against. There's that patriotic bosh, and the talk about national honor, and the German wars and all —all for the benefit of the State, and the bosses, and the existing condition of things. What call has a Frenchy to go and cut a Dutchman's throat—or I an Irishman's? He's my mate, just as the next fellow is. I say, what we've got to do is, to fight; but not fight each other. We've got to fight the aristocrats, or the bosses, or the capitalists at home. I tell you these bond-holder fellows are all over the world; they're just as much in Egypt or in Mexico or in Turkey as they are here or in England. We've got to make a clean sweep, that's what we've got to do."

"By God, when a man talks, I like to hear him talk like a man," said another, approvingly; and there was a murmur of applause.

"But what's the use of destroying things?" said a third, of a sparing turn of mind.

"Destroying things! that's the d——dest bugbear of all," cried Starbuck. "Do you know, if everything in the world was destroyed to-morrow, we fellows could put it all back in two years? Aye, and less, if we worked with a will. I tell you, we've got to make a clean sweep, first of all; and when we build 'em up again, we'll build for ourselves this time—and don't you forget it," he added, by way of climax.

"Well, you talk pretty fine for a young fellow," answered one of the older men; and the party got up and exchanging a rough good-night, separated. Starbuck sat a long time with his chin on his hand, pulling at the embers of his pipe. Late at night the door opened and his sister returned; he heard a short colloquy at the door, and then she entered alone, with a flush upon her handsome face. She had the rude, frank bearing and the pitiless smile which belong to the type who take life's pleasures without much regard to its pains or the pains of others; and the strong, full curve of the merry lip grows harder with age, with less of merriment and more of malice. But, withal, such a woman as no man could ever rule; and James felt it vaguely, as he sat and looked at her.

"A pretty time for you to be in o' nights," said he; and the girl laughed loudly; and putting off her hat and shawl upon a chair, went to a little mirror and stood before it, touching her hair with her fingers. Now, a laugh and then silence was perhaps of all things the most exasperating to James Starbuck.

"Who was that brought you home?" said he, rudely.

"I don't know what call you've got to ask me that," said she. "I go with what gentlemen I choose; I don't interfere with you sticking to your workmen, do I? Phew! how it smells of pipes;" and Jenny ostentatiously rattled open the light windows.

"Well, its just here; I can't have you going round this sort of way, that's all," and James banged his white fist upon the table. The girl only laughed, more contemptuously and less merrily than before, and the brother grew furious.

"I can't have it—d'ye hear?"

"Mind your own business," said the sister, "and don't talk nonsense. I suppose you'd have me sit here in the back room and be a poor sempstress all my life. You like your lectures and your laborers' clubs, and your political power that you're all the time talking about—and I like to have a good time, and go out in society. We're quits. What have you got to say against it?"

"It—it ain't right," said James, weakly.

"Oh, ain't it? Well—I like it, then. I suppose you never do but what's right, of course. You're all the time complaining we don't get enough of the good things of this world—I guess you'd get 'em yourself, if you could, anyhow. And I can." And Jennie pulled off a very pretty little glove and showed a single diamond ring, which flashed bravely in the lamplight. "You go ahead your way, an' I'll go mine; an' I guess we'll both get what we can."

James was honest enough in his philosophy, and really without direct personal ends; and the last words goaded him to madness.

"Yes, an' I guess you went your own way up to Allegheny City a little too much," said he. "Where's Charley Thurston now?" (This Charley Thurston was an old friend of Starbuck's, to whom his sister had been once reported engaged.)

"I left Charley Thurston of my own free will, because I wanted to live in New York," screamed the girl, really angry at last. "Look here, Jim Starbuck—I've had about enough of you anyhow. You can't give me the position in life I require; and I've had more'n enough of your talk. This house is mine; and I paid for it, and for every dress I've got to my back—yes—and for this ring, too," she added, noticing her brother's glance. "You just go, do you hear? Clear out——" And the girl tore her brother's coat from the nail and threw it into his lap.

"You don't mean that," said James.

"Yes, I do—I'm sick of you and all your low acquaintances. I suppose you want me to pay for your lodging, do you ?"

James got up, wearily. They had had many such a dispute before ; but, with his feeble health and physical condition he had never managed to keep his temper so long as now.

"You'll be sorry for this, Jennie," was all he said. "You know where to find me." And he went out, and the front door closed behind him.

Left alone, the beauty rubbed her forehead impatiently, and pouted for a few minutes. Then she took out a small case of crimson velvet from her pocket and opened it ; it was a framed and highly colored photograph of herself, on porcelain, and set in gilt, with small jewels inlaid in the frame. As she looked upon it, her mouth unbent at the corners, her lips came back to their usual roguish, fascinating curves. She laid aside her dress, and robed in a splendid pink-and-lilac négligé, unbound her hair and sat for a long time before the glass, looking from it to the miniature and back again to the original. Then she took out a letter and read its contents, still smiling.

And then, for the first time that evening, you might have seen a resemblance—to what ? Why, for all the world—as she sat with her yellow hair falling on her full neck, with the contented, infantine smile, and the fashionably cut *robe-de-chambre*—for all the world, like Mrs. Flossie Gower.

## CHAPTER XIII.

### UNA AND THE LION.

JOHN HAVILAND was a banker down town, a man of much business and of few intimate friends. He was over thirty at this time, and made no sign of getting married; which was the stranger, as his health was good, his wealth sufficient, and he cared less for the pleasures of life than for its happiness. He had no brothers nor sisters; his mother was a widow and he lived with her. Flossie said it was hard to get interested in such people as John Haviland.

Every afternoon at four he left his office and went on a long and solitary walk; thus his days were of a piece with his life. He never chose the conventional promenades: and through the outlying districts, the river villages, the Bowery, the forgotten little parks and green places; by Riverside and Morningside; through the mysterious Greenwich settlement, as well as Central Park, Morrisania, and Fort Washington; in any sort of weather—sleet, snow, rain, or freeze—you might have met the man, striding along like a well-oiled engine, observant of everything, from the street urchins to the signs in the shop-windows. This at an hour of day when he might have gone to teas; wherefore people said he had never been in love. Which is a rash predication of your chimney-sweeper, but happened to be true of Haviland.

One day his wandering took a direction beyond Washington Square. This most characteristic of all New York squares lies bounded on the north by Belgravia, on the west by Bohemia, on the east by Business, and on the south by Crime. West of it are rich districts of individuality, where the bedrock of shabby gentility develops occasional lodes and pockets for the student of humanity. It is a place where the deserving and the undeserving poor are huddled together, both of them inefficient, but neither wicked; and where all the inhabitants make some sort of incoherent struggle against the facts of life, and either, on the one hand, emulate respectability, or, on the other, excuse themselves with the divine license to vagabondage given by Art.

In one of the southernmost and more dubious of these streets, Haviland, steaming along with his mind on everything and a watch on deck—for he was no introspective Hamlet—noticed a group of hulking fellows ahead of him. They were the sort of persons that have no obvious function in the divine economy; persons whose principal end seems to be to get knocked on the head with clubs in street riots, thereby dying, at least, with some poetic justice. Haviland would not have ordinarily noticed them; but he was struck by their unwonted rapidity of motion, and looking, he saw that they were following something; that something being a graceful female figure, dressed in black. John Haviland swung promptly into line behind them; and gaining more rapidly upon them than they upon the lady, he sauntered innocently between two of them when she was still a few dozen yards in front of them. He glanced casually at them as he passed; they slunk away like beaten dogs, and melted, in divers directions, from sight.

In a moment more they had reached a broader street; and John was on the point of diverging his course again from that of his protégée, when, looking at her, he hesitated a second, and then walked rapidly up to her.

"Miss Holyoke?" said he, raising his hat and with an unavoidable shade of surprise in his tone.

"Mr. Haviland? you down here too? Or perhaps you come on the same errand?" And Gracie smiled frankly, as John looked up, puzzled, into her lovely face. "I am visiting some poor families, you know—for the Combined Charities——"

"But surely," he broke in, "you ought not to be down here alone, Miss Holyoke?" They were at Sixth Avenue by this time; and Gracie was looking for a car.

"Usually my aunt lets me have the carriage," said Gracie; "but Miss Livingstone needed it to-day. And I don't like to drive quite up to the doors, even then. It seems so hard to drive up with one's own carriage and horses, and then have to refuse them everything but a little work," she added, smiling. "And Miss Brevier often goes with me."

"Do you mean that you come here often?" asked

John; and she told him that she and Miss Brevier had each "taken" the people on one street; and were seeing that they got help when help was necessary, and that the undeserving had none wasted upon them. John put her safely in the car, and resumed his pedestrian voyage with something new to think of. This personal visiting by refined young ladies was doubtless an excellent thing on its poetic side; but it could not but seem to him that the danger and the exposure were out of proportion to the benefit. He had had much experience among the city poor, and was perhaps a little skeptical as to the advantages to be gained by such devotion. For, as is the way of things so often here below, the selfish, the fraudulent, the undeserving, find it easy to advertise themselves and solicit help; while the saddest cases of all are lost in some modest garret; there they suffer unseen, ashamed to cry for charity, and wear their lives out silently. Except this latter class, and cases of long illness, most of the poor in New York are poor from laziness, intemperance, or crime; and their moral attitude towards society is rather that of sullen and callous defiance, or covetous acquiescence, than repentance. We need to get a better breed of men, not coddle the present one overmuch. Life suits them well enough as it is, if they could only get a few of their neighbors' goods; such goods as they desire and Mrs. Flossie desired, and not the *summum bonum.* If degraded, they do not mind their degradation, but are content with it; money always, clothing and food sometimes, they will derisively accept;

but work they will evade and not perform. Amongst these, thought Haviland, there may be much squalor, even much suffering; but there is little real poverty. Had he told all this to Gracie she would have said that it made no difference; and that one should try all the more to find the true cases, where righteous-minded beings were sinking in the turmoil of the world; and that one such family helped and saved was worth a hundred of impostures. Moreover, Gracie had not a man's fear of being taken in; had she thought of it at all, she would have scorned it; the odium of deception falls on the deceiver, not the deceived; she would not stoop to be suspicious. And mercy will ever be a mystery to mere justice: like the ways of God to human intellect.

Meantime Haviland was walking along, lost in thought. He wandered mechanically through various unknown and afterward unremembered districts, by a strange old graveyard yet undesecrated, through Leroy Street, and Sixth Avenue, until his time was up; then he went home and dined, with his mother. In the evening he had his ward club meeting; this was a thing in which he took great interest, and he went as a matter of course. It was not an easy thing, at this time, to be admitted to the councils that rule in the free city of New York. And, as we have spent some time over pretty Flossie Gower, that flower of republican society, it may not be wasted time to see a little what thing this political club was, which may stand, in a sense, for its root.

If New England, with its offshoots on the Western

Reserve and elsewhere, is the result of an attempt to obtain religious freedom, our whole country, in a still larger sense, is the result of an attempt to obtain political liberty. Our national faith has been that which is, of all possible faiths, the farthest from that of poor James Starbuck; it is government by every one, while nihilism is the negation of any government at all; moreover it is individualism, as opposed to socialism. But in New York there has grown to be a class who, as others could give no time to government, sought to make up for it by giving all of theirs. For what proportion is there between the time of a busy merchant or physician, and that of a professional idler? And the interminable and vain caucuses, impossible to the one, form the delight of the other. These had leisure to make acquaintances; to know each other; to pass their days in bar-rooms, nurseries of political power; and long ere this, they had arrogated to themselves an effective oligarchy. Theirs to make nominations and to mar candidates' careers; and the people, high-placed or low, had no right in their august councils save on sufferance. Thus we dropped aristocracy, and got a kakistocracy; but an oligarchy still.

John Haviland, however, had been admitted. He had had to struggle hard for this honor; and had finally attained it much more by his physical prowess than by his intellectual qualifications. Near his house were the rooms of a well-known "professor in the art of self-defence;" and there he had been in the habit of taking lessons, and occasionally "putting on the gloves" with all comers. Among the frequenters of the place were also many of the local magnates of the party; and Haviland, whose manners were frank and hearty, had thus met most of his ward leaders, and knocked the greater part of them down successively. Thus treated, they took a fancy to him; said that there was no nonsense about him; and one day, to Haviland's great surprise, informed him that he had been elected a member of their local club.

The meeting to-night was not over-interesting. It might have been called less incendiary, but it was certainly more selfish than Mr. James Starbuck's, we have so lately left; while for earnestness and a definite attempt at effecting something, the two were not for one moment to be compared. For whereas the official political organization of the great national party in Haviland's ward was occupied primarily with satisfactory apportionments of the offices among the would-be candidates, and secondarily with beating the rival party at the polls, Starbuck's people went in much more directly for measures than for men, and as for offices, desired none at all.

Haviland found it hard to keep his attention, that evening, on the subject before the meeting. Tom was saying what a good fellow was William, and how the machinations of Richard might be defeated if Patrick were only secured, which might be done if Michael were given a local judgeship. It was pretty unsatisfactory talk at the best, and hardly can have been what the makers of the Constitution, or even what Monsieur Jean Jacques Rousseau, intended. Haviland had often stood up against it, alone; but that night he gave little ear to it, and things went their own way.

From this meeting he went to the Farnums'. He was a familiar in the house, and could call late, if he chose. Mrs. Farnum had disappeared; Mr. Farnum was rarely visible; but sitting in the front room alone, with a sweeping robe of pale-gray velvet across the floor, and head and arm leaning on a low chair, a book discarded lying face downward on the floor, he found the beauty. A moment before he entered, her eyes (purple-gray they were in color) had had a strange look, both proud and longing, both weary and fierce. This was peculiar to them; but it softened a shade as he entered, and she looked up at him.

"Mr. Haviland?" said she.

"Yes—I came to see you because——"

"Because you had nothing better to do," said she, tersely.

"If you will," said John, smiling. "Though it is not kind."

"The world is not kind," said the beauty, with a frown, looking off again.

"For the world you are not responsible," said Haviland gravely. "Tell me, do you know Miss Holyoke?"

"Miss Holyoke? What Miss Holyoke?"

"Mrs. Richard Livingstone's niece."

"No," said Kitty Farnum, curtly. "I don't know Mrs. Livingstone."

"But I thought you might have met Miss Holyoke. Do you not belong to the Combined Charities?"

"Certainly not."

"I wish you did," said John, half to himself. "I thought you and Miss Holyoke might—might find it pleasant to go together."

"I have no interest in them," said Miss Farnum, as if finally. And she looked as if she thought the world too intolerable to herself to dream of trying to mitigate it for others.

"Excuse me," said Haviland; and the talk drifted off into commonplaces. But Miss Farnum's manners were not lenient, and his call was a short one.

Haviland continued to take his afternoon walks; but he was now more than ever apt to lose himself in the district west of Washington Square. Gracie never came to any trouble, all that winter, on her charitable excursions; but, if you had ever met her there alone, you would have very likely met, just far enough behind her, so that she never saw him, steaming along in his usual wholesome way, our friend John Haviland.

## CHAPTER XIV.

### A SOCIAL SUCCESS.

ARTHUR HOLYOKE was making his way. Despite Charlie's admonitions to the contrary, he had succeeded in living within his income; and, after a six months' trial at the office, the firm put him upon a salary. It was small, to be sure; but it was a distinct step toward the home that he was hoping to build. He had joined one club, recognizing that after the initiation the expense was trifling; and that he must be put in a way to meet men. Here he spent much of his time; bachelor lodgings are cheerless.

Business was, on the whole, a disillusion. The firm of Townley & Tamms had formerly carried large banking and investment accounts; but these had not increased of late years; and it gradually became evident to Arthur that all this legitimate business would hardly pay their office expenses. Where they really made their money was either in buying large blocks of securities at less than their value, or, more commonly, in selling new issues, after a long course of artificial demand and advertisement, at very much more than they had ever paid for them. Tamms was the light and soul of the firm. He never went up town into society; he never sought to shine in the fashionable world, and pretended that he did not want to. His largest social orbit did not transcend the society of the Brooklyn church to which he belonged; in the city of churches he lived and had his being; and he was in all respects a most reputable citizen. Old Mr. Townley might come down at eleven or at nine; Arthur might leave at three or at five; but they always met Tamms at the office, or left him there, curled up over his private desk, silent, in his formal black coat, with his restless eyes shining like a spider's; and he seemed to have a spider's capacity for living without fresh air and exercise. The deacons entrusted to him the church funds, and even, occasionally, made a long or short sale of stocks, on private account, at his advice; for Tamms, even by these aspirants for the kingdom of heaven, was reputed a man of remarkable business sagacity on earth. And in these days, when even the church must have its secular foundation and its corner lots, the laying up of treasure on earth is not to be avoided; what we need, therefore, is some really sure preventive of moth and rust, and some wholly efficacious precaution against those thieves that break in and steal. Although there is, I believe, no text telling us that thieves need be always with us.

But the tendency of the times is toward a fiercer battle in the struggle for existence, and weaker laws to keep the rapacious in check. Of the ever smaller surplus that the world's work wins, a larger share is every year being demanded by the laborer, and aggregated capital, organized monopoly, growing hungrier as it has to take less, thirsts each year more greedily for all that is left. And the middle class, which has ruled the world so long, is being ground to pieces by these warring Titans.

Tamms perceived this, not so dithyrambically, but more practically, and he profited by it. No one could turn in and out of corporations more cleverly than he; or turn them more adroitly to private ends, or drop out of them more apropos. Such an ingenious contrivance for clever men are these; more ingenious than the law which governs them. Indeed, the law has now dropped far behind, standing where it stood in the Middle Ages, when corporations were few and simple, and it stares agape at the Frankensteins of its own creation. But these same soulless monsters afford to their masters unlimited power, without interest or responsibility; and Tamms revelled in them. And Tamms was a self-made man, and a smart one; and the public deified him for both attributes, as is its wont; and his church would have canonized him, had his business needed a saintship instead of a seat in the Stock-Exchange.

Arthur's head grew dizzy at the corporations, and syndicates, and pools and other unnamed enterprises that Tamms's busy life was wound up in. Head and chief was, of course, the great Allegheny Central Railroad; this was the chief gold-mine that they worked; for in it Tamms could make his own market and buy and sell at his own price. But there were many others. And of these, the stock of the Silas Starbuck Oil Company had grown lately prominent.

The Stock-Exchange was no longer a strange sight to Arthur; he had grown familiar with it, with its moods, its dialect, its very battle-cries and interjections. And here he had seen the Allegheny Central bought and sold, and bought again; and of late he had been sent to out-of-the-way holes and corners, auctions, and even to the up-town houses of retired merchants (Mrs. Gower's among the number, only Mrs. Gower would not sell) in search of the share certificates of the Starbuck Oil.

"Governor's up to something," said Charlie. "Don't believe anybody knows what—not even the old man." The "governor" was Mr. Tamms; Mr. Townley was the "old man." And it was true the latter had little to do with the business of the firm. He had been a conservative, prominent banker in his day; and still carried much weight with the multitude; but, though he bore his gray head with much dignity behind his white choker, there was little in it —as Townley might have said. Little remained of the once active spirit behind it but a fixed belief in Allegheny Central and a strong taste for landscape paintings of the French school. However, no one had found this out but Tamms, not even Mr. Townley himself, though Charlie, as we have seen, suspected it. And Mr. Townley was a merchant of the old school, whom all the world delighted to make trustee for its posterity. He had a great box in the Safety

Deposit Vaults, crammed with the stocks and bonds upon which others lived; and these he administered carefully and well.

But one great day there was a "corner" in Starbuck Oil stock; for some mysterious reason the once common certificates had disappeared, like partridges on the first of September. Madder and more extravagant grew the demand for it at the board; scantier still the supply offering; one per cent. a day was bid, even for its temporary possession, so highly were the shares suddenly prized. There were vague rumors of "plums," "melons," and consolidations; meantime the Starbuck Oil stock had disappeared from human vision. Then, one morning, came the news; the Allegheny Central had absorbed the Silas Starbuck Oil Company; two shares were to be given for one, and in addition, to cover terminal facilities, connection, etc., five millions of six per cent. bonds were to be issued. Townley & Tamms, it was announced, had taken them all, and offered them to the eager public for 105 and interest. "Thought the governor was up to something," said Charlie. "What do you suppose we paid for them?—the bonds, I mean," said he to Arthur; and he put his tongue in his cheek and looked very knowing.

Arthur was kept busy, writing personal letters to the more valued clients of the firm, calling attention to the merits of the bonds in question; and preferred not thinking of the matter at all. He solaced himself with human sympathy; that is to say, the delights of society as offered in balls and dinners; and soon grew so accustomed to the stimulant as to take much pleasure in it.

For do we not see every day, gentle reader—that is to say, fashionable, fascinating, admired reader—how great and potent is the charm of this life? Do we not see men ruining themselves, girls giving themselves, for this alone? How dull, how short-sighted must our forefathers have been, who flattered themselves that we, their clever children, would content ourselves with the rights of man! What we desire is the envy of mankind.

Humanity has indeed labored over a thousand years for these simpler things, ever since that crowd of uncultivated Dutchmen came down on Rome, and the feudal system adopted Christianity unto itself and strangled it, or sought to do so. We have tried with brain and sinew, through blood and fire, to get this boon, that our lives may be respected, and our liberty of person not constrained. And now, in the nineteenth century, we have got it; and lo! society is bored. Languid and dull—too dull to hear, in its liberal mass, that low and distant murmur, too skeptical, indifferent, to see the dark low cloud, just forming, now, to the West and East—is it a mighty swarm of locusts, or is it merely storm and rain? Here and there a tory sees it, dreading it; here and there a radical, dreaming of it; their imagination aiding both. And the multitude, who are not indifferent, and who are never bored, have little time to look at the weather, still less to read and think; or, if they read, it is no longer now the Bible, which, they are told, is but a feudal book, a handy tool of bishops and of premiers. Moreover, modern enlightenment teaches that it is a lie; there never were twelve basketfuls of fragments left from loaves and fishes on the Mountain; therefore what words were spoken on the Mountain cannot be true.

The world is free; and ninety-nine per cent. are miserable, and the other one is bored. So, we remember, Flossie Gower was bored, when she got all her wishes, and had liberty to do what thing she chose. But surely, liberty being the greatest good, it follows she must choose to do good things? But to-day the light of the sun does not content us, nor the fragrance of the woods and fields, the breath of free air and the play of mind and body, love and friendship, and health and sympathy. These are but the tasteless water of life; the joys of possession and of envy are the wine. The early pagans were happy with these indeed, benighted creatures; but what though the ancient text says, What does it profit a man if he gain the whole world, and lose his own soul? Others will envy us the world; but our own souls pall with us. We moderns have invented *amour propre.* What matters being happy? The true bliss is, that others think you so. We have realized equality; and all these good people (even to Jem Starbuck's sister) struggle to escape from it. Jem Starbuck was a nihilist, and their logical counterpart. What did Flossie care for her two horses and Russian sleigh and silver mountings and black and white furs and waving scarlet plumes? If Central Park were the wastes about the Northern

Pole, do you suppose she would care to take her sleigh-ride there, and show off to old John Franklin's whitened bones alone? Is it the light, and the air, and the motion, that makes her pleasure; is it the mere child's delight in brilliant colors that makes her flaunt her trailing scarlet plumes; or is it the subtile intoxication of the world's notice of those things the world desires? And Mrs. Gower's equals see these things and do homage; and their daughters wed for these, and their husbands work; and in pretty Jenny Starbuck's head, walking on the roadside, the homage turns to envy; and in James her brother's heart, to gall.

Arthur went in this sleigh many times, and enjoyed it, and said pretty things to Mrs. Gower in exchange. He had a poet's delight in rich and beautiful things, in show and speed and glitter. Shine, not light, attracts your women, says Goethe; and the old courtier-poet might have said the same of men, himself included. And Mrs. Gower lolled back, beautiful, her yellow hair shining strangely through the snow; so Helen in the Greek sunlight; so Faustina in the streets of noble Rome; so Gutrune, by whose wiles twelve thousand heroes and the gods went down to darkling death. All these were blondes, and smiled and charmed and had their adoration and their joy of life. What call had Flossie to trouble herself with the eternal verities, or man's past or future? She was not eternal. She was, furthermore, a skeptic and a cynic—if a butterfly can be said to be skeptic of eternal life. She had no real knowledge of the things she won. She would have liked the sword of Siegfried for a panoply, to put the Grail in her cabinet of rare china. She would have liked to possess these things, and money and fans and dresses, and have other women know that she possessed them. She would have liked to possess men's hearts.

Not that she was wicked. She was no tragedy queen, no evil heroine of romance; she had no desire, so far as she knew, to injure any one. She would have paid a fortune for a picture that other people admired; but she would have exchanged it for a ball-dress, had there been but one ball-dress in the world; and she simply did not believe in the Holy Grail, or the sword of Siegfried, or men's hearts. So a rude conqueror thirsts for the great King's talisman, and barters it for an ounce of colored glass, and wears the latter on a ring in his nose. But yet this glass is not the ultimate reality, despite its wearer's pride.

So some air-dwelling German has told us, long time the world slumbered unconscious, wrapped in a dreamless sleep. And the gold of the Rhine still slumbered in its waters, and the gods kept guard. Then all things broke to consciousness, after a myriad of cycles of years; and their first awakening was a joy; and men arose, and lived in the light of the earth. But shortly, after some few centuries, this consciousness became a blight; and they turned, and knew themselves. And the gold was wrested from the deep waters by an evil race of men, forswearing love forever; and the love of the world turned to avarice, and the love of man to the love of self, and the love divine was forgotten and whelmed in the dusk of the gods. And so the pessimists of the day must follow out the old myth, and tell us that the end and cure of all is this darkness of the gods, the death of all things, the black waters that well again from earth, the rising waves of the dreamless sea.

But behind Zeus and Prometheus and Hera lay Fate, a power not themselves, to whom both gods and men must bow. And beneath Wotan and Loge sits Erda, in the heart of Earth, silent; and the web of things to come is spun, slowly, by the silent Norns.

## CHAPTER XV.

### THE DIVERSIONS OF FINE LADIES.

ARIS had palled upon Mr. Caryl Wemyss, and in February he returned to New York. Paris, he found, had deteriorated since the Empire. Moreover, his social position there was not wholly satisfactory. In London it was better; but even there they did not sufficiently distinguish between him and other Americans; between him, son of the famous poet-dramatist, minister to England and man of letters, when there were no other American men of letters, and, for instance, the present minister, whom Wemyss did not consider a gentleman at all. So his friend, the young Earl of Birmingham, wishing to visit America, Wemyss had returned with him; and was now piloting that nobleman through the maze of New York society.

But this proved a more difficult task than Wemyss anticipated; for the Earl was quite unable to recognize any distinctions, and evinced a most catholic taste for all beauty, unadorned by birth, and pretty faces without pedigree. And now the Farnums had presumed to give a ball in his honor; and Birmingham was there, and Wemyss, of course, had had to go there with him, and Flossie Gower had come to keep him company.

A man may be a peer of England and wear a coronet; but a man's a man for a' that. And as the pudgy, little, sandy-haired Englishman, with his scrap of whisker, his red eyes and his white eyebrows, stood beside Miss Farnum, it was easy, at least for Wemyss and Flossie Gower, to see that he was much impressed.

If one had to name the potent quality of Miss Farnum's presence, I should call it majesty; you, perhaps, might call it scorn. Her walk was that of Juno, over clouds; beneath her coronal of red-brown hair her eyes were great and gray, now looking out beyond you, over all things, sphinx-like—now introspective, but disdainful still.

Mrs. Gower could see that she treated Birmingham as a high-priestess might some too importunate worshipper; and the noble Englishman was, for once, embarrassed of his person—and by hers.

"Who is that girl?" asked Mrs. Gower of Wemyss. "The daughter of our host?"

"A fine piece of flesh and blood," said he.

"A fine piece of soul and spirit, or I am much mistaken," retorted Mrs. Gower. "See, she positively dares to be bored, and the Earl is at his trumps at last. Really, I must have her at my house——"

"She'd be charmed to go, I've no doubt," said Wemyss, with the gesture of a yawn. "But come, you surely don't expect me to talk to one pretty woman of another? Tell me of yourself."

"What is there to tell? Look at Baby Malgam's violets—they are lovely."

"The loveliness of violets," said Wemyss, "is a fact established some years since, and which I am ready at all times and seasons to admit. Your own loveliness is a more inspiring subject."

Mrs. Gower took absolutely no notice of this, but continued to watch Miss Farnum, as a vampire might study a torpedo. Wemyss was seeking a more gracious simile, when Charlie Townley came up and ousted him. "You are coming to Tony Duval's supper at the ball, Mrs. Gower? Tony has got the Earl and Mrs. Malgam——"

"Oh, I am going—if it will not shock Mr. Wemyss here," laughed Flossie. Wemyss cast at her one look of grave reproach, and bowed his own dismissal. To suppose that anything done by others could ruffle his own breeding—he, a polished patrician of the *décadence!* (The *décadence* was a favorite theme of Wemyss; perhaps it was pleasant to think that the society in which he had not been a success—at least, not a popular success—was rushing to its own failure.) Townley sat down by Mrs. Gower.

"But seriously, Charlie, don't you think it may be a trifle *risqué*—this opera ball?"

"*Qui n'a rien, ne risque rien,*" said Charlie, bowing. Flossie laughed; he was one of her ancient train, discarded; a privileged character. In reality this ball, advertised to be improper, was very decent and very dreary, for the most part. And they could draw the curtain of their box, like peris in paradise overlooking gehenna, and turn aside from the multitude below.

But perhaps we shall see more, if we go with Jenny Starbuck. For he had asked her, too; and she was going, masked, upon the floor. She had hesitated much; and refused an invitation from Mr. Dave St. Clair. Probably it would have given her more moral courage had she known that Mrs. Levison Gower was going too.

Her brother James she had not seen for months; not since that night when she had turned him into the street. She did not care; he was but a common fellow, and she meant to be a lady. For some time she had taken lessons for the stage, as being the quickest path to elegance of life; but she was a stupid woman, intellectually, and had not mind for this. In mind she was not like her unknown cousin, Flossie; but she could only imitate her in what she saw. Her quilted satin cloak was very like Flossie's; and she too could get into a coupé and tell the coachman to drive to the Academy.

An immense board floor had been laid over the entire theatre; scattered about this were orange and lemon trees in green tubs; and among them walked perhaps a couple of hundred people—nearly all in fancy-dress and many with false noses or fantastic wigs. They looked like the chorus of an opera just dismissed, except that they appeared more low-spirited and ill at ease. Many of the women were in men's costumes—Magyar uniforms, Cossack, Austrian; some even were in jocose dresses, making a burlesque of themselves; and Jenny, dressed like a lady, looked on these with scorn. Here and there a quadrille was being danced, and among these were a few paid dancers whose kicks and gyrations were supposed to indicate spontaneous gayety and exuberance of joy. Taken all in all, it did not so well imitate Paris, even, as Flossie Gower and her following, London.

But Jenny stood waiting at the dressing-room door, and did not venture on the floor alone. It was still more than half empty, and though the great orchestra rang out in most exciting rhythm, the crowd seemed cold. But above, in the tiers of boxes, every box was full; here the women all were dressed like Jenny, and a few were even masked.

She waited there, in vain; till, finally, Mr. St. Clair saw her and offered himself as escort, magnanimously. Jenny was glad enough to take his arm, and they made the tour of the floor. He laughed at her for wearing her mask, but she insisted still. The band broke into a waltz—fiery, intoxicating; the floor filled with dancers, glancing by them in gay colors, fancifully dressed; but there were more diamonds in the boxes, and bare necks, and men in ordinary evening dress. In front of her was a large box, with three or four ladies, masked; one, her breast all covered with a diamond rain. The box was just above the place where Jenny stood; and she looked at the necklace enviously. Its owner gave a little scream, and Jenny heard the words, how shocking! Jenny followed her glance; beside her on the floor were two girls in satin tights. Then as she looked back to the box, she saw Mr. Townley bend down and speak to her; Jenny lifted her own mask a moment and tossed her head at him and smiled, then leaned heavier on the arm of Dave St. Clair.

Charlie got over his confusion in a moment; but not too quickly for a chorus of delighted laughter from the ladies near him. "Who is she, Mr. Townley?" laughed she of the diamonds; "she's *very* pretty." And "tell us all about it, Charlie—we won't tell," roared Tony Duval.

"You're welcome to all I know," said Townley, coolly. "She's a dress-maker on Sixth Avenue, and makes dresses for my aunt." Tony only laughed the more at this, and good-natured Lucie Gower led Charlie out of the box. "Come," said he, "you must introduce me to her; I'm sure she does business with my uncle." In the back of the box a little, red-haired Englishman was talking to a younger lady, sitting in the shadow; and she was glad, when everybody's attention was drawn to a masked figure in the box opposite—a lady whose green tulle dress and very low corsage bespoke her also fashionable. "What superb emeralds!" cried the black-haired lady, in front.

"I'd have thought Mrs. Hay would have known better," said the other. "But there's no mistaking the emeralds—on those shoulders——"

"What! you don't say its Mrs. Wilton Hay? Where did she get them? I asked Jack for a set not half so fine, and they cost a fortune. Who gave them to her?"

"Mr. Hay, of course," laughed the other.

"You did not know diplomacy had been so profitable?" said Tony Duval. "See, there goes your husband—he has just been introduced to the blonde beauty."

"Not really? 'Pon honor, I didn't think he had it in him," said she. Then Tony Duval began to relate to his companion an anecdote of a nature that seemed to Arthur most surprising; he was sitting behind the *rivière* of diamonds; and the rest of the company seemed bored.

"Positively, Mr. Wemyss, there is nothing new under the sun," answered the blonde in front. "After all, the flowery paths seem quite as stupid as the straight and narrow way."

"It's very slow," answered he addressed. "They've too much conscience for it still."

"Perhaps," suggested another, "we could give them lessons."

It was Van Kull who spoke; and in the pause that ensued came the point of Duval's story, accentuated by the silence; and Wemyss tactfully called attention to an adjoining box, where the ladies were sitting with their feet upon the railing, smoking cigarettes.

"Come," said she of the diamonds, rising; "we have had our moral lesson; it is time to go."

From the floor, Jenny Starbuck had watched this box, until she saw them rise as if to go. She stayed at the ball many hours later. But Arthur, in the back of the box, was witness of a little scene that she could not see.

The elder ladies went out first, passing the Earl, who seemed busied with his companion's opera-cloak. She was standing, leaning upon the back of an arm-chair, with her weight upon one round, bare arm; and as Arthur went out of the door he was almost certain that he saw their noble guest lay his hand upon her arm, familiarly.

A second after, and Arthur had dropped his opera-glass; it rolled back into the box, and he went back for it. There was no change in Kitty Farnum's attitude; she was still leaning on the chair, but looking at Lord Birmingham: her face cold and fixed, like some scornful face of stone. She gave her arm to Arthur and walked out.

## CHAPTER XVI.

### IN MAIDEN MEDITATION.

RACIE was sitting alone in her own room; she had been reading—the "Faery Queene" the book—but it had slipped from her hand—and now she was thinking. Not of herself, but of others; Arthur, perhaps, principally. For she had given her heart to him; and in a perfect maidenly love there is always some foretaste of the maternal, a fond solicitude as of a mother for her child. Perhaps even Arthur did not know how much she thought of him: and Mrs. Livingstone was too much bound up in Mamie, and Mamie too much in herself, to notice it; Miss Brevier alone had seen it, and had held her peace. Gracie fancied that no one knew it, save Arthur himself; though for her and Arthur it had changed the world. The world itself she did not understand; all things did not look clear to her that winter; the people of her acquaintance puzzled her. It almost seemed as if she would not have their sympathy in all ways; but this could not be proven, for Gracie never made a confidante. Now Mamie Livingstone, on the other hand, confided everything to her; and then, apparently, forgot it all, much as a Parisian lady may be supposed to forget the substance of her last auricular confession; for

Gracie noted a certain repugnancy or incoherence in this young woman's heart history of which the heart's possessor was unaware entirely.

Mamie was intensely a metropolitan girl; the exquisitely sensitive product of a great social nerve-centre. She did not know her Emerson, and was wholly untroubled with "the whichness of the why:" but she had mastered her own environment at an early age. And she had—except, of course, as against young men, her natural prey—a frank disposition and a warm heart.

The great event of her life, her appearance in society, was to take place in the season following; and all through this winter Mamie was in a state of electric anticipation. She was already laying, in an innocent and girlish way, her wires. What Gracie failed chiefly to understand was these very love confidences, above mentioned: for though Mamie talked most ardently of the qualities of her successive swains, they seemed to bear a much more definite relation to her own self-love than to her heart. But then, it was her self-love that was the source of motive to her; her heart was an amusement only. And Mamie knew the world, as has before been hinted, *à priori;* she was a girl of transcendental mind, who saw through the copper-plate formulas of her study-books to the realities around her; with innate ideas and tastes as to what was fashionable and really fine. She alternately patronized and petted Gracie, who was three years older than herself; yet Gracie had more influence over her than anyone else. As for the parental authority of her father and mother—the phrase is too grotesquely mediæval to be completed. Mr. Livingstone was an old gentleman with a million and a half of property, whose manners had outlived his mind.

Gracie was looking—if I could describe to you the manner of her look, you would all men be poor Arthur's rivals, I am sure; the direction of her look was simply to the northward, through the window. The manner of it—perhaps even Arthur never wholly noted it; may be he thought all girls had it; may be he even preferred the scintillating alertness of Pussie Duval's or Baby Malgam's—people now called her Baby with a touch of malice—which was more new to him. It was a deep and holy radiance, as if the look's object were not yet quite found, and a certain questioning withal. Gracie was almost sure to have it when alone; perhaps a certain exquisite if unconscious tact restrained it, with other girls, lest they should call it pose; but no man—that is, no *man*—ever saw it fairly, but his soul was turned to fire. Medusa's look it was that turned a man to stone; but there seems to be no metaphor for this opposite one. Perhaps because the Greeks had never met with it; it is found since Hamlet and since Gretchen, and grows mostly in the country, with books, sweet thoughts, and solitude. I have more rarely met with it in crowded colleges; yet it is not absolutely inconsistent with a knowledge of Greek.

"You do look so sweet, cousine," cried Mamie as she tripped into the room, "but awfully poky. I've got such a thing to tell you about Mrs. Lucie Gower.

And oh, do you know? Charlie Townley called here to-day. And somebody else too—aha?"

"Who was it?" said Gracie.

"Who was it, Ma'am Soft-airs, indeed. Cousine, do let me try a bit of rouge some time—that blush was so becoming to you. Mr. Haviland, of course; and I peeked through the crack of the door when the servant said you weren't at home. But tell me, Gracie dear, do you think it would do for me to ask Mr. Townley to dinner next time? You know, I've had all the younger men, and he dances like an angel."

"Why, Mamie, you don't mean to have a dance?"

"No, no, stupid, but for next winter, I mean. I'm determined to have Charlie lead my german, you know; they say all the young married women are fighting for him. And the only other man is Daisy Blake, and he's too slow for anything. Besides, I'm dead in love with Townley, you know."

"Oh," said Gracie.

"I heard he gave a supper-party last night, and both Mrs. Gower and Mrs. Malgam were there, and the Earl of Birmingham; and afterward they all went in masks to a public ball. Wasn't it horrid? And just think what fun it would be to get him away from those married women? Why, Marion Roster told me last year that the debutantes had no chance at all. I'll see about that." And Mamie stamped her little foot and tossed her pretty head defiantly; and indeed it looked as if the filly might make it hard running for the four-year-olds. And Charlie Townley, had he seen it, might have felt that he had gotten his reward on earth. For I doubt if any poet's bays or any soldier's laurel were more highly prized by maid or wife than Mamie, the rich, well-bred, well-born, rated Charlie Townley's style of excellence. *Le style c'est l'homme*, says some old, grave writer; what then is style to a giddy young woman? And I doubt if either bays or laurel be so marketable. And Charlie was a man of the world, familiar to its stock-exchanges; who did not mean to marry, but meant to marry well.

Gracie looked at Mamie Livingstone with some faint wonder; and then the young girl laughed loudly, as was usual, and kissed her, and called her a dear old thing; and laughed again, as if she had been jesting. And so the other one supposed it, and smiled back through Mamie's many kisses.

"Look here," Mamie began again, with a gesture of triumph; and she pulled a note from her pocket, and waved it triumphantly in Gracie's face. "I've got a note from him already!"

"Oh, Mamie——"

"'Sh, Ma'am Prunes and Prisms—it's only about a summer fan. I asked him to get a kind which I knew had only been made at one place down town, and they were all sold out, so he had to write and tell me so. See, isn't the signature nice? 'your devoted servant, Charles Townley'—and such a nice manly hand." And Mamie roguishly made pretence of kissing it, the while her eyes danced with merriment. Gracie looked at her—puzzled; and Mamie only laughed the more. "There, there, don't look so grave, you delightful old darling; it's not so awfully serious, after all—yet." And with the final burst of laughter that accompanied her last word, Mamie danced from the room.

Left alone, Gracie's smile, which had reflected Mamie's, changed to a deeper look, a look that Mamie's face could never mirror. Yes, it was a puzzle, in a way; people so rarely seemed to care for the essentials of things. Gracie's notion of a man was enlightened heroism, of a woman perfect bravery and trust, and the light in the lives of both the light of the world that comes from another, like the sun's. But to these young ladies and gentlemen, the light of the world was the light of a ball-room.

So she sat there, looking northward over the roofs and steeples, to the bright sky-line; and perhaps, if an eye were at the other end of that ray of light that slanted through space to meet her own, it saw a human soul. But to the telegraph wires and brick chimneys, to Mamie and the men near by on the roofs, it was a girl with a pretty face like another.

Human nature, they tell us; and another says, people are all alike when it comes to the point; and the motives of mankind have ever been the same, says a third. The course of history is thus and so; it is human nature to do this, and take this bundle of hay rather than that; and we are all alike, they repeat again; scholars, men, and books repeat again, until we do become human nature—or drown ourselves in preference.

But it is a lie. Humanity is not all alike; it is as a broad plain of grass or weeds; and this is alike. But among it, here and there, there flames a poppy, and above it, here and there, stands up the glorious lily, like a halo on a flower's stem; and beneath it breathes the sweet and gentle violet. Hard by grow the weeds, and dock and hardy thistles; on one stem perhaps with these, unconscious of them.

So mankind is a great crowd composed of common units, all alike; but with them walking, mostly alone, there journeys the hero, and there the martyr, and the woman with a soul. And the hero looks straight ahead, sad and strong; the martyr looks up to heaven; and the soul looks about it and breathes its fragrance to its fellows.

But the crowd is so great that these three, though they are many, yet seem few. And they journey as they may, and work, and do, and die; but ah me! they are lonely, for they seldom meet, each one the other; they are fortunate if they see each other's radiance dimly, through the crowded field.

## CHAPTER XVII.

### A CULTIVATOR OF THISTLES.

SPRING had come. Theatres were fuller, the opera not so full; dancing parties were less frequent, and there began to be talk of races and of country parties; it was no longer a rule without exception that the men wore dress suits who were dining at Delmonico's. Besides this, there were also the green buds, and the crocuses, and the twitter of the birds in Central Park.

Arthur Holyoke looked like the spring, as he sauntered down the steps of his lodgings with a light stick and betook himself, swinging it, to that temple of a modern Janus, the railway station. Ah, you may talk to me of rialtos and bridges of sighs, of moonlit pavilions and of temples, court-rooms, and shrines; but the great stage of humanity, of catastrophes, partings, and dénouements—is it not now the railway station? Here the jaded head of a family, tired of struggling, beheads himself by abandoning his middle-aged wife and her six children; here Jack, fresh from college, goes down to that country party where he shall meet Jill, and proposes to her, the very next night but one, on the piazza above the tennis-ground. Here mamma comes home, or papa goes away; or we leave for India, or Grinnell Land, or school. This is the portal to pleasant long vacations, and to dreary working days; here Edwin and Angelina begin their new life, and murderers escape; and old men come home.

Arthur had gained decision, alertness in his manner; he wore a spring suit of a most beautiful delicate color; if he had luggage, it was all disposed of, and he looked like a poet hovering above earthly cares. In the one hand he held an *Evening Post*, in the other a cigarette; and as he took his seat in the parlor-car he opened the one and threw away the other in a manner that betokened his content with himself, and, consequently, with the world. For he was going on a week's visit to La Lisière, the country-seat of the Levison-Gowers, at Catfish-on-the-Hudson.

Arthur looked about to see if any of his fellow-guests were on the train; but there was no one who looked like a likely member of so select a party as all of Mrs. Levison-Gower's were known to be. There was a maiden with a gold ornament at her neck, and a pot-hatted and paunchy personage with a black coat and tie—both quite impossible. Arthur gave them up and buried himself in his newspaper.

At Catfish he alighted, and standing with his luggage, on the outer platform, looked about him inquiringly. A groom, who was standing by a pretty little dog-cart with a nervous horse, touched his hat. Arthur walked up to him. "Can you tell me how to get to Mrs. Levison Gower's?"

"Mr. Holyoke?" said the groom, touching his

hat again. "This is to be your horse, sir," and placing the reins in Arthur's hands, he lifted the leather trunk and overcoats in behind. Arthur got in front and the horse started at a jump, the groom catching on as they turned. "Beg pardon, sir,—first turn to the left, sir," said he, as Arthur held in the horse and hesitated at the first dividing place of roads. Thus directed, they soon came to a high stone gate, clad with ivy, each post surmounted by a stone griffin which Arthur recognized as belonging to the Leveson-Gower arms. (The American family, said Mrs. Gower, spelt it with an i.) Through this they passed and by a lodge with a couple of children at the door, who courtesied as he drove by; and then through quite a winding mile of well-kept park and green coppiced valley. At last they reached the house; in front of it was a level lawn and terrace bounded by a stone balustrade, and beneath this lay the blue Hudson and the shimmering mountains beyond.

Arthur was given a small room, in the third story; but it had a view of the river and a comfortable dressing-room; from the window of which he caught a view of a most glorious sky as the sun went down behind the purple mountains. This passed the time very pleasantly; for it took him only a few minutes to dress, and he had a certain delicacy about appearing below, while it was yet sunlight, in his dress suit. The scene even suggested a short poem to him, the gradual fading of one mountain-crest after another as the sun left them all in turn; something about the sun of love illuminating and then leaving sombre the successive ages of man. But the clangor of a gong interrupted his first stanza; and he went down-stairs.

Here, too, they were admiring the beauties of nature. Several of the guests were assembled on the lawn-terrace before mentioned, and talking in subdued tones about the scenery; among them two or three lovely women, flaunting their fair heads in evening dress and laces. Arthur recognized Miss Farnum, and Mrs. Malgam, and who was that lovely creature in the corner with Charlie Townley? A most radiant and perfect blonde, whose yellow hair was luminous in the twilight. He would ask his hostess. She was standing in the corner of the terrace, leaning over the stone balustrade and looking into the still depths of the forest beneath; a man was beside her. She turned as Arthur approached, and held out her hand frankly to him.

"So glad to see you, Mr. Holyoke," said she. "Mr. Wemyss I think you know."

Arthur did know Mr. Wemyss; and admitted as much to that indifferent gentleman. "A beautiful place you have here, Mrs. Gower," was all he could think to say.

"Perfect," added Wemyss. "Look at that mountain—not the first one, but the second, half lost in the gloom, beyond the bay of bright water—I have rarely seen a mountain placed with more exquisite taste."

"You are very kind," replied Mrs. Gower with a slight smile. "I think I may say, with Porthos, that my mountains are very fine—'mon air est très-beau,' you know."

"Tell me, Mrs. Gower," said Arthur, "who is the lady talking with the man I do not know; the dark man, with broad shoulders?"

"Don't you know him? That is Lionel Derwent, the great English traveller—writer—soldier—socialist—what shall I say? And she is Mrs. Wilton Hay. You must indeed know her, for you are to take her in to dinner. Shall I introduce you?"

Mrs. Hay was one of those apparent and obvious beauties of whom all young men are rather afraid. How could his poor attentions content so experienced a shrine? Still, it was in a state of rather pleasurable panic that he went up to her, was presented, and made his due obeisance. Mrs. Hay did not snub him; her mission was to fascinate; and from this and other points about her, Arthur divined that she was English. English beauties are less coy than ours, and more eager to please: all professional manners must be equable. And even Mrs. Flossie Gower's photographs were not sold on Broadway; though perhaps she sighed for that distinction.

"I am told I am to have the pleasure of taking you in to dinner," said Arthur. Mrs. Hay had dazzled him a little, and he could think of nothing better to say.

"What a pity you had to be told!" laughed she. "It would be so much nicer if one could choose partners, you know. It's almost as bad as marriage, isn't it? All the spontaneity of the companionship is destroyed; and you haven't any escape—at least, until after dinner." Now, this was a clever device of the siren by which she bound Arthur to her band of adorers for the whole evening. He was nothing loath.

"Marriage!" he answered vaguely. He started to tell her she would rob the grave of its terrors, let alone matrimony; but it seemed rather sudden. So he laughed; and swore to himself as he felt that he had laughed sillily. Was he such a country-boy as to be afraid of this woman because she was handsome and he saw it?

Dinner was announced; so he offered her his arm and said nothing until they were seated. Then they both looked around; and it was the occasion for those whispered confidences about the general *coup d'œil* and the appearance of their fellow-creatures which form so quickly the little bonds of mutual likes and dislikes.

And, truly, it is a fine and a suggestive sight—a dinner party—custom cannot stale, to the thoughtful guest, its infinite variety; however age may wither it. For are not here collected, in one carefully arranged bouquet, the single flowers of our vast society? The newest varieties, the brightest tints and rarest hybrids. Here are twelve of the few who have wealth to bloom and give fragrance, leisure to cultivate, develop, and adorn; they are fretted with no cares until the morrow; their duty but pleasure, to be happy their one endeavor, to please and to be pleased. I am afraid to say how many folk have labored that this hour should be a pleasant one to these; shall we say, a thousand? The table is snowy and sparkling; about it sit these six men, whose chief virtue seems conformity, those six women, whose merit seems display. They do not eat, they dine; a daily sacrament of taste and studied human life. So, far above the cares of earth, feast leisurely the careless gods—do they not?

Who are our gods and goddesses? Well, first, there *is* Mrs. Levison-Gower; she is in gray silk and silver, *pétillante* with *esprit* (how does it happen that she always makes one go to the French for epithets?). On the right, Lord Birmingham, who looks bored; next him (to Arthur's slight surprise) is Kitty Farnum. Then John Haviland; then Mrs. Malgam; then Caryl Wemyss at the end, looking irritable. (Mr. Gower was away.) On his right, Mrs. Wilton Hay (black velvet is her dress, without lace or collar, from which her blond neck bursts, like a hot-house bud)—then Arthur; next him, little Pussie Duval and a stranger; beyond him, Miss Marion Lenoir, a dinner beauty, and Lionel Derwent, on his hostess's left, and scowling at Lord Birmingham. Five—yes, six beautiful women; half a dozen picked men. A veritable round table, with women's rights, in this castle by the storied river, "Tell me, who is that next you—a fine-looking man?" said Mrs. Hay.

"I believe his name is Van Kull," said Arthur, indifferently.

"Oh, indeed?" said she, with interest; and honored our old acquaintance with her eyeglass. "I heard he was such a favorite with the Prince." And as we have not seen Kill Van Kull for some years, a hint as to his past would not be amiss. Only, you mustn't refer to his recent past, beyond the last two months. The fact is, Van Kull had a way of disappearing, under complicated circumstances; but as he always returned alone, after a few months, society pardoned it. Particularly when he came back with a man, a lord, or fresh from a visit at Sandringham—New York tries hard to be virtuous; but what can it do when an offence is condoned by London?

"I tell you, you should read your Bibles," broke in a voice, like a heavy bell. The sentiment seemed *mal à propos;* but the voice was Lionel Derwent's, and it continued speaking without the slightest tremor of consciousness that it was producing a sensation. "You are none of you Christians—not one." Derwent was addressing Mrs. Gower; but, in the sudden silence, his remark seemed addressed to the entire company. The remark did not seem to offend anybody, coming from so handsome a man with so sweet a voice; but there was quite a little chorus of shocked dissent.

"Do you suppose," said Derwent, gravely, "that the Christian church, when it reorganized society, meant—this sort of thing?" And with a sweeping glance, that was as definite as a wave of the hand, but not so discourteous, Derwent indicated the table and its brilliant occupants. No one seemed quite ready to defend herself, as there manifested; as for the men, they sat all withdrawn from the fray, with the feeling that, as they made no religious pretences, it did not concern them. Perhaps Miss Lenoir's reply served the purpose as well as any other.

"But surely, Mr. Derwent, we are all church members," said she, simply.

"The church itself is not Christian," said he, as simply. "I doubt if it ever has been, since it got established in Rome, it or its Eastern and Western successors. The fact is, the only two high religions of the world have both rested on the abnegation of self: the Buddhist, by quietism and annihilation; the Christian, by action and sacrifice. But the Jews and Mahometans founded their ethics upon the development of self, upon visible rewards, slaves and flocks and herds, personal aggrandizement; and these things they obtained by wars of conquest, by the church militant, as rewards of the holy zeal that made converts by physical victory. Then Christ came; and it was his only work to remove this idea, to change this life, not as a king of a victorious people, but as a vessel of divine spirit. But this one work and faith of Christ, this only thing that made his teachings new, regenerative of the world, is just alone what all our churches, Protestant and Catholic, unite in evading, in dodging, in interpreting away. The one thing they will not follow Christ in is his unselfishness."

"But we cannot all be saints and martyrs," said Mrs. Gower.

"If we were all Christians, there would be no martyrs," said Derwent.

"I think," said Wemyss, softly, as if he were studying the painting of a fan, "I think that Mr. Derwent is historically right. Such was undoubtedly the pure doctrine, the face of the pale Christ as it first appeared, palsying the hand of art and civilization, unnerving the arm of war, bleaching life of all color and flower, whelming the sunlight of Greece in the pale artificial cloister, quenching the light of the world in an unsane, self-wrought asceticism.

> 'When for chant of Greeks the wail of Galileans
> Made one whole world moan with hymns of wrath and wrong.'

We may know the gods are but a beautiful fancy; but it would almost prove a devil's existence, that humanity had hardly found itself at peace with itself in a fair and fertile earth, fanned by sea-winds and warmed by summer suns, when some devil's instinct made it fashion for itself a cruel fetich, oppress its brief mortal hours with nightmares of immortal torture, curse itself with grotesque dreams of Calvaries and hells." And Mr. Wemyss snuffed at the rose-bud in his hand, as a Catholic might sprinkle holy-water.

"But, my good sir," answered Derwent, and his voice rang with the disdain of the athlete for the æsthete, "Christ has not taken from you the flowers of the field nor the breezes of the sea, although his curse be on your factories and mints, your poison-stills and money-mills, your halls and courts and prisons. He has given you the soul of a man for the life of a dog. Any pig may possess, an ape can dress itself in trinkets; but only souls can dream, think, do, be free. Assert your souls in freedom, not weight them down with things. Think you that beauty, glory, love, and light come from possessing tangible objects?"

Caryl Wemyss made no reply; but raised a glass of Yquem to his lips and sipped it slowly. The rest were not in it at all, as Van Kull good-naturedly whispered to Pussie Duval. In his simple way, Kill Van Kull suspected that he would some day be damned; but he took it in good part. John Haviland made answer. "You, too, think Christianity is communism?" said he.

"Not necessarily that," said Lionel Derwent; "and much more than that. The New Testament makes no direct attack on property but as the root of other evils. Property would be harmless, if it did not foster the self-idolatry; this is the true curse. Even that poor cynic, La Rochefoucauld, saw that *amour-propre* was the principle on which our social fabric rests. The truth is, that the moment you have counters, everybody makes getting counters all the game. Now, the true game is emulation of the soul, or, even, of the body; of the real self, not the factitious one. Let us have healthy bodies, brave men, heroes, and poets; beautiful women, kind hearts, noble souls; not dukedoms and visiting-lists, landed-estates and money-appraisals. If diamonds are intrinsically beautiful, wear them, paste or real; but do not wear them because they are things difficult for the country curates' daughters to get. But flowers are prettier, after all. And even then, it is the beauty, not the trinket, we are right to seek. God made a woman's neck; the devil made the diamonds upon it."

"It is a far cry from the New Testament to woman's fashions," said Mrs. Wilton Hay, maliciously. Mrs. Hay was a hunting woman and followed the hounds; and her neck had frequently been praised in the society newspapers. But Derwent took it innocently.

"True," said he, simply; "and I say our churches do not dare to preach the words of Christ, but awkwardly fashion them into parables and symbolisms; in effect, they say, 'Christ said it, but did not mean it.' The Roman church, too, enriches itself; but this is nearer Christ, for she gives a part away. But our dissenting churches encourage their director-deacons and produce-exchange elders in taking what they can unto themselves, and even whitewash their methods for ever so slight a share of the plunder. But when Christ made that remark about a rich man, a camel, and the eye of a needle, he meant a needle's eye, and not a paddock-gate. And when he said, 'Sell that thou hast, and give to the poor,' he meant now and here, not in some future state of civilization, nor yet by charitable devise. And when he said, 'take no thought for the morrow—for where your treasure is, there will your heart be also—and your father knoweth you have need of these things,' he had in mind both the future course of stocks and the necessity of brown-stone fronts and widows' life-assurance. But our churches imply to us, 'Christ was a good man; but he was no political economist. He did not foresee these things. Life has grown a more complex art than he could comprehend.'"

Mrs. Gower had shown signs of rapidly increasing distress throughout this harangue; and now she gave the signal for the women to depart. "It is so interesting!" whispered Mrs. Malgam, as she swept in front of Derwent. "Do tell me more about it after dinner." Derwent bowed; and the six men resumed their seats; Van Kull and Birmingham talking horse; Arthur and Wemyss near Haviland and Derwent.

"I do not object to your conclusions, Mr. Derwent," began Wemyss, languidly, "but to your remedy. Christianity is so far from being this, that it is the cause of that decadence we both see. And what more natural than that Christianity, having destroyed civilization, should perish, like another Rienzi, in the conflagration itself has kindled?"

"And I," said Haviland, impatiently, "object not to the remedy, but to your conclusion. That, I take it, is communism. Now, communism is no part of Christianity."

"Neither," said Derwent, "is property. Christ, from his principle of non-resistance, admitted property in others; but his own disciples were to do without it. There have been two great religions—religions in the true sense religion, transcendental faiths, looking from this world to the next—and each was followed by a so-called religion which was really not religion, but looked to this world alone. Both the two religions aimed at the annihilation of the individual; the Buddhist by passive abnegation, the Christian by active emulation in the doing of good to others. The one is the negation of self; the other is its apotheosis. Therefore, Christianity has naught to do with property, which is the accentuation of self, by aggrandizement, by appendages. Christ recognized persons, not personages. Christianity came with a commercial civilization, and as an antidote to it, after the Jewish religion, which had asserted a divine recognition of property; and set up an earthly kingdom, that had to do with flocks and herds and landed estates. And after Christ Islam came, with wars and conquests. So the Jews never recognized the Messiah; they looked not beyond into the next world."

"And as a compensation," interposed Wemyss, "they seem likely to obtain all that there is of this. But we are told that finally the Jews, too, shall become Christians—which lends a terror even to the millennium." There was a general laugh; of which Derwent seemed to be unconscious.

"So the gospels," Derwent added, "recognize no property save in the soul. This is what we are adjured to preserve, though we lose the whole world besides. A man's truth and love, his sense of goodness and beauty, his courage and his pity, are his alone. Even his body is only his secondarily, and temporarily; his broad acres, his trees and rivers, are no part of him at all."

"But it remains property—even if you sell it all and give it to the poor," said Haviland.

"Not if they give it over again to whomsoever has immediate need," answered Derwent. "In this broad world there is room for all; and there are fruits in plenty, ample food, and raiment always ready. Let each one take what he needs, and have no fear of getting no more when these are gone. Why, the labor of all men for some few minutes a day will suffice to bring them all things they can need and use. Property is unnecessary. But men are like rude children at a public feast: each one fearing that he shall not get enough, they trample one another forward, and the foremost few lay hands upon it all."

"No one of us who thinks," said Haviland, "would object to communism if it were practicable. But I must have an overcoat, or a roof, or a horse; is anyone coming along who prefers my coat, my roof, to his, or to none, to take it? And, in the second place, men are not unselfish enough to work, even those few minutes a day, that all humanity may live."

"They are, if they have souls," said Derwent. "And if not, we are beasts; and let us perish like them. And as for the first objection, it is a trivial one, soon forgotten in practice. There will naturally grow up an unwritten respect for one's personal belongings; so far as it is necessary that there should be. If a man needs a coat so much as to filch mine, it is better he should have it. Free men will no more stoop to take a neighbor's coat, or roof, or hat, than a prince will steal a pocket-handkerchief. And as to great values like statues, paintings, libraries, they are for all the world, and not to be monopolized by a vulgar money-maker. He truly owns a picture who enjoys it; not he who buys it. The pleasure in these, by divine law, is not selfish, not individual; only when a man loses himself in the contemplation of a beautiful picture does he really enjoy it, really make it his; it is of as little moment who has the title to the canvas and frame, as it is who owns the wide prairies and the mountains that the poet roams over. So there need be no vulgar property in these things; and they are all that is worth enjoying. As to exotics, and waste land, and dozens of houses, and yachts, and palaces, and game-preserves—these are social crimes."

"Exactly," said Wemyss, with a well-bred sneer in his inflection. "You wish, like all the rest, to abolish civilization. All communists hate excellence; because they do not themselves excel. They say, since we cannot all be princes, let us all be savages."

"What they say, Mr. Wemyss," cried Derwent, fiercely, "is this: Instead of the vulgar democracy of crass possession, let us have the noble aristocracy of merit, mind, and soul. Let no man excel by owning the souls and bodies, the waking and the sleeping, the getting up and the lying down of his fellow-men. And this whether it be done directly, by chattel slavery, or more secretly and dangerously, by corporate control, monopoly of land, monopoly of that fateful thing that men call capital. Money is the devil's counters; a treasure accursed, thrice cursed when welded into the ring of power, like that fabled Rhinegold, which only he may win who for it lays aside all love, both human and divine. Let men enjoy the light of the earth, the noble teachings of art and letters, the health of the body and the freedom of the soul; but these without the virus of self-appropriation. It is this that makes barbarism; it is not civilization. Look at your Yankee money-grubbers; they give, and greedily, ten thousand dollars for a common painting, which they may ostentatiously make their own; they would hesitate to give a dollar for Dante's Divine Comedy, if he wrote to-day, because—of course, they do not care for it—and they cannot lock it up as theirs and bar it from their fellow-men. And even if, as you insinuate, the future were to be what you call barbarism, the morning chase of the free savage after the wild creature on whom he feeds is more ennobling than the grimy greed of a stunted humanity for these counters that are worthless in themselves. I have seen Australia and Hawaii, and I have seen Sheffield and East London; and I say, better a thousand-fold the heathen savagery than such Christian civilization as are these."

"I have hitherto failed to observe, among socialists or knights of labor, or their wives," said Wemyss, dryly, "any newer or other impulse than a rising desire for these same counters that you scoff at, or the gin and brass jewellery that they may purchase with them."

"Ay," cried Lionel Derwent, "you have seen little yet but a blind, instinctive striving for the drugs and poisons you have fed them on; for the treasure you have kept, and welded to the ring of tyranny that held them down. So, when you lift a stone from the ground, or hurl the roof from some long-lived-in Bastile of humanity, the sudden sunlight streams in, and the prisoners, poor insects that they are, crushed by a thousand years of oppression, blinded, dazzled by the light of heaven, grope vainly and mechanically for the things of earth they have been wonted to, and which want and custom and your own example have taught them, too, to prize. No, they are not better than you are, yet; not until their souls have come to life that you so long have robbed them of. But give us light and love, and the word of Christ, and we will see. But, as I said in the beginning, your priests have tortured even this to suit their ends."

"Well, Mr. Derwent, I wish you success in your mission. Civilization has got to go, one way or another; and I don't know that it matters much which. I confess that your way strikes me as rather a novel one. Most of your radical friends, however, if what you say be their true aim, show a singular predilection for atheism, free-love, and omitting their daily baths." With which climax and a slight yawn, Wemyss walked over and joined the group in the other corner.

John Haviland had for a long time been silent; but now he spoke. "I am afraid, Mr. Derwent," said he, "that I so far agree with Mr. Wemyss as to feel that three essentials of civilization are so bound up together that with leaving either one we may lose the rest—I mean, my right to my property, my right to my wife, and my right to personal liberty. The same radicalism which, on the one hand, sets up a tyranny of majority government to tell me what I shall think, what I shall eat, what I shall spend, is that which, on the other hand, tends to the age of reason and the regulation of property out of existence, and women's rights to lose themselves as women, and absolute liberty of divorce. Property and marriage and personal liberty—they go together. There is no argument for freedom but the inner light of the mind; none for monogamy but that it seems farther from the beasts; none for property but that man creates it for himself. And the age of reason, which denies a divine sanction, will yet require a divine sanction for all that it does not destroy."

"Man does not create the air, nor the ocean, nor the surface of the earth," said Derwent.

"No; and man does not hold the surface of the earth for himself, but for all humanity. Is it not better that you should make a garden of a hundred acres than that it should lie a common waste? You hold it, not for yourself, but in general trust; sooner or later, if you fail to make the land bear fruit for all of us, it will be taken from you. If you are not a good steward for the people, you will, sooner or later, fail. Christ said 'Sell that thou hast, and give to the poor;' but is it not doing the same thing to keep what I have, and use it for the poor?"

Derwent paused a moment; and before he could reply, Wemyss came back.

"Shall we join the ladies?" said he.

All the gentlemen got up, some hastily finishing their coffee, others taking a last whiff of their cigars.

"He paid twenty thousand," said Van Kull, hurriedly, to Birmingham. "He bought him for the Duval stables."

## CHAPTER XVIII.

### A DAY'S PLEASURE.

ARTHUR awoke the next morning with a confused consciousness of splendors and regret; a mood which seemed superinduced by some forgotten dream. His first perceptions, however, were of the glory of the morning and the budding, bursting season. The shade had been drawn up by a servant; and from his bed he saw through the open window mile after mile of the country-side, and beyond it the broad, gay river, wearing, like a new gown, the blue of early summer. What nests of men might be in sight were lost in the white glow of blossoms; but the birds made their presence vocal, singing in the close boughs unseen.

No man with a trace of sap left in him could lie inert at such a time; and Arthur rang the bell and asked the servant when they might have breakfast.

"There is no bell, sir," said he; "the ladies mostly breakfasts by eleven, and the gentlemen when they like. Have you found your things, sir?"

As everything of Arthur's had been laid out and brushed in most attractive order, he had; and he dressed and sought the breakfast-room. Here was no one but Mrs. Malgam, who, attired in a diaphanous material of many folds and pale tea-rose ribbons, was standing at the window like a thing bereft. But as Arthur came in, her face mantled with smiles that could have hardly "been much sweeter for the blush between." "Oh, Mr. Holyoke, I am so glad you've come," said she. "It *is* so poky, breakfasting alone."

Mrs. Malgam sat down to make the tea; and Arthur sat down beside her. "What pretty hands she has," thought Arthur; "I never noticed them before." And just as he thought this, her blue eyes fixed his, looking suddenly up from the tea. "One lump or two?" said she. "One," said Arthur, gravely.

A word should be given to Baby Malgam, as many thought her likely to be Flossie Gower's rival; that is at some day, for as yet our heroine still distanced her. It is true, Flossie was a nobody, by birth; so was Mrs. Malgam; but her first husband had been Mr. Ten Eyck. Flossie was rich, but so at this time was Mrs. Malgam; Flossie was no longer young, while Baby's ivory skin still was smooth with youth and pleasure and lack of care. Baby had been poor; and now she had three houses and four horses and forty ball-dresses and a young and fashionable and careless husband and an opera-box, and the grace and *cachet* of her own to properly adorn all these things—a grace which had been almost a trial to her when, already conscious of it, she had feared it was to be never used, but born like a blossom of the fields, to die there, and not in a china vase. But now she had her china vase, and was happy, and fast forgetting the fields, and him who had wandered with her in them; and regretted, not that he was dead, but that she was growing stout. And it was very coscy and charming for Arthur to be sitting with her so prettily at breakfast.

"Is nobody else up?" said he. But he did not say it in regret; and Caryl Wemyss would not have said it at all, as Arthur thought with a pang just afterward. Mrs. Malgam smiled a little, but she said:

"Mr. Derwent has been up and disappeared long since. Mr. Haviland has gone to the city. Flossie never appears until luncheon. About the rest, I don't know."

"What are we to do to-day?" said he, by way of conversation.

"Anything we like—that is Mrs. Gower's rule. I fancy she and Mr. Wemyss will take a drive;" and she laughed a little again. "Mr. Van Kull and Mrs. Hay thought of riding. That is, Mr. Van Kull spoke of it to Mrs. Hay; and Mrs. Hay proposed it to Lord Birmingham. But I fancy his lordship will ride with Kitty Farnum." And again did pretty Mrs. Malgam laugh a little.

"Are there horses for all of us?" said Arthur.

"Oh, yes. Mrs. Gower has a way of providing for us, you see."

"In that case," said Arthur, "will not you drive with me?"

Mrs. Malgam would and did; and a lovely drive they had of it in the fresh May morning, over the range of hills back in the high country behind the Hudson. Mrs. Malgam's conversation was most charming, and instructive, too, to a young man; it is unfortunate that so much of its merit consisted in the manner and personality of its owner as to be quite incapable of transcription. They talked of the day; of the place; of Mrs. Gower, of Mrs. Gower's friends; of love; a good deal of himself; a little of herself; of the time for luncheon; and of the immediate future. This last topic was called up by Mrs. Malgam's asking whether Arthur was invited to the coaching party; and it turned out that Mrs. Gower had in immediate contemplation a drive in a coach-and-four from Catfish-on-the-Hudson up to Lenox. Lucie Gower was coming up from town to drive them; and Mrs. Malgam, though she had not yet received her invitation, was in hopeful expectation of one. It must be confessed that the prospect was enviable; and Arthur most ardently joined in the wish, so kindly expressed by the pretty woman who was his companion, that he might be one of the party.

Civilization has cruelly made up for making our luncheon regular and certain by depriving us often of any desire for it; but one of the brightest attractions of the upper circle of humanity, in which our hero now moved, is perhaps its return to this primitive condition. It is a pity that fresh air and idleness, cleanliness and exercise, do not necessarily bring with them health for the soul; but they bring health for this world, which is already something. Arthur and the pretty woman returned at two, impelled chiefly by a desire for food; and found others of the company, similarly inspired, already sitting at the table. Wemyss alone, whose dyspepsia seemed to be the last relic of his inherited puritan conscience, was not hungry.

"I do not know what we can do for you, lovely Jills, this afternoon," said Flossie. "Three of our Jacks have disappeared. Mr. Haviland and Charlie Townley are in town, and Mr. Derwent has gone to the Mills village. Pussie, where's your young man? Your acknowledged one, I mean—Jimmy De Witt?"

Miss Duval blushed and smiled. "Mr. De Witt is in town, I suppose. His address is the Columbian Club."

"Yes, dear," said Flossie, laughing. "Well, I've written to him. Then there's Sidney Sewall coming to dinner," Flossie went on, as if she were counting her chickens. Sewall was the famous editor of one of the great papers of the day.

"He's awfully clever, and improving and all that," continued the critical Mrs. Malgam; "but he's no good in the country. What's become of Mr. Derwent, did you say?"

"He's passing the day at the Mills down in the town, studying the condition of the laboring classes, I suppose. He's always doing that kind of thing."

"Much more likely he's found a pretty face there," said Van Kull. "Those cranks are all humbugs."

Miss Farnum looked at Van Kull while he spoke, and then looked about as if for someone to answer. Her eye fell upon Marion Lenoir. And Miss Lenoir was magnetized to speak.

"Oh, how can you say so, Mr. Van Kull?" she cried. "When he talks so earnestly, and fixes his eyes upon you so, they bore you through and through. I could fall in love with a man like that, I am sure."

Miss Farnum rose and walked to the window. "Yes, and he bores me through and through," Van Kull had retorted; but there was a general noise of rising and sliding back chairs, and no one noticed his little joke. Jokes were rare with this big fellow; a fact to which he owed much of his popularity.

Arthur stood at first with Miss Farnum for a minute; but she seemed unresponsive, and he was soon swept out in the wake of Mrs. Wilton Hay. The broad terrace was bathed in the pleasant May sunlight; but over the end opposite the house was an awning slanted down to the stone balustrade. The great river lay still; far to the south, where the light blue vanished in the gleaming, was a solitary sail.

The air was full of the singing of birds and the fragrance of spring blossoms; it was like a scene from Boccaccio, thought Arthur, the stone terrace and the flowers, and the distant view. Caryl Wemyss seemed to have like thoughts. "If life were only this, how simple it would be!" said he. But even this speech was too analytical for the company in its present mood.

"It only rests with us to make it so," he added, as if expecting an answer.

"I don't see what you mean," said Mrs. Hay. And she did not. Wemyss smiled bitterly, or smiled as if he meant it so. Flossie laughed. Lord Birmingham came up and leaned over Mrs. Hay's chair; then Van Kull came up on the other side, and Arthur had to go over to Miss Farnum, who was standing alone, looking over the parapet into the deep gorge in the forest, that led down toward the river. Mrs. Malgam and the other two girls were laughing together, standing at the other end of the terrace. Miss Farnum seemed to Arthur more *blasée* than any girl he knew.

"Why does your friend Mr. Haviland come here so much?" asked she, suddenly. Now, Arthur could certainly give no answer to this. And he remembered his first discovery of John's secret, as he had thought.

"It is a delightful house to visit," said he. "Did you have a pleasant ride this morning?" And he remembered the scene in the opera-box.

"I hate Englishmen and foreigners," said she, inconsequently; and just then Birmingham came up. "Lovely day, Miss Farnum," said he. "Ah, would you not like a bit of a walk? The park, down there, looks most inviting."

"I don't know," said she, listlessly. "What are the others going to do?"

"They're playing tennis, I dare say, or something like," said he. "I got off, you know."

Miss Farnum turned toward the house; and just then the others joined them. "You play, Mr. Holyoke, I know," said Marion Lenoir, "and Mr. Van Kull is such a dab at it." Van Kull looked anything but a dab at it, but rather an oddly sophisticated lamb being led to the slaughter; but then Miss Lenoir was, as she expressed it, "a tennis girl." And certainly she looked it, when Arthur met her on the lawn, her lithe young figure robed in a blue and white tennis dress, her black hair shining in a tight coil.

"Fie, what would Jimmy say?" said Mrs. Gower to Miss Duval as they passed her. "Jimmy may say what he pleases," said that young woman, with a shrug of her shoulders.

They had played several sets, and Miss Lenoir so well that she and Arthur had won most of them, when there was a ripple of excitement among the two married women, who had been sitting on a shady bench watching the game. Mrs. Gower had disappeared; Mr. Wemyss had sauntered up from time to time, to say a word and disappear again. "I do believe it's the men come back!" cried Mrs. Hay, as a carriage stopped at the door of the house.

The game came to an end; and Arthur walked back with his partner to the terrace. Charlie Townley was there, and a middle-aged man who was Mr. Sewall, as Miss Lenoir told him; and a stout man with a red face, who bore a little clumsily his introduction to Mrs. Hay, and then turned with a "Well, old fellow—what do you know?" to Kill Van Kull. It was our old friend S. Howland Starbuck. He had changed more than Van Kull, and seemed ten years older, with a bloated look in his face. Van Kull, as he stood there in his light scarlet tennis-jacket and white flannels, was still a model of manly strength, with features pale and clear-cut, and a look of race about him. Probably he had led a far worse life than simple Buck Starbuck, as they still called him; but Van Kull's beauty deathless, like a fallen angel's. "So good of you all to take pity on us lone women," said Flossie Gower, as she approached with Mr. Wemyss. "Mr. Sewall, thanks for leaving the administration so long unwatched. How are you, Si?

Tell us what to do, Mr. Townley. Shall we take a sail?"

"A sail would be delightful, I think," said Sewall, affably. "Mrs. Hay, I hope you got safely home the other night? Lord Birmingham, I am very glad to meet you; I had the pleasure of knowing your father, the late Earl."

"Come, young women!" cried Flossie, "run and get your things on. I've ordered the lunch to be ready at five."

Arthur was much impressed at the prospect of going on a pleasure-jaunt with so great a man as Sidney Sewall. He was one of those who really seem to shape the fortunes of the country; his newspaper was a political power throughout the land, and he made and unmade candidates at will. People of wealth and fashion were getting familiar to our hero; but the companionship of men of power was a social summit he had never yet climbed. Flossie Gower liked to get such men about her, as a child plays with chessmen.

There was a break to take them to the river; but most of the company preferred to walk. Mrs. Gower led the way with Mr. Sewall, and Arthur was close behind with Marion Lenoir. He was struck with the elaborate air of pleasure-seeking that Mr. Sewall assumed; he made himself a perfect squire of dames, for the nonce, and his talk was of other people and their misdoings. As they turned from the lower footpath-gate of Mrs. Gower's place into the main road, they met Derwent, striding homeward in his knickerbockers; and Flossie introduced him to Mr. Sewall. Then they all went on and soon came to the river, where the Gowers' pretty little steam-yacht lay at a private wharf. Derwent was full of his day at the Mills; and began talking of it to the great editor. "They are nearly all French Canadians," said he, "not Americans at all; and their wages are quite as low, except the few skilled workmen and foremen, as at Manchester."

"They were even lower last year," said Sewall, "at the time of the worst depression. The mill has really no reason for being, except the tariff; and, of course, in the bad years the laborers are ten times worse off than if there were no tariff at all. But it attracts Canadian cheap labor; and our ignorant workmen think they are being protected all the same."

"Surely, you would not abolish the tariff and wipe out the mill entirely?" said Wemyss, who had taken a seat close by. Sewall shrugged his shoulders. He was the editor of a great protectionist newspaper. "There is no use riding against a herd of cattle," said he. "If you want to lead them, you must ride their way." Arthur opened his eyes at this, for Sewall's paper declared itself the great representative of the laboring classes; but he soon found that "cattle" was a milder term than the popular editor usually applied to his constituency. "The secret of statesmanship," he went on, "in representative government, is to do nothing yourself until driven to it by the rabble, and in the meantime make capital out of the other fellow's mistakes."

"Ay," said Derwent; "but it is not the people, but the selfish middle class that rules as yet. Anarchy, even tyranny, may be the mother of men, of high thought and noble deeds; but the lights of the Manchester school are matter and greed, dry bones and death."

Sewall looked at him quizzically. "Oh, dear," said he, good-naturedly, "here's another terrible fellow who believes something!"

"But," hazarded Arthur, with a blush, "will not representatives do something, and think something, when we make our politics something more than a game for party stakes?"

"Young man," said Sewall, impressively, "this country cannot be governed without parties and organizations. And if the organizers are not paid for their trouble, they wont organize. I've never known a man with a principle that was worth his salt in politics yet; how can you expect parties to have them? This great country of ours is on the make, just now; and it doesn't trouble itself about much else." And Mr. Sewall suddenly dropped his professional tone and, turning to Mrs. Gower, resumed his air of an *homme du monde.* "Lovely country, after all, is it not, Mrs. Gower? Look at that purple twilight stealing in under the western mountains; I've just got a Daubigny with exactly that feeling in it. Only Frenchmen can paint in the half lights, the minor tones, after all."

Mrs. Gower still patronized art, though she successively had given over most of her special protections for the patronage of human life in general; but Sewall was an amateur, and was famed for his galleries, his cellars, and his orchids. Derwent looked at him from the corners of his eyes, but kept silent; meantime Kill Van Kull, Si Starbuck, and Marion Lenoir, sitting forward, had brought out their banjos and struck up a Southern melody, very soft and sweet. "What a pity we have no folk-songs," said Wemyss. "Great art is, after all, impossible without the nursery songs and tales of many generations, without the legends and delusions of the people."

"I am glad to find you need the people for something," said Derwent, dryly.

"But they have self-educated it away," said Wemyss. "They have driven beauty out of the world with the three Rs; and now they are about to cut one another's throats for its mere goods and raw material."

"True," said Derwent. "But is it they that have done it? or we that have taught them?"

"Speaking of the people," laughed Flossie, "there they are." And she pointed to an excursion-boat coming up the river; it was filled with a holiday party—clerks, upper mechanics, small tradesmen, and their womankind. The latter were resplendently dressed in new bonnets and bright shawls; the husbands looked dingy and jaded. Wemyss took out his opera-glass and scanned the decks for a minute or more, then laid it down wearily as if exhausted. "I have no doubt they are most of them virtuous," said he. "But they all wear glass diamonds in their ears."

"Nay," said Sewall, without cynicism, but as if merely stating an obvious fact. "There are the people." And he pointed to a huge three-decked barge, coming slowly down stream before two tugs. It was covered with long streamers; the largest bearing, in flaring white letters, "The P. J. McGarragle Association;" and on smaller ones, "6th Ward." All the decks were black with people; and all the people were waltzing to the loud rhythm of several brass bands. A few dozen of the younger men on the lower deck yelled at the little launch as it went by; they were tipsily singing an obscene song. "Mr. McGarragle has just been elected to Congress; and he is giving a free picnic to all his supporters in his district."

"You were one of his supporters, Mr. Sewall, I believe?" said Derwent, calmly. "But you are both wrong. These are the American people, if I understand them right." And he pointed to the night boat. The upper decks were crowded with men, intent on their newspapers, regardless of all else—business-men returning to Chicago or the great lakes. And in the bow and main deck were groups of emigrants bound for the prairies; ploughs, sewing-machines, and bales of Eastern goods. This great steamer swept by them with a certain majesty; and Mrs. Gower's little yacht lay for some seconds, rolling and tossing in its wake.

It was after seven o'clock when they got back from the sail; and all the ladies hurried into the break, lest they should lose that calm leisure before dinner which a perfect toilet demands. Mr. Sewall and Lord Birmingham and Caryl Wemyss were further specially honored with seats therein; the others walked, Townley with Van Kull and Starbuck, Arthur with Lionel Derwent. "What a different man is Sewall from what one would suppose," said Arthur.

"Sidney Sewall is the most guilty criminal in America," said Derwent, vehemently. Arthur started a little at so superlative a characterization; which Derwent went on to explain. "There is a man with all the birthright of light; with the inherited instinct of truth, the training of character, the charm of breeding; with power of intellect and cultivation of the finest that your country gives; and if there is a malignant lie to be disseminated, a class hatred to be stirred up, a cruel delusion to be spread, a poisonous virus of any subtler sort ready to be instilled into the body public and politic—there stands Sidney Sewall, of all men, ready and willing to do the devil's work. And he does it with the genius of a Lucifer; and all to get his personal luxury, and his orchids and his wines, and a little power, and revenge for personal spites. Mephistopheles himself was not so quick at seeing the evil side of any human error, the wrong that may be wrought from any chance event. And yet it does not even pay; or pay any more than if he chose the good and served it with half that intellect of his that now seeks to sap his country's soul!"

Poor Arthur had not thought to reap such a whirlwind with his little conversational seed, and stood aghast.

"And he doesn't really care for money either; he

knows its worthlessness, deep down, as well as I do. And he hasn't even, or he says he hasn't, the devil's motive of ambition to make a reason for his wrong. And he's married a rich woman, like any common adventurer. I tell you I have spent years in this country of yours; and the people have a heart, and a soul, and in their clumsy way they blunder ahead upon the right. But Sewall! He has no heart, nor soul, but only stomach and cerebral matter, like a jelly-fish. In his intellectual Frankenstein way, when fresh from his Ohio farm, he was once a communist; just as he might be to-morrow a dynamiter. But if to-morrow there comes to the polls a well-meaning, honest man, and against him a very figurehead of that greed and cynical materialism which bids fair to blast your country in its bud, this man will hasten to bid the people to choose Barabbas, that Cain and Abel's strife may be on earth once more."

By this time they were walking up the avenue to the house, and on the terrace they met their hostess, already dressed and waiting for them. "Ah, you philosophers!" said she. "You must make haste. By the way, you know I count upon you, Mr. Holyoke, for our coaching party! Mr. Derwent has already promised." Arthur was, of course, delighted.

"I am so glad——" he began.

"There, there," said she, "you must run and dress or you will be late to dinner. And Mr. Sewall is very particular about his dinners, I know."

After Derwent's outburst, Arthur went in to his dinner with some trepidation; but Derwent had too often dined and lodged with Arab chieftains, or other persons who had designs upon his life the next morning, to show his personal feelings in his demeanor. Arthur took in Miss Duval; and she asked him if he had been invited on the coaching party. She was going, and Mrs. Hay, and Kitty Farnum. Mrs. Malgam had not been asked, after all. "She is perfectly furious," said Pussie; "and wanted to go home to-night." And Arthur himself felt a slight pang at the absence of his fair companion, such a mitigated pang as one must feel at the exclusion of others from a paradise open to one's self.

"What men are going?" he asked.

"Oh, Lord Birmingham, and Mr. Wemyss, and Mr. Van Kull—and—and Mr. ——"

"Derwent," said Arthur. "I know."

"Mr. Derwent? dear me," said Miss Duval. "I wonder what he's going for!"

"But where's Mr. Gower?" asked Arthur.

"I don't know," said she. "He can't come, I believe. Kill Van Kull is going to drive."

"You can't fancy what terrible things Mr. Derwent has been telling us, Mr. Sewall. We quite needed you last night. He has been saying we are none of us Christians." It was Mrs. Malgam who spoke.

"We are not," said Sewall. "Christianity is a very fine thing; but, like many another, quite too fine for this world. If people could practise it, there would be no need of it; it would be heaven here and now, and a divine revelation quite superfluous."

"And are you really going to drive, Mr. Van Kull?"

said Mrs. Hay. "You are such a dangerous man, I shall not trust myself with you—on the box seat." And she cast down her eyes, while Van Kull gave her one of the dark glances that made his pale face so famous.

"Would you confess as much in your paper, Mr. Sewall?" said Derwent, in answer to his speech.

"Certainly not," said the great editor. "You know the natural failing of the middle classes is hypocrisy; and we still have a large constituency with them. They like to think they are Christians, while they make their money; just as they like to have full reports of divorce cases, and call it news."

"Hypocrisy, in the end, is of all vices the one least suffered by gods and men," said Derwent.

"Quite so; and sooner or later the people will arise and wipe out the middle class in this country, and leave nothing between them and us," said Sewall, placidly. "That is why I am anxious to have my paper appeal more and more to the masses."

"But when that day comes, we—that is, the people—will destroy you, too," said Derwent.

Sewall looked again at Derwent, with his expression of polite curiosity, as at a misplaced mummy. "Our grandchildren, you mean," said he. "I haven't any."

"All thinking men are agreed as to the coming *déchéance*," put in Wemyss. "They only differ as to the feelings with which they regard it."

"Well," said Sewall, in a tone of finality, "we can get a good time out of this world as it is; those to come may amuse themselves as they like. What do you think, Mrs. Gower?"

"I think you are all pessimists," said she. "Surely we live in a most enlightened age; consider the progress that has been made in a few years! Why, in my grandfather's old house they hadn't even carpets. Now the very poorest can have everything."

"Everybody has a chance to make money now," said Baby Malgam. "Just think how many self-made men you meet in society!"

"You wouldn't have us go back to those days, surely," said Flossie. "Just think how narrow people were! And everybody thought almost everybody else was going to be damned. But we are growing more liberal every day.

"Ay," grunted Derwent. "We are above the revelation of Christ; but our clever women talk glibly of theosophy, and go into fashionable crazes over imported Buddhist priests; and nobody is afraid of being damned."

"What *is* theosophy, Mr. Derwent?" said Marion Lenoir. "Something to do with spirit-rapping, isn't it?—or palmistry?"

"I am sure," said Mrs. Malgam, "I was always brought up to go to church; but when I was first married, Mr. Ten Eyck didn't care for it."

"The only advantage should be, that the general smash gives us at least a chance at personal liberty. But most of these fads start in my place; and in Boston the masses are more philistine than almost anywhere," said Caryl Wemyss.

"There is some strength in Philistinism," said Sewall, curtly. "What I can't stand is the critical crowd, the cousins of the nephews of the friends of Emerson, who now talk sagely of the fine art of their boarding-house literature, of the tea-table realism school—what Poe called, the Frog-pond weakly school. They are too delicate to take life straight, at most they can only stomach a criticism of a critique of humanity, as we give babies peptonized preparations of refined oatmeal. Their last fad is pure government. Pure government!" repeated Sewall, with a snort of disgust.

"It is the literature of the decadence, of course," said Wemyss; "an emasculated type, product of short-haired women and long-haired men, gynanders and androgynes. I have often myself thought of writing another novel—if only for the sake of putting a great, horrid man into it. But gentlemen should all the more have courage to reassert their essence. It is an age, after all, when one may lead a full life. There is a fine passage somewhere in Zola, where the lips of two lovers are unsealed at the approach of death. So we, on the eve of the destruction of society, are free to live our lives elementally; enforced to idleness, like patricians in the fall of Rome."

"Mr. Wemyss, do you know my definition of a Boston man?" cried Sewall, who had had an evident struggle to repress himself during this speech.

"No," said Wemyss, respectfully sipping a glass of Yquem.

"An Essay at Life," said Sewall, hurling the words at Wemyss like a missile.

There was a certain pause and then Derwent was heard softly quoting Dante's "gran rifiuto."

"So there is nothing for us, you both think, but to make 'the grand refusal,'" said he, sadly. "To take no office in our human life, but wait for death; amusing ourselves as best we may."

After which, Lord Birmingham was heard saying to Miss Farnum, "I should so like to show you Noakes Park."

"No," said Sewall, taking up the thread of the conversation again, "what's the use of breaking lances on windmills? The simple fact is, that everybody wants about a hundred times his individual proportion of the world's labor; and some few fellows have got to have it, and the other ninety-nine be deprived of that little which they have. Therefore the more toys we give the rabble to play with the better. When they find them out, they'll break the toys and our heads with them."

"I'm sure," said Mrs. Malgam, "I don't see what there is so very terrible. I like real lace shawls; but my Irish servants prefer red and green ones. And what would be the use of taking a scrub-woman to the opera? She wouldn't understand it."

"It's astonishing how soon those same scrub-women catch on," said Charlie Townley, who sat next. "I see two or three at the opera every night."

Derwent muttered something about the lust of the eyes and the pride of life; and Mrs. Gower said there was one in the box next her. "She has red arms and diamonds as big as a hotel-clerk's," said she, with a fine scorn. "But of course there must always be such people trying to get in."

"Kehew entered her; but she was scratched for the Derby," said Van Kull to Si Starbuck, who was on the other side of Mrs. Wilton Hay. "De Mora told me she was safe for the Grand Prix."

"Kehew? why, that's the very man who has entered his wife, too—at the opera," laughed Flossie.

"He's a great friend of the Duc de Mora," said Si Starbuck to his sister. "I don't see what there is bad about the old woman, and the daughter's capital fun."

"Kehew's a wonderful man," added Townley. "He turned up from some road-hotel just out of Chicago, and the next thing we knew he put through that Wabash deal."

"What a name," sighed Wemyss—"Kehew! how it expresses the sharp, lean-faced Yankee of the day, who doses his dyspepsia with whiskey-cocktails, and bores you through with his dull, soulless eyes! 'Brainy,' the newspapers call them, I think."

"But they are making the country, and they make the government," said Sewall. "It's all very well to talk about the greatest good of the greatest number; but government is going to be run in the interest of the successful man, and not for general philanthropy."

"Ah!" said Lionel Derwent, sadly. "You have done a good deal, in your country. You have done away with rank, and chivalry and the feudal system, with established churches and bishops, priests and deacons—except, perhaps, the Pope of Rome. You are independent of authority and experience, and enforced respect—Aristotle's 'Ethics,' and Plato's 'Republic,' to say nothing of Montesquieu and de Tocqueville, have become 'chestnuts,' as your phrase is. 'You have eschewed a titled aristocracy and abolished primogeniture; you elect all your officers, from judges up to President; your laws run in the name of the people, instead of in the name of a prince; your State knows no religion and your judges wear no wigs!'—and for King Log you bow to King Stork; your God Baal is money, and you have lost individual liberty into the bargain."

Mr. Sewall chuckled to himself a little, but said nothing, like an Augur with a sense of humor; the collective individual liberties of the land made power, and power was his. It was left to Mrs. Malgam to respond.

"I am sure," said she, "I think money is very nice; and those who don't want it needn't get it."

"Money," said Wemyss, "gives us the very individual liberty Mr. Derwent wants."

"Money," said Flossie Gower, "is certainly necessary to get married on; else married people would have to be together all the time."

"Oh," said Marion Lenoir, "I think love in a cottage would be just charming. Do you know I saw such a lovely household last winter in Florida——"

But here Mrs. Gower gave the signal; and the men were left to their own reflections. Derwent rose abruptly, took a cigar, and walked out the open window to the terrace above the river. Wemyss and Arthur followed; and the other four were left about the dining-table.

Derwent was puffing his cigar violently, and did not speak to them; but after a minute or two he took the path leading down into the valley and disappeared in the wood. Wemyss and Arthur sat down in one corner of the terrace and lit their cigars comfortably.

"Derwent," said Mr. Wemyss, "is one of those fanatics who do more harm, from their position and education, than any leader of the proletariat. But all women rave about him; for women are all hero-worshippers."

"Mrs. Gower has asked him to go on the coaching-party," said Arthur, secretly flattered at being thought by Wemyss worthy of hearing that gentleman's opinion. He made no reply to this, but frowned obviously. Pretty soon the others came out and joined them, and they had cognac and coffee; the ladies, too, were out on the terrace, at its other end, attracted by the beauty of the night; and gradually the two groups came together and intermingled. But it was the man's hour; and they made bold to keep their cigars, even when, as soon happened, each one joined his fair one and took to walking with her. Wemyss walked with Mrs. Gower, Birmingham with Miss Farnum, Van Kull with Mrs. Hay, Charlie Townley with Miss Duval, and Mrs. Malgam with Si Starbuck.

Arthur found himself with Miss Lenoir. She was a pretty girl, with fine black hair and gray eyes, and an ivory-like complexion; and her dress was the perfection of style and enlightened civilization. It was the most glorious night; a night made for the imaginative and idle, for those who have read the world's literature and looked at paintings, and whose women are fair ladies, bravely dressed. The great pathway of the river lay open to the dark sky, walled by ebon mountain-masses; to the east the azure shaded into blue, where the stars were sown less freely, tremulous, luminous with the rising moon. The moon's light was pleasant, too, on the figure of the pretty girl beside him; and the others, as they passed and repassed, seemed like the gay ladies of Boccaccio's garden, and looked, each pair, as if they had been lovers.

Down in the factory village, too, the night was fine; perhaps a few old men, smoking, enjoyed it, dumbly, as such people do. For these do not comment, in diaries or print, upon such things, nor analyze the moods they bring. But most of the women who were stirring made only a convenience of the moonlight, lighting the uncertain hazards of the dirty street; and the young men, smoking and drinking, were quite unconscious of it, for tobacco and whiskey had more direct action upon their consciousness, besides having a money cost, which the beauty of the night had not. But here, too, were some few young men wandering afield with young women, and perhaps upon these the moonlight had its unconscious effect. Up at Mrs. Gower's the love-making, though not inartistically done, was rather like a play; here it was more earnest. Yet, as it seemed to Lionel Derwent, there was not so much difference between these two places, laying aside mere dress and manner, as there should have been.

But to Arthur, the softness and good taste and beauty of framing seemed inspiration fit for any poet. If the evening was not one of true happiness, it was an excellent worldly counterfeit. After Miss Lenoir went in, he stayed out alone, watching the river. The other guests, successively, sought the drawing-room; and soon he heard Mrs. Hay's voice, singing a simple Scotch ballad, and singing it very well. Now, any cultivated foreman's daughter, in the factory village, would have sung in bad Italian, and not sung well.

As Arthur stood leaning over the balustrade in the terrace, he heard low voices; and looking down, he recognized, in the moonlight, Mr. Caryl Wemyss and his hostess. Their talk seemed to have come to an end; for as she rose, he seized her white hand and imprinted (as the dime novels say), with studied grace, a kiss upon it.

## CHAPTER XIX.

### A COACH AND FOUR COUPLES.

SEVERAL days passed by in much the same way; and truly a pleasant way enough it was. Arthur went now and then to town; but it was easy to get vacations in Townley & Tamms's office, and the inmates were mutually conceding upon this point, particularly when the absence was known to be connected with people likely to be valuable, as clients, to the firm. And perhaps Arthur had a secret notion that his visit at Mrs. Levison Gower's was an advancement more speedy and notable than anything that was likely to come to him in the office while he was away. For, after all, in her society he was getting the ultimate result of all labors and seeing what it was that people realized when they were successful here on earth.

Townley urged Arthur strongly to avail himself of Mrs. Gower's hospitality to its utmost limit. It was a principle of his philosophy of life that it was the part of a clever man to take things directly rather than attain to them gradually; to grasp the fruits, and not cultivate the tree. "Any country bumpkin, any ordinary mechanic, can do that," he would say. "But we in New York, in Wall Street, sit at the counter on which is poured the net earnings, the savings, the symbols of title to all the creations of a mighty nation. Ten thousand men may work to build a railroad, for instance, and ten thousand more to run it; and the clean result of all their toil and trouble, free of all dross and surplusage, is turned into our hands, portable and convenient, in the shape of a few engraved certificates of stock, or bonds, or bank-notes. Presto! change! and some of them are in my pocket, and some in yours, and perhaps a new bit of paper, issued by us for the balance." Arthur found Charlie a much more intellectual fellow than he had thought at first.

Guests came and went at Mrs. Gower's, all with some charm of person, or of fashion, or of successful mind; applied intellect, not perhaps the pure kind. Arthur spent a few days in town, to prepare for his longer absence on the coaching trip; Tamms was moving down to his summer quarters near Long Branch, and old Mr. Townley hardly ever came to the office now. He had a private room upstairs, where he used to spend some two or three hours a week, looking after his trusts. Charlie was neglecting his business more than ever, but seemed to make up for it by his devotions to Mamie Livingstone, which were almost getting, for him, exclusive. That young lady was "coming out" the next autumn, and already making elaborate preparations for it. Arthur saw her when he went to call on Gracie Holyoke, who was going, with Miss Brevier, to the old place at Great Barrington for the summer.

Mrs. Malgam had gone away, and Haviland, and Miss Lenoir; and the party had gradually settled down to those who were invited for the drive. As their numbers were narrowed, a feeling of increased intimacy sprang up among those who were to go through so much together; and they were fond of talking of it and consulting maps as to roads and stopping-places; and they grew confidential about outsiders. "But I thought Mrs. Malgam was to go with us, too," said Mrs. Hay one day to Pussie; the two women were sitting on a new-mown hay-rick on the lawn, that had been cut for ornamental purposes, too soon to make good hay. Arthur was lying, with a volume of poetry, at their feet.

"Oh, dear, no," laughed innocent Miss Duval. "Flossie and Baby never could abide each other. You must know Mrs. Malgam is a very dangerous person, for all she looks like a pan of cream."

"Oh, indeed," said Mrs. Hay, compressing her rich lips. She had recognized in Mrs. Malgam her American counterpart, and was slightly afraid of the violet-eyed brune, to whose deeper beauty her own made but a tinsel foil.

"Yes, indeed," said Pussie. "You know a man shot himself for Mrs. Malgam, once, they say. Isn't it exciting?"

"What, really?" put in Arthur. He had been forgotten for the moment; and Mrs. Hay drew up her red satin brodequins with a start. "Here comes Mrs. Gower," said she, "suppose we ask her?"

"Oh, don't," put in Pussie, rather frightened; but

Mrs. Hay was not to be repressed. Flossie Gower barely raised her eyebrows at the question. "There was a man, a Mr. Vane, who shot himself," said she. "But it was from overwork, and not for Baby Malgam, I suspect. He was nothing but a money-making machine."

It was a glorious day, when it finally arrived. Nature seemed, as usual, to smile on Flossie Gower's plans. The party met at breakfast, all the women radiant in the neatest of dresses, with the gayest of coaching umbrellas; Caryl Wemyss and Van Kull in brown frock-coats with rosebuds in their silk lapels, and Derwent and Birmingham informally in knickerbockers. Breakfast was a longer meal than usual; and the warm June air came in through the windows, laden with roses. Then the crisp and rapid sound of many horses' feet was heard upon the ground, and they all ran to the door to inspect the coach.

The women ran away to get ready, and the servants were busy packing every conceivable kind of a wrap, shawl, waterproof, mackintosh, rug, cloak, cape, ulster, or other similar garment yet devised, together with various little leather and silver travelling-bags, contents to Arthur as yet unknown. Of course, there was no room for real luggage in the coach; this went behind in the wagonette. But the inside of the coach was quite choked up, as it was, with some bales of these and similar trifles; so that when any lady had a headache and had to ride inside she had to lie upon the cargo, the seats being lost some two feet beneath it. Behind stood the wagonette, with four extra horses, in case of need, loaded with the luggage; and besides all this there was an extra servant, or postilion, riding a "cock horse," or tow-horse, for the pulls up-hill.

At last all was ready; on top of all inside was thrown a bundle of the morning's papers, which were to lie there unopened through many sunny days; the light steel ladder was brought out, and Miss Duval and Kitty Farnum were inducted with much ceremony to the highest seat, Derwent and Lord Birmingham their companions. Mrs. Hay went behind with Arthur and Caryl Wemyss, in front of the pair of servants—an old stout one and a thin young one, both well trussed up in their plum-colored broadcloth. But these were not there yet, and only their neatly folded coats, showing the two brass buttons with the well-known crest of Levison-Gower, betokened their future presence. Mrs. Gower herself climbed lightly into the box-seat, scorning a ladder; Van Kull took the reins beside her, and with a rapid leap the four horses took the road. As they passed out the coachman and groom came climbing up behind; the latter seized the horn, and a long and joyous peal of coaching music woke the echoes of the sleeping woods and lawn.

It seemed this gay *fanfare* had loosed their tongues, for at once a clatter of laughter and merry voices began. Van Kull, the horses being fresh, was busied with his driving; but Mrs. Gower turned to talk with the four behind her, and soon Miss Duval's flow of animal spirits was set off and exploded in shrieks of shrilly laughter. Miss Farnum, too, said something to make Birmingham roar his catastrophic bass guffaws, and Wemyss took up the cue with Mrs. Hay. Only the two servants sitting facing them maintained the severe aspect which decorum of them demanded.

They were already sweeping down the dewy ravine in the forest, and in a minute more had come to the gate of Mrs. Gower's demesne; it flew open, the porter bared his head, the porter's wife and children bobbed up and down behind him; and between the armorial pillars they rolled out upon the common road. A dusty, sleepy road it was, giving no hint of its much use; for, early as it was for them, the people that travelled by the highways, the morning tradesmen's carts and factory operatives, had long since passed over it to their daily station in life. You would be surprised if you knew how busy this same road could be in the hour or two that followed sunrise. But now it stretched away in silence through the broad green country, and its dust lay heaped in ridges undisturbed. The horses trotted smartly down its gentle slope; and then, breaking into a joyous gallop, rushed them up the other for a mile or more. Here was the factory village; and they swept through it triumphantly, but almost unseen, for all the world was now indoors. A few dogs barked; a few street-children, too young to work in the mills, cheered at them, or jeered, it were hard to say which. There was a great whirring of wheels from the mills, however; and the two free leaders took fright at them, and almost broke away from Van Kull, who held them hard, the big veins swelling in his throat. The coachman facing Arthur leaned far out and looked forward at them anxiously; but no one else minded. Such was the exhilaration of the air and motion, they might have run away and Pussie Duval have but sung her song the louder, while the others laughed the more. At last Van Kull pulled up his smoking team on the face of a big hill, the town a mile or so behind them. It was a very steep hill, or they would have carried it by assault; but now the groom on the cock-horse rode up and hooked his harness to the whiffletree, and the five horses set their necks into the collar, and took the summit slowly, as by siege. As they rose up, the country all behind them was unfolded, ridge by ridge, like a map; Arthur from his back seat faced full toward it. Gradually the chimneys of the factory village sank down into the bosom of the valley; the hills breasting it rose up behind them, until they overlooked their highest ridge; now the village was nearly hidden in the green floor of the valley, and all beyond were faint blue films of mountains; then, as they rose still higher, the rift of luminous air between the near hills and the distant mountains was seen to be paved with the blue flood of the river. The horses paused a moment to take breath; it was marvellously still; now and then the cackle of a hen came up from the valley; a train was crawling along its other side, but it moved as noiselessly as the white specks of sails upon the river.

The sunlight began to be hot, and Wemyss was

sent within to fetch the larger sunshades from the "cabin," as Miss Duval pleased to call it.

"Now you men," said Flossie, "may go behind and smoke; and Mrs. Hay can take a place in front. You have none of you had your morning cigars, I am sure." They had not; and after due demurrage the change was made. Four blue clouds arose to heaven from the after-seat; the four fair women grouped together in front; and Van Kull looked now and then askance and backward, as if in envy. And surely if ever an approach to godlike Nirvana is realized on earth, it is when one is moving rapidly through a broad June morning, looking down upon the roundness of the world, and blowing clouds upon it dreamily.

When Lord Birmingham took Van Kull's place upon the box, giving the latter his seat in the smoke-room, as he termed it, most of the party felt, if they did not show, a delightful drowsiness, which was only dispelled by their arrival at a town and rumors of luncheon. A wild burst of the coaching horn electrified the main street, and they drove up before the principal "hotel," a vast and ill-aired wooden structure, quite inappropriate to a coaching party, or even to the more civilized usages of life, as Mr. Wemyss with much particularity pointed out. But a private room had been engaged for them, and in this, with some local chickens and the resources of Mrs. Gower's cellar and grapery, they made out not so badly.

After luncheon the men smoked, and the women retired to their especial quarters, where, it is to be presumed, some took a nap, and others, having sent for the little travelling-bags before mentioned, performed mysterious rites therewith. Wemyss, Lord Birmingham, Miss Duval, Miss Farnum, and Arthur went to walk about the town, and became the subjects of considerable admiring comment. In the country, on the contrary, such had not been the case; *nil admirari* was a motto faithfully practised, and the old farmers would hardly hitch their trousers and turn about for the loudest horn or the most rattling pace. When they came back to the hotel and found the coach drawn up to the door, there was assembled a considerable concourse of immature populace, who had already passed from the open-mouthed stage to the derisive one, and were making sarcastic and injurious comments upon the coach and its equipment, with that tendency so noteworthy in young America to deride or decry what it does not itself possess.

Off went the horses—the two wheelers were nearly fresh, having only been in the wagonette in the morning—the coachman wound a rapid call upon his horn, attended by an obligato of small boys, and they swayed and swung through the winding street of the hot little town, out into fields and hedgerows again. The hedges were in front of the lawns and villa residences that surrounded the town; and the road was well arched over with elms just breaking into leaf, under which the afternoon sun slanted.

It seemed to the party almost the perfection of life, as the little disconnected comments and the absence of any effort of conversation indicated. Simple being was enough; there was no sicklying over that day's air and sunlight with any pale cast of thought, as Derwent said. Again they were high up on the slope of the country side; but the great golden bay of the Hudson had become a river here, and close beyond it the blue mountains of the highlands loomed up bold and near.

Now they came down close by the shore of the river; its salted waters were lapping, lapping on the round, weedy shore-stones, and over against them, in the skirt of the hills, lurked already the night. The stream's broad bosom glowed motionless, bearing here and there a bark or boat; but no Sidney Sewall spoke of these to-night, or cared to trouble with intellectual speculation. Arthur remembered with unconcern that in the past there had been such things as the city, business, hour of duty; what mattered this to them, the chosen ones, bright beings in a world apart? And certainly everyone of the party had a charm our hero had not realized before; even Mrs. Hay, with her strong, sensuous beauty, lent a richness and a color to the grouping.

"It is lovely, after all," said Miss Farnum, dreamily, voicing his thoughts. Here they were entering a high hanging wood; on the lower side of the road a lofty hewn-stone wall, all overgrown with moss and ivy, surmounted with old-fashioned stone urns now chipped and crumbling away. Over it they could see the winding leaf-heaped walks of a forgotten garden, untended lawns, and old stone garden-seats swathed in moss and mould. "It must be the grounds of some gentleman's old country-seat," said Miss Farnum. "Everyone goes farther from the city nowadays." There was a something begetting thought in this suggestion; the warm sunlight sank sleepily down in the cup there between the woodlands, and the old garden looked like a place where one might take a nap for half a lifetime—say from youth to early old age. It was evidently a place of the old Idlewild, Ik Marvel, Porte-Crayon days, when peopled lived in their country, wrote of Dobb his ferry, and were as yet unacquainted with Englishmen and other foreigners. There must have been a strong home-fragrance in our life in the forties or thereabouts, before the few found out that we are provinces, or the many that we are all the world. . . . Now they came out by a little water-bay, or lagoon, reaching inland, where the water lay still and a salt crust was on the long plashed grasses. "I suppose the people who live here go to Mount Desert, nowadays," said Miss Farnum. "I wonder why they left here?"

"Malaria," suggested Wemyss.

"There always seems something unreal, impossible about malaria here," said Arthur. "Malaria is languid, tropical, unsuited to our bleak Northern, Puritan, hard-worked hillsides and meadow bottoms. Consumption, not malaria, is the typical disease."

"It is only lately creeping into New England," said Wemyss, dryly. Just then a merry burst of laughter was heard from the front; Arthur looked behind him, but there seemed to be no one speaking.

The laugh had been from Miss Duval; she turned around at the same moment, her black eyes sparkling from her rosy face. "Isn't it delightful?" said she to Arthur. There seemed to be no other reason for her laughing than this; and Arthur laughed in accord with her. It was delightful.

Now they were up in the highlands again, bowling along a hard straight road between the rows of trees. Continually the merry horn was sounded to warn the slow teams ahead to turn aside, or wake the sleepy milkmen, or pedlars in their carts. The sun, across the river, had already set behind the purple mountains; but eastward, to the right, the hills were light.

They entered into a high wood, filled already with gray shadows; along the edge of the road still lay the last year's leaves, thick-matted, making the sound of the wheels soft. What light there was came from the violet sky above the tree-tops; and against it Kitty Farnum's profile shone pale and clear-cut. Arthur was humming a German song to himself, and looking at her and wondering about her: what she was, what was her secret of life.

So the night came on them, in the wood. It was evening when they came out of it and rolled along, low by the river-shore; opposite, the great black mass of the Storm King, and beyond it, farther to the north, the mountains sank into a long low line, and above the dark ridge the sky was saffron, and in it hung and trembled one large liquid star, reflected larger and softly in the calm river. And they all looked at these things and were silent.

## CHAPTER XX.

### THE CHARIOT OF THE CARELESS GODS.

THE coach drew up at the little wharf at Garrison's, and the party got into the ferry-boat and were carried across the river. The great hotel at West Point had been opened ; the waiters were spick and span ; the wooden floors were varnished, and slippery like glass. In the hall were two or three pretty girls, overdressed in white tulle dresses, low-necked, with their cavaliers who served for the nonce and their noisy younger brothers. This bright company crowded to the porch, curious, when the carriages drove up ; and Arthur heard one of the pretty girls say to another, "It's the coaching-party—from New York."

They went out and wandered on the cliffs above the river ; the beautiful moon-washed mountains stood about them, and below them slept the Hudson with its salt flood, deeper, nobler than any Rhine. But there were no castles here, nor Lorelei ; and the sunken gold had long since been robbed from its depths and was circulating in the hands of men.

Arthur fell to Miss Duval's share, a position he always found a somewhat uncomfortable one ; for how could he replace another man like Jimmy De Witt, and that one her acknowledged lover ? But, had he known it, Miss Pussie, who was looking forward with intense and hungry anticipation for the joys of worldly pleasure and a fashionable marriage, and regarded this coaching party as an earnest of them, would have blushed at herself if she had been so out of the mode as to be unable to flirt with anyone but her future husband. It must be owned, therefore, that she found our hero slow; she tried to talk to him of hunting, and he to her of books, both things of which they were reciprocally ignorant. Then they walked up and down the great piazza, and amused themselves by looking through the windows into the great parlors, where the hotel girls (*puella tabernensis Americana*) were dancing with some tightly buttoned cadets. Just then Lionel Derwent came up, alone with his cigar. "Let me join you," said he. "I went downhill and I came upon Birmingham, in at attitude full of unconscious humor, addressing Miss Farnum; I came uphill and blundered upon Van Kull and Mrs. Hay. From these I retreated in disorder only to make myself *de trop* with Mr. Caryl Wemyss and our charming hostess. Shall I be so here?"

Miss Duval laughed. "I was just going to bed, Mr. Derwent; so you and Mr. Holyoke can fight it out alone. Good-night—good-night, Mr. Holyoke." And she left them in the doorway and took her way up the great staircase. Arthur and Mr. Derwent looked at one another inquiringly. "Shall we go and smoke?" said the latter, at last. "By all means," answered Arthur. "Where shall we go—out upon the cliff?"

"I am afraid it is too densely populated there for

such a wild man as myself, already," said Derwent, laughing. "Come down to the billiard-room." They went down there, and sat at a table, opposite a bar, where they were not, as Derwent expressed it, "troubled by the moon," and here they smoked their cigars and pondered.

"Mr. Van Kull seems rather devoted to Mrs. Hay," said Arthur, at a venture.

"And well he may be," said Derwent, gravely. "He prefers the flowers of evil; and she is a most glorious one."

"Evil?" said Arthur, incredulously. "She seems to me a kind-hearted creature, fond of show, no worse than thoughtless."

"So is a nightshade blossom fond of sunlight, and bright-colored and innocent of harm," said Derwent, with a smile. "Mrs. Hay is a luxuriant animal—a woman of the world, as other women are women of the town; and her life is one continual sermon unto these: 'Look ye; I am rich, happy, high-placed; I have all the opportunities and advantages, all the taste and teaching, that the best can give; and I have not one single taste, or thought, or aspiration that the worst of you have not; nor have I lost one that you have, except, perhaps, the fondness for domestic life which some of the best of you may once have had. I, too, still care for dress and show and the longing glance of many men; these things, that you are foolishly told have ruined you, are just what I, too, prize in life; I, Mrs. Wilton Hay, the great high-born beauty whose photograph you have seen in the shop-windows!' I tell you," ended Derwent, savagely, "but for a little poor fastidiousness, her soul resembles theirs as do two berries on one stem. But consciously, 'tis true she does no harm; possibly she has not even sinned; as well attach a moral guilt to some gaudy wayside weed, growing by mistake in a garden among the sesame and lilies!"

"But Mrs. Gower seems very fond of her——"

"Ah! Mrs. Gower!" answered Derwent, dropping his voice. "She is a different sort of person entirely. Fannie Hay is but a soldier of Apollyon; but Florence Gower is a general-of-division."

"I don't see why you live with them," said Arthur, boldly.

"Ah, Holyoke, I live everywhere; I see these, and others, too. That night when I came back from the factory village, I had been talking with the men, and with some of the young girls there. And I could fancy Mrs. Hay going there, good-naturedly as she might, and saying to them: 'Don't care for dresses, or to lure men's love or women's envy, or to dazzle your neighbor Jenny or break her Johnny's heart; read books, look at pictures, enjoy the beauties of nature, seek the beauty of holiness.'—'Does your ladyship?' say they.—'Well, at all events, be clean,' answers Fannie Hay, shocked.—'But cleanliness costs money, my fine lady.'—Christ solved the question once; but now Christ is forgotten; and the sphinx looks out unanswered over the desert sand."

"Surely you can say nothing against Miss Farnum, at least?"

"She is caught like the others, in their web," said he. "But come, it's late indeed to be troubling ourselves over these two or three. What are they to the million?"

Arthur thought much of Derwent's talk; but he seemed to him a morbid fellow, unpractical and vague. And still more morbid it all seemed in the morning, when he woke and saw the sunlight and blue sky above the mountains of the river. Dressing was a delight, with such an outlook and with such a day before him; and coming down he met Miss Farnum looking fresh as a rose with the dew on it. Caryl Wemyss was standing talking to her with that air of distinction of which he was so proud; and just after, Mrs. Hay and Miss Duval came bouncing down the staircase, arm in arm. So they went in to breakfast, without waiting for Mrs. Gower, hungry, and in high glee for want of a chaperone. "Oh, I don't consider you a chaperone," said Pussie Duval to Mrs. Hay. "Nor do I," added Kill Van Kull, hastily.

Theirs was the central table in the dining-hall; and each lady found a dozen roses at her plate. These were from Lord Birmingham, who appeared late, and was duly thanked for them. Every man asked his neighbor for one rosebud as a boutonnière: and just then Flossie came in, dressed in the airiest of summer gowns; and there was a great arising and scraping of chairs among the gentlemen.

Soon they were down at the river, and crossing the river again. Such a wealth of brown sunlight as was in the air! The bold mountains rose up on either side, not soft and purple with heather, as in England, nor brown and sharp with rock, as in Italy, but green and shaggy, as in a new country, with a growth of timber; the deep, swirling waters, brown where you looked into them, shaded off to blue farther from the boat, where they gleamed smooth beneath the cloudless sky. And the sparkle and the stillness of the morning gave one the feeling of a truant school-boy.

"There is something about an American landscape that reminds one of the pictures in omnibuses," said Wemyss. No one replied to this; for they were nearing the wharf, where the coach and four were standing, as if it were Fifth Avenue. Again there was the shifting of rugs and wraps in the body, and the courtesies of the steel ladder, and the pleasant twinkling of neat ankles as the ladies alertly mounted it. The four men hove themselves up anyhow, with Lord Birmingham and Miss Farnum on the box; and then with a swing the heavy drag was swaying under way, and the four shining chestnuts took the hill at a gallop. They were passing a row of square wooden houses where poor people lived, and Mrs. Hay turned about and called to Wemyss. "One thing I notice, Mr. Wemyss—in America you have tenements, not cottages."

"Yes," said he, "and 'elegant residences' for gentlemen's houses!"

"Now, in Devonshire," said Mrs. Hay, "those cottages would be smothered in roses and fuchsia vines. Don't you have any cottage improvement societies? My cousin, Lady St. Aubyn, at Hartland (near Clovelly, you know), has been most active in them; and one of her tenants took the prize for the county!"

"These people are nobody's tenants," said Wemyss; "and they decorate their houses as they damn please, American fashion; with goats and tomato-cans, if they prefer."

By this time they had entered the forest that clothes the slopes of Breakneck Mountain. The road was none of the best, and the top of the coach careened violently, almost shaking Derwent, who was idly smoking with his face in the sunlight and his eyes half closed, off the back seat. "Come, let's walk," said Pussie Duval; and as the coach halted a moment upon one of those ridges across the road imaginatively designated "thank-ye-marms," she nimbly dropped herself over the side and sprang back into the daisies and buttercups. Arthur, Mrs. Hay, Flossie, Van Kull, and Wemyss followed; Derwent Mrs. Gower ordered to remain upon the coach and play propriety; whereupon that gentleman stretched himself quite lengthwise upon the warm back seat, pulled his cloth hat over his eyes, and to all appearances went to sleep.

"We can cut off a mile," said Van Kull, "by cutting straight through the woods to where the road strikes the river again. Now then! each his own way, and the coach will wait for us there, if it gets in first." So they disappeared; Van Kull with Mrs. Hay making for a pine grove on the high land, Wemyss and Mrs. Gower going lower, where there seemed evidences of a path, and our hero with Miss Duval taking a middle course through a rocky pasture, sweet-scented with fern and heathery blossoms, and dotted with dwarfed and obsolete apple-trees. This gave Lord Birmingham a chance of devoting himself entirely to his driving and his companion upon the box. For an hour or more the coach lumbered on; its driver talked incessantly, but drove very badly, and Lionel Derwent slumbered in the rear.

In the woods, the day was a very warm one. What breeze there was could not be felt. It would take too long to follow the devious ways of every party in all their wanderings; suffice it to say that shortly before noon Arthur, with Pussie Duval, came out upon the road close by the Hudson, where they sat upon a fence and waited. Arthur was getting every day more used to her society; and Mr. De Witt was no longer so continually upon his mind. Here they were met by the other two couples; and finally, when the coach came thundering down the hill with a wheel in a shoe, the whole six were sitting on the fence, *à la mode du pays;* and Wemyss was even whittling.

"Well, you *have* been long," said Van Kull.

"Ah, you can't make up for lost time with cracking of whips and horn-blowing!" laughed Mrs. Gower.

"What have they been doing all this time?—without prejudice, now, Mr. Derwent?"

"I don't know, Mrs. Hay—I've been asleep," said that gentleman.

"Come, now, I'd like to know how long all of you have been here—that's all," growled his lordship, blushing obviously. "Get aboard there—I'm hungry as a bear. Where do we stop for lunch, Mrs. Gower?"

"At Fishkill," said that lady. "It's only a few miles ahead." And in an hour or so they stopped before a sleepy old inn, low and rambling, with a Rip-Van-Winklish look about it. There is a lazy luxuriance, a sort of slatternly comfort, and a Southern coloring about these old New York villages, bespeaking material ease and an absence of moral nervousness; perhaps nervous morality would better express it. "I never look at a place like this," said Wemyss, "without thinking that the most vigorous-sounding word in the Dutchman's language was Schnapps!"

After luncheon the day was warm, and the ladies inclined to sleep. Only Derwent wished for a walk, and Arthur went with him, while the others smoked. They sauntered through the little town's unkempt, painted streets; and Derwent sent a telegram. Arthur noticed, with some surprise, that it was addressed to Haviland. Then at three they returned, and found the party for the most part wrapped in dreams.

They put to and were off, but the order was changed, as usual, and Pussie Duval rode with Derwent on the box. Caryl Wemyss would not drive, for he never did anything that he thought he did not well; so he and Mrs. Gower and Birmingham sat on the back seat, with Arthur, Van Kull, Mrs. Hay, and Kitty Farnum on in front. The drive to Poughkeepsie was straight and uneventful. The long hours were only diversified by Mrs. Wilton Hay's uncertain efforts on the coaching-horn.

Poughkeepsie is a brick-built city, with horse-car lines, an opera-house, and a court of justice all its own. Here they had a suite of rooms, with long lace curtains, black-walnut furniture, and Brussels carpets, equipped "before the dawn of taste, in poor imitation of a poorer thing," said Wemyss; "how different from an English inn!" The rest of the adornment consisted, in each room, of a steam-heater and a pitcher of ice-water! "I believe they even bathe in ice-water!" said he. "Dear me!" said Birmingham, simply. "I rang and could not get a tub at all."

They had dinner in Mrs. Gower's parlor, and a telegram was brought in to her during the dessert. "Oh, I am very glad," said she, as she laid it down. "It is from Mr. Haviland; and he says he can join us to-morrow." Arthur looked at her, and then at Derwent; but that gentleman made no sign; only, Lord Birmingham looked disgusted. The others expressed a polite gratification, and then the question came up what they were to do in the evening. Already a great intimacy had sprung up among the party, and a certain feeling of youth, born of much outdoor air and freedom from care. Some proposed ghost-stories, others, games. "I bar kissing games," said Pussie Duval, with much aplomb, "in the absence of Mr. De Witt." Kisses were debarred, being, as Van Kull expressed it, too serious things to be made game of; but forfeits, twenty questions, even dancing, was indulged in. When all these failed to satisfy their souls, it was rumored that Mr. Derwent was "up" in palmistry. "Oh, do tell us our fortunes!" was the cry. "We must have a regular gypsy tent."

"Now," said Mrs. Hay, "it's no fun unless we all tell. Agree all of you to tell us what he says!"

"Girls, girls" (the women of Mrs. Gower's set had a way of still addressing each other joyously as "girls")—"suppose he reveals the secrets of your hearts?"

"'Pon my soul!" cried Mrs. Hay, "I've quite forgotten what they are! Who'll go in first?"

A shawl had been hung across an open door, behind which Derwent took up his position. No one seemed anxious to make the first try; and at last the voice of the company fell upon Arthur Holyoke, "as having," said Mrs. Gower, "the most future before him."

Arthur went in and came out laughing. "I have had," said he, "a very terrible horoscope, as Derwent says. Everything that I really wish for is to happen to me!"

"I don't see what there is so very terrible about that," said they all; and the others were emboldened. Mrs. Gower went in next. "Speak aloud, Mr. Derwent," cried Mrs. Hay, "so we all can hear—we can't trust the garbled statements of the culprits."

Derwent's voice was heard, in sepulchral tones, from behind the screen. "I see the hand of a woman who has done whatever she has meant to do——"

("Dear me," interjected Mrs. Hay, "how successful we all are!")

"She may come near doing more than she meant to do; but her will shall conquer everything."

"How delightfully enigmatic!" laughed Pussie Duval.

"You must go in next, Miss Pussie—you spoke," said Van Kull. But Pussie wouldn't; and the choice fell upon Kitty Farnum. She disappeared, and there was several moments' silence. At last—

"Ein Jüngling liebt ein Mädchen,
Die hat einen Andern erwählt;
Der Andre liebt eine Andre
Und hat sich mit Dieser vermählt.

"Das Mädchen heirathet aus Ärger
Den ersten besten Mann,
Der ihr in den Weg gelaufen;
Der Jüngling ist übel dran.

"Es ist eine alte Geschichte,
Doch bleibt sie immer neu;
Und wem sie just passiret,
Dem bricht das Herz entzwei——"

"Good heavens!" laughed Flossie. "Come, you go in, Mr. Van Kull."

"I can tell more of this man's past than his future," said the voice.

"There has been a voyage across the water—perhaps to Brighton, or to Cannes. And there is a fair maiden and a dark maiden; and both have had but little influence on his life. And there is to be another yet, I see——"

"There, there," interfered Flossie, "if you make poor Van such a Don Juan, we shall have to send him home again, in our own protection. Mrs. Hay, you go in."

But this the beauty flatly refused to do. And after much chaff at her expense, the party betook themselves to their several slumbers.

The next day was Sunday; but, as Wemyss said, to leave Poughkeepsie was a work of necessity and mercy; and they were early under way. Here they left the river, and they struck inland; the country grew more rural and primitive, and their spirits rose proportionately. Haviland appeared by the early train, and shared the back seat with Birmingham, Mrs. Gower, and Kitty Farnum. He brought the news of the day, which no one cared to hear; and some gossip of the town, which interested everybody. "How can you have the heart to bring him up?" Wemyss had said at breakfast; and Flossie had laughed, and said that she expected a very entertaining day. "He must go back Monday evening, you know," she added.

They had another perfect day, and by this time all of them, even to Caryl Wemyss, were charged with ozone and overflowing with animal spirits. Even practical joking was in order; and Arthur had caught an instantaneous photograph, which he exhibited with much applause, of Van Kull assisting Mrs. Hay over a stone wall. Conversation was unnecessary; it was quite enough to live and laugh. Much amusement was caused by a rustic, at a farm-house where they stopped for milk, who first insisted that they were the advance-guard of a circus, and then would have it that they were "travelling" for something—"jerseys" and men's clothing, he first suggested, and then parlor organs and patent medicines. And all the women were so pretty, and so stylish, and so sweet-tempered, that Arthur began to feel a little bit in love with every one of them.

"But one gets tired of women, after a while," said Caryl Wemyss to Arthur, at Washington Hollow, where they lunched. The inn was an old roadside one, at the "four corners," smelling of dusty leather and the road, with a large bar-room, fit political centre of the surrounding district; but the country was robed in beautiful green forests, into which the others had plunged, and came back loaded with wild flowers, Mrs. Gower with Lord Birmingham, and Haviland and Kitty Farnum last of all. For a wonder, Derwent had done the polite, and wandered off with Mrs. Wilton Hay. Van Kull and Miss Duval came back laughing over some quaint epitaphs they had discovered in what he termed a "boneyard" opposite. "What a jolly place this must have been in the old days!" said Flossie. "Look at the splendid great chimney-places and the old ball-room!" And Arthur's memory suddenly went back to the ball-room at Lem Hitchcock's. But it was summer now, and the place was civilized; some stranded woman-boarder was playing, upon an old piano overhead, one of Beethoven's sonatas. And Derwent took up a curious old stone jug, in which they had had milk, and read:

"He who buys land, buys stones;
"He who buys meat, buys bones;
"He who buys eggs must buy their shells—
"Who buys good ale buys nothing else."

But, after all, no stops were like the rapid riding; the sense of freedom and delight of sweeping high over the rolling country, making a panorama of it, and being in a little republic of their own. Two small roans were leaders to-day, and the chestnuts, being a little used up, were in the lighter baggage-wagon, in "spike team" with the cock-horse; for no great hills were expected that afternoon.

Arthur settled himself again to the pure delight of life, gazing joyously from sky to forest and from forest to the wide green carpet of the fields, sweeping by them with the changing angles of the long Virginia fences. Arthur and Pussie Duval were the least *blasé* of the party; and both drank in the very moments with enthusiasm. And when he was tired of looking at the swelling hills and spaces of the sky, it was pleasant to look in her fair face—or, for that matter, at any other of the beautiful women about him. As for Miss Duval, the world was like an opening treasure-house to her; she saw before her all she wanted, and had only to grasp her fill with full hands. Ah! saints and cynics to the contrary, this world has happiness for some—thought Arthur. But what he said was, "How lovely that long edge of the forest is, Miss

Duval! See how boldly the high trees rise out of the meadow; I suppose it's what the poets call a 'hanging wood.' *La lisière* they call it in French; I have always thought it was such a pretty name for Mrs. Gower's place."

"But you weren't really thinking of that, Mr. Holyoke," said she. "You weren't looking at it."

"I was looking at your eyes, Miss Duval, if you will have it," said Arthur. It will be seen that our hero was making progress.

"Dear me!" cried Mrs. Hay, who overheard this speech, "I shall certainly write to Mr. De Witt. Why don't *you* say such intense things to me, Mr. Van Kull?"

"Because I daren't," said Van Kull, meaningly.

"Please—I'll promise not to write to Wilton," retorted she. "Poor Wilton! he must find it so hot in Washington."

How pleasant it is to feel ourselves moving above the world like gods! How pleasant it is, like gods, to make of our own rules of conduct our laws of good and evil! And what responsibility have we for the rest of humanity? They should not all attempt to be in fashion. Fashion is for us alone—us few, who transcend common laws.

Yet it is relying on the many abiding by the humdrum rules of gravity that the few can flutter and glitter freely on the surface. In the evening there was a moon (which shineth alike upon the just and on the unjust; particularly the latter, for moonlight has no conscience), and the warm night attracted them forth from the dreary hotel parlor. They wandered up the hill, through pastures, to where there was a cliff, above huge chasms of a quarry, carven deep into the living rock. Here they met some Italian laborers; they were living in little wooden huts about the quarry, with their womankind, richly, upon seventy cents a day. Their views of life were much the same as their own, thought Derwent, looking at the merry party; with only, perhaps, a little less morality, a little more religion, these day laborers, than had they.

Caryl Wemyss conversed with them a little in their own language, at which they were greatly pleased. They were citizens, and had come over to make their portion of our great democracy; but they sighed for the sunny skies of Sicily as yet.

Wemyss was walking with Mrs. Gower, and as they turned back they found Haviland sitting with Kitty Farnum on a stone wall in the long grass; the moon lit up her fair face and her eyes, which were shining; and all about them lay the petals of a rose that she had pulled to pieces. "How like Faust and Marguerite!" said Mrs. Gower.

"Say, rather, Psyche with her Dipsychus," said Mr. Wemyss.

"Who is Dipsychus?" said Flossie Gower.

"Have you never met him, then?" said Wemyss. And coming back, she took his arm across the fields.

Wemyss pressed it gently, and began to analyze himself, whether he was in love with her or not. It rather flattered him to think he was.

## CHAPTER XXI.

### ARTHUR GOES HOME.

THE days were growing unnumbered by this time, measure of time being only necessary when one has daily petty duties, and existence is not a continuous, untroubled joy. Arthur positively bloomed; even Derwent seemed a shade less anxious for the souls of men, and Mr. Wemyss a point less analytic. And the morning was one to bring a bit of fresh color to the cheek of a very Tannhäuser who had been long years jaded with Venus's joys, his dull eyes rested with the lights of earth again, his ear soothed by notes of spring and human love. The land was beautiful with bud-promise, the air steeped with joyous light of life. And the girls came down to breakfast, looking each and all a Hebe.

For the will of the world comes out in this—that all that has to do with life, new life, charms and attracts us; that all that speaks of over-thought, of over-soul, if you will, is wan and weird—either positively uncanny, or laughable, like the chorus of old men in Faust! Instinctively, we all turn to the flower, to the fresh looks of the young girl, to the rosy lips, full of the promise of future life. No wrinkled wisdom, no sorrowful lines of character, can make up for this.

The first thoughtless girl we meet shows her *beauté du diable* more than a match for all the crow's-feet of the intellect. And this is the magnetism of vitality; it is your full-blooded man that the masses of the world delight to follow. The unthinking are repelled by too much consciousness, as by disease.

We all have known such sunny mornings, when we that are living live, and the dead lie dead in their churchyards. Gayly the party mounted; and the strong horses galloped over the roads. They were still in the broad valley of the Hudson; far behind them lay the river, unseen, but farther still was visible yet the blue film of the Catskills. They crossed a broad intervale, and ahead of them was a gap in the hills, over which the road wound in a sort of pass. And now as they galloped up it in the shadow of the elms it was as if they had gone through a narrow door into a different country; the scene changed, the hills grew small, rugged, and broken; the vegetation was less rich; they were in New England. So marked was it that Wemyss pointed out the change; even the color of the houses was not the same, nor the look of the barns. They were small and neat, and painted sternly white; the very gates were better hung, and the sidewalks more neatly trimmed; the squalid, unkempt look was gone, and with it the greater luxuriance. One no longer felt the vastness of the Continent, but seemed to be in an older corner of it, the bars not yet let down, where elbow-room was less, and ideas and conventions artificially preserved. The hills were smaller, and the trees looked stunted; human habitations had a look like an old dress which the wearer in her penury still struggled to keep neat. Arthur was reminded at once of the look of the land about the hill-town to which he had driven on that day with Gracie. They had crossed the line into Connecticut, and the boundary was more marked than is usual in political divisions. Even in New York there had been a suggestion of the Western prairies; here was none. But there was a greater vigor in the air, which had a sort of moorland sparkle in it; and the talk was livelier than ever. They had a long and breezy drive of it, and the cock-horse was used many times in pulling up the grassy old road, which led uncompromisingly up the barren, ferny hills. For lunch they stopped at a little place called Lakeville, nestling in the hills between two clear blue ponds; and here John Haviland (having performed his errand) had to leave them to take his train back to the city.

In the afternoon Arthur was allowed to try his hand at driving; he sat on the box-seat with Miss Farnum, who was very silent, and Mrs. Gower and Wemyss had the rear seat to themselves. Kill Van Kull was allowed to get into the "cabin" and go to sleep, a refreshment which he averred the country air made most needful to him. Behind him on the middle seat the party were very noisy, and Arthur had much ado to keep his attention on the horses, who seemed also to feel the tang of the keen soft air. As they were going down a crooked hill, longer than he had expected, so that no shoe had been put on, the horses got almost beyond his control. He gathered the four reins together and pulled his best, and just managed to keep them in the road. The people behind were laughing and talking, unconscious of what was going on; and Arthur had already begun to congratulate himself upon his escape, when, as they were nearing the bottom, he got too far on the outer curve, and the heavy wheels sank deep in the gravel, still wet with the spring rains. One awful moment of suspense, and then the ponderous vehicle swayed heavily, rolled majestically over on its side. A shrill scream resounded behind him—it is not the custom for American girls to scream—and Mrs. Hay threw her arms wildly around Lord Birmingham, with the feminine instinct to embrace something in emergencies. But it was of no avail; and they all sailed gracefully off into the long grass, Arthur still devotedly hanging to the reins.

No one was hurt; and after a bare pause for reflection, everybody burst forth in a roar of laughter. Loudly and long they laughed, holding their sides; they were laughing too much to get up; one horse was down, and the others rearing and plunging. Van Kull put his head ruefully out of the window of the coach that was uppermost and contemplated the scene. His hat was crushed, he was nigh smothered with shawls and veils, and his hair hanging down over his eyes; and his head protruded slowly, like a disabled jack-in-the-box, amid the merriment of the company.

"Perhaps, when some of you damned fools get through laughing," said he, without undue emphasis, "you'll find time to attend to those leaders."

Van Kull's remark, though over-forcible, was undeniably just; and Derwent was already at their heads. The groom was also there; and in a few moments the horses were taken out, the coach set upright again, and all damage repaired. Everyone agreed that the accident was in nowise due to Arthur's driving, but entirely to the soft bit in the road.

"These things will happen, you know," said Birmingham, good-naturedly.

"It's half the fun, I think," said Pussie Duval.

"I thought you'd 'a dumped 'em, sir," said the groom, "when I see that ere soft bit in the road." And as a mark of special confidence, Arthur was allowed to drive the coach the rest of the way into Great Barrington, where they were to stop for the night.

The merriment consequent on their disaster did not cease during the afternoon, and Arthur was many times maliciously thanked for the diversion he had afforded the party. But Miss Farnum, who was still his companion on the box, seemed fortunately as much inclined to silence as he was himself. Indeed, she had been strangely silent all the day.

The country roads gradually drew themselves together and made themselves into the broad, straight avenue that is Great Barrington's main street; and up this they swept gayly, about an hour before sunset. They did not pass the Judge's old place; but as Arthur heard Mrs. Gower's light laughter behind him the old scene in the garden recurred to him at once. It was not yet a year ago: and he remembered now that the man she had been driving with was Wemyss.

They drew up merrily before the village hotel—it seemed so odd to Arthur to be there in his own town; he had never associated it with so gay a party—and after a few minutes of preparation they started out to see the place. Miss Farnum made pretext of a headache and did not go; but the others sauntered along beneath the overarching elms. To the left the setting sun lay across the intervale in broad gold bars. Arthur was walking with Lord Birmingham and Mrs. Hay.

Coming back, they met Mrs. Gower at the dinner-table. "I am sorry," said she, "Miss Farnum has to go home."

"Dear me, I'm so sorry," said Mrs. Hay, politely.

"What, you don't mean she's going to leave us?" said Lord Birmingham, blankly. He looked from one to the other of the party, as if asking an explanation. "She said nothing to me about it," he added, naïvely.

"I have telegraphed to Mrs. Malgam to ask her to join us," said Mrs. Flossie, hurriedly checking the general inclination to laugh that had succeeded his lordship's last speech. "You need not look so blank, you men—no Jack shall be left without a Jill."

"*A* Jill," said Wemyss, maliciously, accentuating the indefinite article, and looking at Mrs. Hay.

"'Pon my word, I think you're very insulting," broke in Mrs. Hay, savagely. No one could exactly see why; whereupon Van Kull, with much social dexterity, looked upon Mrs. Hay and sighed. Further comment was checked by the arrival of Miss Farnum herself, who bore her fine face quite as unconsciously, a shade more coldly, than usual. And then the finer emotions gave place to food.

Arthur was honored by a seat on Mrs. Gower's left; but he was silent through the meal, a fact which was maliciously attributed to the events of the afternoon. "Don't look upset, Mr. Holyoke, please!" cried Miss Duval. "We have quite regained our composure." Arthur had not been thinking of the accident at all; but he did color again, to be reminded of it. "It was a soft spot in the road, you know," said he.

"A soft spot in your heart, I much suspect," laughed Mrs. Gower. "Miss Farnum, you should not have sat with him."

"Who?" said the beauty, bringing her gaze to a focus. "Oh," she added, indifferently. "I?"

"'Pon my word," screamed Mrs. Wilton Hay. "You two are too delicious! But you're positively too absent-minded to be trusted together. Aren't they Mrs. Gower? They might not have presence of mind enough not to elope, you know."

Soon after this Miss Farnum left the table; and when Arthur followed, he found her out upon the doorstep, talking with Lionel Derwent. The sun had gone down now, and its last radiance came down upon them from some scarlet clouds. Miss Farnum went in almost immediately, leaving him with Derwent alone.

"A lovely evening," said he. "Will you take a tramp?"

Arthur hesitated. Then he spoke with decision.

"Yes. I have a call to make—won't you come with me? Miss Livingstone, you know, and my cousin, Miss Holyoke, are here—do you know them?"

"No," said the other; "but I shall like to."

"Come along, then," said Arthur. And they went up the long village street until the road began to twist among the apple-orchards and they got into the dusk that was already at the base of the wooded hills. Derwent pulled out a brierwood pipe and smoked it, and they walked in silence.

At last they came in front of the dignified old house, wearing, like a wig, its high-pitched roof and white balustrade, with its terrace for silk stockings and its dressed front of quaint old flowers as a ruffle of old lace. The gate creaked in its wonted way; and they walked up the familiar gravel-walk. "The ladies were at home;" and the two went into the large living-room, and found Gracie and Mamie Livingstone together. Arthur shook hands with Mamie, and then, after introducing Mr. Derwent, sat down by his cousin, leaving Mamie to his friend, a proceeding which the latter noticed. Derwent talked nearly all the time to Mamie, whose little self he read at once, but his eyes wandered more than once to Gracie and her cousin. Now, Gracie Mamie thought a character far simpler than herself. They all sat so near that when either pair was silent the other's conversation could be heard. Their call had lasted nearly an hour, when Miss Brevier came in, who was there, matronizing the young people, for a few days only. Then the conversation became more general, save that Derwent talked some half an hour, at the end, with Miss Holyoke. It was after ten before they rose to go.

"So you are going to Lenox to-morrow," said Gracie. "And after that?"

"After that, I don't know; perhaps I shall come here?"

"I don't think you could bear being at the Barrington Hotel," said Gracie, with a laugh. Arthur bit his lip.

"Well, I suppose a fellow can go somewhere," said he. "I may have to go back to the shop. Where do you go, Derwent?"

"I am going out among the Rockies of British Columbia, hunting," said he. "I wish you'd come," he added, turning to Arthur suddenly, as if the thought had then first struck him.

"Thanks," said Arthur, ill-naturedly. "Unfortunately, *I'm* nothing but a broker's clerk." But his *amour propre* was soothed by the evident increased consideration that Miss Livingstone had shown him; and even to the last moment she pressed him with questions, and hung admiringly upon his history of the trip.

"Who did you say was with you on the box when you upset?" she said, as they lingered at the doorway. The moon was up by this time, bleaching all the colored roses of the terrace in its yellow light.

"Miss Farnum," said Arthur. "But I believe Mrs. Malgam takes her place to-morrow," he added, carelessly.

"Oh!" said Mamie. "I'm fearing you'll be quite

too grand to speak to me when I'm a bud." And she gave him a look—one of her practised looks—out of her very pretty eyes, a look that Gracie never could have compassed. Arthur returned it, with the skill of a year's experience; meantime, Derwent was taking leave of the others, and they soon were walking home together—that is, to the Great Barrington Hotel.

"A charming girl," said Derwent.

"Who?" said Arthur, curtly.

"Miss Livingstone," said the other, after a pause. "Your young New York girls are such delicate flowers—and yet so hardy, too. And they can be trained to almost anything."

Arthur did not sleep well that night; but the morning was a lovely one again. They had to wait until the New York train arrived, which was not until the afternoon, for Mrs. Malgam. Kitty Farnum had started off quietly, early in the morning, and Derwent had gone with her, meaning to see her safely to New Haven, where her maid would meet her, and then take the return train back with Mrs. Malgam. Lord Birmingham had been too dull to think of this proceeding, and was in a vicious humor all the day in consequence. Arthur was in two minds about going to see Gracie in the morning. But as Birmingham sulked all day, there were not men enough without him; so he went to walk with Mrs. Hay instead. Mrs. Hay was one of those women whose flirting was less intellectual than the American type; she delighted chiefly in appealing to men's senses; and her company was not ennobling.

But in the afternoon appeared Mrs. Malgam, clothed in the loveliest of smiles and spring dresses. If she had any grudge against Flossie, she did not show it; but spoke to her caressingly, and with a certain deference, as from a giddy young girl to her chaperone. And then, as if her conscience were safely in Flossie's charge, she inaugurated a most audacious and ostentatious love-affair with the peer; that is, she caused him to inaugurate it. Baby Malgam never inaugurated anything; she only looked as if she understood it. A pan of cream, indeed; not milk and water; opaque, unfathomable to the eye, and yet, perhaps, not deep. Wemyss talked with Arthur about it. "You are the only fellow left whom one can talk to," said he. "Birmingham's too dull, and Derwent's not a man of the world." Arthur's heart warmed to him at once. "Baby Malgam," said he, "means to beat Mrs. Gower on her own ground."

This was said on the way to Lenox. At five the horses were brought up to the door; the brilliant party were again in their familiar seats, and bowling briskly over the well-made roads. And our hero was himself again; and the exhilaration of the motion, and the bright eyes and pretty dresses, and the trained flattery of their most desirable owners, and the admiration of the populace—to him as to them, was the breath of his nostrils.

"A woman's looks
Are barbèd hooks,
That catch by art
The strongest heart,"

says the old Elizabethan poet; but they swallowed the hooks in those days.

So they came to Lenox; Lenox of the sleepy hills, and sweet wild roads, and shady green seclusion. Here were the first good roads they had seen since they left Mrs. Gower's home; and Van Kull "let out" the horses, and they galloped like a summer storm. And the gayety seemed redoubled since Mrs. Malgam's arrival. Lord Birmingham was evidently drinking her in like some new sort of wine; Derwent alone was silent and abstracted. So they were none of them sorry when he told them that he, too, must leave at Lenox. In the evening, he got a long walk with Arthur, and spoke most bitterly about them all. "As for Mrs. Hay," he said, "she's hardly worth considering; she only injures men, and men who are her mates. But Mrs. Gower is a woman who has successively sought and successively attained, or appeared to attain, every height, every good thing, and every great place in turn, in order that she might vulgarize it. She has mounted every summit but to make it hers. Do you see how Mrs. Malgam, and Miss Duval, and all the others ape her?"

Arthur thought him very ill-bred and rude to this most charming hostess, and almost dared to say so. Derwent pulled out his brier-wood pipe, and they walked on in silence.

"Now," the other went on, "take another sort of girl—a girl like your friend Miss Holyoke, for instance——"

"I don't see what Miss Holyoke has to do with the case," said Arthur, goading himself into a passion. And the walk ended—purposely, so far as Arthur was concerned—in a sort of quarrel. Coming back, he found Mrs. Malgam walking in the lawn of Mrs. Gower's cottage, and joined her, and found solace after the Englishman's asperity.

Mrs. Malgam was dressed in a faultless summer gown, and wore the famous pearls that she had bought with the estate of her first husband. Arthur revenged himself by repeating to her all Derwent's conversation.

"I am glad he's going," said she. "He's the most cynical person I ever met; and I hate cynicism."

"Who's that you're talking of?" said Wemyss, coming up.

"Derwent," said Arthur. "We're both glad he's going."

"Oh, Derwent is quite impossible," said Wemyss. "He's well enough at a dinner where they feed the lions, but quite out of his place in society. The fellow's a crank, too; just the sort of a man who ends by marrying a woman of the demi-monde."

"By way of reformation, I suppose," laughed Mrs. Malgam. Arthur walked with her some time, as Wemyss left upon this last *bon mot;* and the next day, when they came together after breakfast, there was no trace of Derwent.

"Do you know he's a friend of Chinese Gordon?" said Lord Birmingham.

"I should think, quite possible," said Wemyss. "I

hope we'll get a better fellow in his place—a gentleman, at least," he added, *sotto voce.*

"They say he belongs to one of the oldest families in Northumberland, do you know," said Mrs. Hay.

"All rot," said Wemyss; "I believe him to be a mere adventurer—nothing more."

"Well," said Flossie, "I've written to Tony Duval in his place."

"Oh, dear!" cried Pussie. "I hate to go about with Tony; or, rather, he says he hates to go about with me. He says he can't have any fun while I'm around."

"He hates to flirt before his little sister," laughed Mrs. Gower. "Never mind, dear—I think you'll soon be even with him." And when Tony Duval arrived, all his simple soul went out to Mrs. Hay. "She is the finest woman I ever saw," he would say to Arthur, almost with a sigh. And he sent to Long Island for his two best blooded horses; and the first day they rode out he spilled Mrs. Hay over a four-barred fence, just as they were returning, and brought the fair burden home in his brawny arms. Her eyes unclosed soon after she was in the house; and she was not seriously injured. And Arthur, who had indited a telegram to Wilton Hay at Washington, sensibly put the despatch in his pocket.

So the days went by delightfully. Arthur had fears that he was sometimes the odd man; but after all, they seemed to like him pretty well; and if even Pussie Duval failed him, there were other fair in Lenox with no cavaliers imported, like the fruit in the hampers, from the city. So June waned toward July, and everyone almost cheered at Flossie Gower's proposal that they should have one more drive—to Lake George—before they parted. This new excursion was duly chronicled in all the newspapers, where Mamie Livingstone, eager, and perhaps a little envious, saw it. Arthur wrote and got his leave of absence extended at the office. They were easy-going people at the office.

Meantime, Derwent was "hunting big game" out in the Rockies, and Charlie Townley was sweltering in the city—"working like a dog, by Jove," he would say—at the affairs of Messrs. Townley & Tamms. And Gracie Holyoke was in great Barrington, alone.

## CHAPTER XXII.

### A HOUSE BUILT WITH HANDS.

CHARLIE TOWNLEY'S ways were not like the ways of other young stock-brokers. He worked at the most unusual times, and usually made ostentation of idleness. Many others much delighted him by thinking him a fool, chiefly because he wore a single eye-glass; and had a drawl, up-town. He had begun the summer —in the latter part of May, after Arthur had gone to Mrs. Gower's—by showing a considerable amount of attention to no greater a person than Miss Mamie Livingstone; thereby delighting her (as yet rudimentary) soul. The rest of his mind seemed given, as usual, to his person, his other equipages, and the various fashionable meetings of the season. His homage to Miss Mamie had been of the ostentatious variety, rendered at races and at horse-shows. He had even invited her to drive out to the Hill-and-Dale Club with him in his dog-cart; and it had only been as a favor reluctantly accorded to Gracie that she had not gone. Mamie was convinced that such an expedition would make her the most talked of débutante of the coming season; and she knew that in society (as perhaps in other things to-day) the main element of success is advertisement. When an article has once attracted notice, a clever person can make that notice favorable or the reverse almost at will.

But Gracie was gaining a very powerful influence over Mamie—almost as powerful as all the world outside. Her parents possessed none; they were not only of a previous generation, but *ex officio* prejudiced advisers; the girl of the period holds their evidence almost as cheaply as the business man holds his minister's upon theological subjects. Herein also was she a girl of our age, when men go to Ingersoll and Tyndall for their theories of the unknown God, and their wives to faith-cures and esoteric Buddhism for the practice of Christianity, and leave the outworn Scriptures. Still, a nature like Gracie's had its effect, even upon a girl like Mamie. She was too quick not to be conscious of this, and sought to make it up by chaffing and patronizing her elder cousin.

When Gracie persuaded Mamie to go with her to Great Barrington, Charlie was left entirely to his own devices. Some reader may say, his vices; but Charlie was not more vicious than another. He was almost alone—always excepting Mr. Phineas Tamms—in the office that summer. He showed, nevertheless, no desire to get away, but manifested a very strict attention to business. If Arthur had but known it, he had only been asked in Charlie's place upon the coaching party; but Charlie was one who never made himself the cause of another's knowing a disagreeable fact. He had his room permanently taken at Manhattan Beach; and he divided his leisure between this and divers clubs, urban and suburban. Occasionally he passed a Sunday on the yacht of an acquaintance.

Old Mr. Townley still dropped into the office two or three times a week; he still fancied their reputation unchanged, and the business the same as in the old concern of Charles Townley & Son, before they had helped young Tamms out of difficulties and given him a clerkship in the firm; and he bobbed his gray head sagely over Tamms's exposition of his plans. Business was quiet enough. But after the old gentleman had fairly gone to Newport for the summer, things seemed to take a little start. Tamms's family were away, his wife and two showy daughters travelling in Europe by themselves, and spending a great deal of money. Tamms himself lived at a small hotel down at Long Branch, where he had his private wire, and where he would occasionally rest a day in rustic seclusion, having his mail and stock-reports brought down to him to read. For Tamms never read books: like Mrs. Gower, he preferred the realities.

One day early in August Charlie was invited to go down and spend the night with his master, "the Governor," as Charlie termed him. He marvelled much at this, and went with much curiosity, never having witnessed any of Mr. Tamms's domestic arrangements. He knew that Tamms's womankind were travelling abroad; for he had had frequent occasion to cash their drafts. He had often speculated at their lack of social ambition on this side the ocean, and had come to the conclusion that it was either because they thought it easier "over there," or because Tamms deemed the time had not come for that as yet. But if not, why not?

Charlie took a little leather satchel with him, filled with railway reports, letters, telegrams, prospectuses, and other business documents. The boat was crammed with excursionists, clerks and their female friends, common people, as Charlie would have called them, evidently going down and back for the sail. Charlie secured a stool upon the upper deck, lit a cigar, and buried his thoughts in the stock-report of the afternoon paper; while the steamer made its way down the teeming harbor, by the base of the statue of Liberty, then being erected, past a Russian man-of-war, and through the green-shored Narrows.

To a patriot turned pessimist, there is something typical in the Jersey shore, the first American coast one sees in coming from the other world. Think of the last coast you leave—Cornwall, for instance—with its bold rocks, its glorious cliffs, its lofty castles that have been strongholds, at least, of courage and of faith; fit selvage for a land which sometime felt the nobility and the sacrifice of life. And then look at the long, low, monotonous strip of sand, the ragged, mean bank of crumbling clay, where the continent merely seems, as it were, sawed off, and ends with as little majesty as some new railway embankment. On the little bluff a gaudy row of cheap, undurable houses and hotels; even the sea seems but an anticlimax, a necessary but uninspiring end of things, devoid of dignity if not of danger. But the Jersey shore is not the coast of all the continent, nor is the city of New York America.

Charlie was not troubled by these things; they seemed as natural to him as the pink strip that marks the boundary of an atlas map. New York was an excellent place to make money in; and these things go well with materialism. The boat made its landing, and Charlie walked up the long pier through the crowd—a crowd of summer boarders, seeking rest, and who, finding rest a bore, had come down to see the evening steamer land, for the sake of excitement. The great rollers foamed in beneath the pier, lashing the piles indignantly; and the sea on either side was speckled with bathers—children, men, and women, the last looking their unloveliest in bathing-gowns.

The avenue at the pier-head was crammed with carriages—ladies, bored with the long day, who had come there for the last faint simulacrum of pleasure that the being seen in their own equipages still afforded them; other ladies waiting for their tired husbands from the city. In a handsome victoria with two long-tailed horses Charlie made out his host; and throwing up his overcoat and satchel, took his seat beside him.

"Hot in town?" said Tamms, laconically.

"Beastly," answered Charlie.

"We might as well take a drive, I suppose; there's nothing else to do before dinner."

Charlie silently assented; and they took their way along the red-clay road; on the left the wooden walk and railing above the gullied bank that met the sea, on the right a long succession of eating-houses and candy stores; then huge barracks of hotels, then fantastic wooden villas, which wildest fantasies of paint and stained shingles had sought to torture into architecture. Not a tree was to be seen; and the vast assemblage of human habitations in the sandy plain resembled more a village of prairie dogs than anything else a traveller's mind could have suggested.

"Land is immensely valuable here," said Tamms. "That's Deacon Thompson's place; he paid thirty thousand for it two years ago, and he says he's been offered fifty since." Charlie looked at the red-and-green structure, with its little paddock of lawn, and felt that it would not satisfy him; and yet he possessed not even thirty thousand dollars. "Pretty place," said Tamms.

Charlie assented. "Now what does a man like that want money for?" he argued to himself. But Tamms, having paid this tribute to the æsthetic side of life, proceeded to open his telegrams, and cast a hasty eye on the stock reports in Charlie's paper; then they both conversed of stocks and bonds. And after driving some three miles above the water (which made continual murmur at their feet) they drove back the way they came. At Elberon, Tamms pointed out the cottage where Garfield died.

"I see the Starbuck Oil has declared its usual dividend," said Charlie, watching his chief closely. "The boys say it wasn't earned."

"I don't suppose the directors would have paid it

if they hadn't earned it," said Tamms, sharply. Now Tamms, since they had purchased the control, was one of the directors.

"I suppose not," said Charlie. "I was merely saying what the boys say."

"Humph!" was all the reply his host vouchsafed to this; and by this time they were driving into the carefully pebbled avenue of "The Mistletoe," which was Mr. Tamms's abode. It was a small hotel, partly surrounded by glass galleries, in one of which three young men were sitting at a lunch-table, over claret and seltzer and liqueurs, though it was after six o'clock. The house was most ornately furnished; a little yellow-haired girl of twelve, dressed in pale lilac silk, with a short skirt, and mauve silk stockings on her long little legs, was standing at the counter talking to the clerk. All the servants were in livery, and Charlie made a mental note that the place was unexpectedly "swell."

"You want to go up to your room before dinner, I suppose," said Tamms, as if making a concession to Charlie's juvenile weaknesses. Charlie found his room a small apartment, with a rather expensive carpet and a most overpowering wall-paper; and it had the unusual luxury of a dressing-room attached. The sea was quite out of sight; but his room looked out upon the dusty street, and a printed placard on the wall informed him that its cost was twelve dollars a day. There was neither view, nor hills, nor country, nor even trees (save a line of petted young oaks that gave the place its name), in sight; but in every direction the eye was met by scores upon scores of wooden houses; and on the clipped grass that struggled with the red-clay plain the sun's rays still beat mercilessly.

They dined sumptuously; and had champagne, which was, with Tamms, the only alternative for water. A score or so of richly dressed ladies, with their husbands, were at the tables, including the little girl in lilac silk, who drank champagne also. The mother of the little girl—a magnificent woman, with black hair, carefully dressed, like a salad—sat opposite them; and her husband leaned his elbow on the table and his beard upon the palm of his hand, and talked to Tamms, between the courses. Charlie was introduced as "a young man in my office," and was treated by the lady with undissembled scorn; indeed, she condescended even to Tamms. And Charlie felt all the delight of some explorer landed among savages, who prefer colored beads to diamonds. "Positively," thought Charlie, "she does not even know that I am Charlie Townley!" Mrs. Haberman certainly did not, and would have refused him her daughter's hand in marriage, that evening, had he asked for it. And again it occurred to Charlie that wealth was the one universal good, after all.

Tamms certainly thought so; and when they got out on the piazza, began to talk about it. "Mr. Townley," said he, "I think I have observed that while you are not over-attentive to the business, you can keep a secret."

"You are very kind, sir," said Charlie.

"The fact is, the Starbuck Oil Company has proved a very bad investment indeed for the Allegheny Central Railroad Company."

"Dear me!" said Charlie, sympathetically, but as if inviting further confidence. Tamms looked at him for a moment, and then went on:

"The oil works showed the usual profit, but upon closing the accounts of the first year of the new terminal enterprise, we find that the property has failed to pay even its running expenses. In fact the company will probably default on the next coupon of the Terminal bonds.—How many of them have we left?"

Charlie was silent a moment, as if to count.

"Only a little over a hundred thousand," said Charlie, "not counting those we are carrying for our customers."

"You will of course have to look after their margins," said Tamms, absent-mindedly. "Sell at once if they do not respond."

("The old Shylock!") thought Charlie. "Certainly, sir," he said. "Shall I sell the hundred thousand we have left of our own?"

Tamms looked at our young friend sternly. "And profit by our official knowledge of the coming default? Certainly not, sir. We will bear our loss with the rest." And Tamms drew himself up and placed his right hand in the breast of his black frock-coat, much as if he were addressing posterity—or a newspaper reporter, as Charlie reflected. This sudden high moral attitude was admirable, if inexplicable.

"But," said Charlie, "the bonds being guaranteed by the Allegheny Central Railroad——"

"Guaranteed by the Allegheny Central?" interrupted Tamms, in astonishment, his whity-blue eyes opened to their fullest extent.

"That was certainly my impression, sir," faltered Charlie. For he remembered that he himself had composed a newspaper item to that effect.

"Here is the original circular under which the bonds were issued," said Tamms, with dignity; and Charlie cast his eye over it timorously. There was certainly nothing in it about a guaranty, though Charlie had a distinct impression that when the bonds were "listed" on the Stock Exchange this had been the general understanding. "You must be thinking of some mere newspaper rumor," added Tamms.

"Very possibly, sir," Charlie replied, meekly; and just then an elaborately dressed woman of rather flamboyant appearance passed through the glass-covered piazza in which they were sitting, and Mr. Tamms scrambled hastily upon his feet and bowed. Charlie followed suit, though surprised at this unusual demonstration of his impassive principal; and as he looked at him, he fancied that he saw the faintest trace of some embarrassment.

"She is not a guest of the hotel," said Tamms. "Her name is Beaumont, I believe; she owns an adjoining cottage."

"Dear me!" said Charlie. "That is very bad for people who own the stock."

"Own what stock?" said Tamms.

"The Starbuck Oil," said Charlie, in a tone as if adding "of course."

"Oh, ah, yes," said Tamms. "It is most unfortunate. Still, they should have exchanged it for Allegheny Central when we gave them the chance."

Charlie suddenly remembered that all the stock had not been exchanged.

"I suppose our people hold a majority, of course," said Charlie. And again he looked at Tamms.

But to this Mr. Tamms vouchsafed no answer; he apparently did not hear it, for he was already rising and putting on his gloves. "Shall we take a stroll?"

"I should like nothing better," said Charlie, heartily; and Tamms having sent for two cigars (for which, as Charlie noted, he paid fifty cents apiece), they took their way across the close-cropped lawn.

"That, I am told," said Mr. Tamms, pointing to a gayly lighted pagoda opposite, "which they call the Maryland Club, is in reality nothing better than a gambling house."

"Dear me!" said Charlie.

"It is an outrage upon our civilization that such social plague-spots are openly tolerated;" a sentiment from which Charlie could not withhold his assent, though he was glad the darkness prevented Mr. Tamms from seeing the smile which accompanied it. Nothing more was said between them for some time; Mr. Tamms was evidently wrapped in thoughts of business, and Charlie for his part was considering that previous state of her existence, in which he had known Mrs. Beaumont before.

So musing, they came to the plank-walk above the sea; it was almost deserted of promenaders, and below it, from the darkness of the night, came in the long ocean rollers, shining whitely on the shallow beach, as if gifted with some radiance of their own. They leaned some time over a railing by a bath-pavilion, and watched the breakers in silence; some women were in the sea—it was the servants from the hotel, bathing in the only hour that was allowed to them. And from the great hotel behind them came some vulgar music from a band.

"They are having a ball at the Beau-Monde to-night, I believe," said Tamms, at last. "Would you like to look in?"

Charlie professed his willingness; and they walked across the dusty street to the huge caravanserai, its hundred windows flaming with light. They found the veranda crowded with perhaps a thousand people, sitting in groups, the ladies in white or low-necked dresses, their diamond ear-rings flashing thick as fire-flies above a summer swamp. Among them were numerous Jews and Jewesses; the latter, at least, a splendid, full-blooded, earth-compelling race, though their males more wizened. In the great ball-room some score or more of children were dancing to a waltz, but no grown people as yet. These were as elegantly attired as their parents, only that they did not wear low-necked gowns, but in lieu of this had short skirts and gay silk stockings reaching well above the knee. Among them was the twelve-year-old miss in lilac from the Mistletoe; and many of these had already diamond solitaires and more than the airs and graces of a woman of the world. Their cheeks were flushed, and their long hair tossing about them; some few were romping frankly, but most were too Dignified for this; and as their silk sashes fluttered and their silk stockings twinkled in the dance, they were undeniably a pretty sight, and might have been a pleasant one, to their mothers. But I think a country hay-mow had been better for them.

But these same mothers were sitting on the piazza outside, not yet too old to flirt, and taking more pleasure in showing off their dresses than perhaps their children did, as yet. And those who were too ill-favored by Heaven for this could at least talk about spending money, and about each other. Tamms soon found a congenial group, a group consisting of Mrs. Beaumont and himself; and Charlie was left to his own devices. He drifted into the bar-room and took a drink, by way of killing time; and thereabout he found the husbands mostly congregated. And, as their wives had been talking of spending money, they were talking about making it; and Charlie listened some time and then went home alone.

When he got to the Mistletoe, he called for a telegraph blank and wrote a telegram to Mrs. Levison Gower. It ran as follows:

"I think you had better sell your Starbuck Oil. Who is attending to your affairs in town? C. T."

Surely, with all his faults, our friend thus proved himself a knight faithful and loyal, *à la mode*. But having written it, Charlie remembered that he did not know where to send it; for Mrs. Gower was off in a chariot which bore no freight of worldly care. Was she not mistress of Aladdin's lamp? She had but to rub a finger, and all things were heaped at her feet. Aye; but the slaves of the lamp, who were they? Suppose they were not faithful; suppose they proved unruly and rose up in revolt? Did not even an Aladdin's slave turn out to be one of the Genii?

Townley liked Mrs. Gower, and did not wish her to be humbled. Socially, she helped him still. Should he say Lenox? He thought a moment; and the upshot of his deliberations was a resolve to do nothing for a day at least. Whereupon he went to bed, and, let us hope, to pleasant dreams.

For he could not quite account for Tamms's virtuous refusal to sell their own bonds before the coming default.

## CHAPTER XXIII.

### THE SLAVES OF THE LAMP.

"YOU had better not go back to-day," said Mr. Tamms to Charlie when he came down in the morning. "They can get along without you at the office; besides, I should like you to drive with me to Ocean Grove." Charlie was always ready enough to get along without the office, even if the converse of that proposition had not been unusual enough upon the lips of Mr. Tamms to excite his curiosity. So the long-tailed fast horses were brought out in the trotting-buggy, and, well provided with cigars and morning papers, the two set forth upon their journey. It was a piping hot day; the glaring surface of the sea lay still beside them, and the straight, unshaded, red-clay road seemed to be rapidly baking into brick. Mrs. Haberman came to see them off, robed still in a sort of gorgeous bedchamber arrangement of pale silk and laces, the inevitable large diamonds still in her ears. For some miles their way was the same they had taken the day before, along the rows of shadeless villas, each "cottage" more ornate and ramifying than the last; then they came to a long rise of the sweltering fields, past a thin grove of pines, a few cheaper boarding-houses, and a swamp with an artificial pond. Beyond this the hotels began again; and they crossed a long lagoon that looked like some breeding-place for fevers and lay between two great wooden cities; these were Asbury Park and Ocean Grove; and in front of them was still the sea.

Many of the cottages were here the merest little wooden boxes, some of them put together still more informally, of canvas and of poles, so that one looked through the whole domestic range, from the front part, which was a parlor, through the open family bed-room to the kitchen behind. These were the abodes of those who (not like the dwellers at Long Branch) came here in search of religious experiences; but Charlie saw, save a Bible text or two in chromo, no visible evidence of the higher life. Paterfamilias was usually lolling, unbuttoned as to waistcoat, in the front part of the establishment; materfamilias, in an indescribable white gown that seemed but a shapeless covering for divers toilet sins, was busied with housewifely duties; and the *filia pulchrior* was commonly set forth in a hammock upon the little piazza, lost in some novel of "The Duchess" or of "Bertha Clay," but not too lost in those entrancing pages to cast some very collected glances at Charlie and his patron's handsome equipage.

There were fewer "saloons" than at Long Branch; but even more confectioners' shops and summer circulating libraries; and plenty of hotels. Before the largest of these, Mr. Tamms drew up his steaming horses, and asked of the sable yet proud young porter if Mr. Remington were in. "Deacon Remington is down at the beach, sah," was the reply; and Mr. Tamms gave orders for his horses to be rubbed and cared for, while they sought the Deacon (who seemed a person of much prominence at Ocean Grove) on foot.

Plank-walks led in all directions through the streets, which otherwise would have been heavy walking, in the heaped-up sand; for there was no turf nor other vegetation, except where an artificial *platebande* of red leaves and greenhouse plants was fostered at the street corners. They took the walk which led seaward, passing one or two huge wooden tabernacles where sermons, meetings, or other Methodist functions were performed every day, as frequent wooden placards informed them. But they were empty now; and Charlie could see the theatre of rows of rising seats, much like the band-pavilion at a beach less sacred than was this. They crossed the end of the fresh-water lagoon, passed a flotilla of pleasure boats, and ascended to the sandy shore; here, from the crest of the beach, the walk led upward still, supported on piles, to the great ocean pier, a sort of sublimated piazza, double or triple decked, roofed, and extending far along the beach before them, with a pier projecting far out over the sea. Here was the population of the place assembled, knitting, reading, or doing nothing to the music of a brass band which, stationed at the outer end of the pavilion, was performing revival hymns. It seemed to Charlie that there must be some thousands of people on this pier alone;

and he saw that there was another deck below, and still below that the beach was strewn, like drift-wood, with humanity. The task of finding Deacon Remington seemed hopeless, and Charlie made bold to ask why they should look further.

"The Deacon is the leader of our church," said Tamms, "and a very shrewd man. He is one of the largest stockholders in Starbuck Oil."

Charlie said nothing more; and in a moment a gaunt man rose up from a little table they were passing by and addressed Tamms eagerly. His upper lip was shaven, but otherwise his beard was unkempt; his sallow face had a worn and weary look which even the perfunctory smile that continually gleamed across it, like sheet-lightning, did not permanently relieve. "How's the madam?" said Tamms.

"My wife is here," said the Deacon; and he jerked his head in the direction of a fat and comely personage, clothed in continual gray, who was placidly knitting at the table beside them. It seemed a pity to rout her up to bow; but it had to be done, for Charlie was introduced, and she rose portentously:

"Delighted to make your acquaintance, Mr. Townley," said she, when Tamms had mentioned him. "Father, where are the girls?"

"You'll find my da'ters down on the beach, I guess," said the Deacon, thus prompted.

"I came to tell you a little about that Starbuck stock, you know," began Tamms; but the Deacon sprang up hastily again, as if this were no place for tidings of moment. "Let's walk along the beach and find my da'ters," said he, "and then you can both come up to the house to dinner," and he led the way back to the pier-head, and then down the stairs to the lower story, where the bathing-houses were. Here the floor was less occupied; possibly because the continual passing and repassing of persons in bathing-dresses and bare feet made it uncomfortably damp and sandy. Charlie looked over the rail, and saw the beach beneath, where it was shaded by the pavilion, crowded with men and women in every conceivable variety of attitude. Many couples had scooped out hollows for themselves, where they wallowed with the sands heaped about them; others lay back to back, a huge umbrella stuck in the sand behind them, the girl usually reading aloud, the young man smoking.. Many still wore their bathing-dresses, though the folds of cloth were now quite dry and it was evident that they had worn them through the morning. One pretty girl was lying with her bare feet and ankles drying in the sun and her long hair spread out upon the sand; a young man sat beside her, in a striped sleeveless jersey and tights, smoking a cigarette. Charlie could not but think of cows upon a summer's day, standing knee-deep in the pool, as he saw these varied groups in age and dress and sex all grovelling in the delicious coolness of the wet sea-sand.

"We have got to default upon the Terminal bonds, you know," were the first words Charlie heard spoken.

"No!" said Mr. Remington, open-mouthed. And

he stood staring at Tamms, his long arms hanging limply to his broadcloth coat-tails.

"Yes," said Tamms; "I came down to tell you. The thing isn't known yet, you know."

Charlie fancied that a shade of color returned to the Deacon's cheek at this announcement. "Dear me!" said he. "But I thought——"

"Come back to the hotel, Remington; we can't talk here," said Tamms, who had some difficulty in picking his way among the outstretched arms and limbs and heads of hair, many of whose owners had closed their eyes, and the way being further complicated by the gambols of playing children, and the wetness of others, in wading to their waists.

"Certainly," said the Deacon, half turning about. "And of course you'll have dinner with us. Only I wanted this young man to meet my girls. Why, here comes Sadie now." And indeed a brown-haired damsel of some twenty summers, just emerged from the sea, was running swiftly toward him. "Sadie, this is Mr. Tamms, and Mr.—Mr. Townley," and the trio bowed at a respectable distance, for Miss Remington was still extremely wet. "Sadie'll show you the shortest way back," said Mr. Remington, "and I'll go back and get the mother." Sadie gave a toss to her mane of hair, which scorned any oiled cap, as if to indicate her readiness; and led the way up the soft banks of sand to the street and its plank-walks.

"It must be very pleasant to be able to bathe so easily," said Charlie, trying hard to walk on the plank-walk beside her and yet keep out of his fair guide's drip.

"Yes, it's ever so much nicer than dressing in the bathing-houses," said Miss Remington. "Did you drive over from the Branch? I'm told it's awfully gay there, this season;" and Charlie admitted that it was. They had now reached the main street of the town, and Charlie could not but admire the genuineness of Miss Remington's constitution, as the hot sun streamed upon her wet face and her salted locks hung heavily behind her. The hotel was now before them, and after indicating the gentlemen's parlor to her guests, she herself disappeared by a side entrance. The great parlor contained nothing of human interest but a leather-bound Bible on a marble centre-table; and Tamms and Charlie Townley soon gravitated to the piazza, where, feet upon rail, and Tamms (who smoked at all times and junctures) with a cigar in his mouth, they awaited the coming of their host. Soon he appeared, with another young lady, more slender and, if possible, wetter than Miss Sadie, walking nervously, Mrs. Remington steaming hopelessly in their wake. "My wife can't stay," said the Deacon, after the first moments of compliment had passed; "she's got to get ready for dinner. And now tell me all about it, Tamms," said he, as he drew a chair up beside them. It was curious to watch the contrast between Remington's evident nervousness and Tamms's entire self-possession; and Charlie watched it.

"Have a cigar?" said Tamms, politely drawing another black one from his pocket.

"You know I never smoke, Tamms. But what's this about the Starbuck Oil?"

"Well, you know about all there is about it," said Tamms, lazily. "It can't pay interest on the Terminal bonds, that's all. They never ought to have paid any dividend, in my opinion." This remark cleverly cut from under his feet the rejoinder Remington had in mind; and he looked at Tamms helplessly.

"This is a pretty state of things," said he, at last. "I thought the Company had consolidated with Allegheny Central."

"The Allegheny Central voted to consolidate with Starbuck Oil, but I don't know that the Starbuck Oil ever consolidated with Allegheny. The Terminal bonds were issued by the Starbuck Oil and properly authorized by the directors; but for the other question, you remember, we never got control." This was a home-thrust; for, as Charlie now remembered, the Deacon held the balance of power in the stock; and he had always refused to commit himself upon this point. "It looks bad for Starbuck Oil—it does, indeed," added Mr. Tamms, thoughtfully, stroking his smooth chin and eying Remington closely. "And I tell you what, Remington: I felt that I had more or less got you into this thing, and I came down to tell you about it while there was yet time. There isn't money enough in the treasury to pay the September coupon; that's certain. But nobody knows it yet."

"Well," said Remington, with an evident effort, "one other thing is certain, and that is that it's nearly dinner-time. Don't you gentlemen want to brush up a bit?"

Tamms answered that it was unnecessary, and Remington left upon that pretext. But Charlie noticed that he took the door that led to the hotel telegraph office. "Remington thought that he was doing a very shrewd thing in keeping that stock," said Tamms, dryly; and he went on smoking, but kept his eyes intently fixed upon an imaginary point in air, about eighteen inches in front of his own nose.

While Charlie was watching him, the young ladies, much transmogrified, came down for dinner. But the dinner was a long and weary meal, made up of many courses; no wine was served, but the hotel made up for this by giving them, at intervals, three glasses of ice-cream.

"You must find it very pleasant here, Mrs. Remington," was Tamms's contribution to the conversation; and "We're not much acquainted yet—I think it's rather too gay," was her reply. The two Miss Remingtons showed an evident inclination to converse with Charlie, but seemed as if restrained by the presence of their elders; and Charlie was not sorry when the nuts and raisins appeared, and they took their leave. The Deacon had seemed greatly preoccupied; but he walked with them to their buggy and fast horses, and Sadie Remington with Charlie.

"Of course, you know, Tamms," said the Deacon, by way of parting, "I'm much obliged to you for the point."

"Don't mention it, Deacon, don't mention it," said

Tamms, heartily, as he climbed in and gathered up the reins.

"I hope, Mr. Townley, now you've found the way, you'll be neighborly and come and see us often," said Sadie Remington. She was really a very pretty girl, thought Charlie; he had done her some injustice in her mermaid garb; and he was able to regret the impossibility of returning to Ocean Grove with some sincerity.

Tamms said very little going home; and Charlie's mind was also active. "The Governor" had certainly made of him his most intimate and confidential clerk; but such was his cleverness that Charlie felt he knew rather less of Mr. Tamms's projects than he did before. Upon one thing, after some reflection, Charlie was decided; and that was to very carefully tear up and throw away the telegram he had written the night before for Mrs. Gower. For Tamms had given too much advice to the Deacon, by half.

The next day Charlie got up betimes, and was driven to the pier by Mr. Tamms. "I need not tell you," said that gentleman, "not to say anything about what I told you, or of our seeing the Deacon yesterday."

"Of course not," said Charlie.

"The Deacon is a very overbearing man in business affairs," added Tamms, absently. "And by the way, Townley, any chance bits of Allegheny Central stock you can pick up—at the board, you may take for us."

"Certainly," said Charlie. "How much?"

"I don't particularly care—ten thousand or so, perhaps—you'll hardly get more than that. But do it quietly."

"The deuce!" thought Charlie to himself; but he held his peace; and by ten o'clock he was back at the office and hard at work. Mr. Tamms did not return; and Charlie had orders to tell everyone that he was temporarily out of Wall Street, taking his well-earned vacation at the seaside.

On that day there began to be a sudden activity in Starbuck Oil. At first the price went up a point or two; and then some thousand shares were thrown upon the market, and it fell more than twenty points. Charlie fancied that the selling came from the good Deacon; but who the buyers were, his sharpest investigations failed to show. On the day after, there were rumors of a coming deficit, and the stock went down with a rush, carrying with it the Terminal bonds. The same afternoon there was an item on the "tape" to the effect that the September coupon would probably have to be funded. The next day was a Sunday; but on Monday poor Charlie was flooded with letters, angry and beseeching, and with irate or troubled customers, who were holders of the bonds in question. He had but one course open to him: to those who paid for the bonds, he regretted that unforeseen expenses had made the Terminal enterprise so unprofitable; and to those who had not paid for their bonds as yet he added a polite request for further "margin."

Mr. Tamms in person dropped in late that afternoon; and Charlie told him the condition of affairs, though he could have sworn that gentleman was paying no attention to any word he spoke.

" Keep at it," he said, when Charlie had got through. "You can tell them that we, too, have a large block of bonds, besides owning nearly all the stock, and are heavy losers ourselves. No one could foresee it, of course. Mr. Townley still at Lenox, I suppose?"

Charlie said that he was, and Tamms departed, saying that he would be in again to-morrow. And Charlie went up to the Columbian Club, and read the following item in *The Evening Post:*

"The late depression in Starbuck Oil securities is believed to have been caused by the fact that the property has failed to earn its fixed charges in the past six months. The selling has come largely from Deacon Remington, through Rawson, Lawson & Co.; and it is regarded as beyond question that the Company will default September 1st upon its mortgage bonds. The banking house of Messrs. Townley & Tamms are said to have lost largely by the failure, as they hold the bulk of the Company's stock."

"By Jove," said Charlie to himself, "I ought to have telegraphed Flossie Gower, after all."

But then he re-read the article and began to reconsider it. Charlie was a young man addicted to much reconsideration. It was a very strange thing that a responsible newspaper should go out of its way to print an item like that—an item which might seriously injure the credit of a prominent banking house. Why (for Charlie had studied law in his youth), it was almost libellous. Tamms had read the paper before leaving the office, and had not seemed particularly disturbed. "Does he want it to be supposed we lost money?—and certainly," said Charlie to himself, "the Governor is a clever fellow."

The next day was the first of August, and Charlie had arranged to begin his summer vacation by going to Newport that afternoon. He was early at the office, but found Tamms there already, dictating to a couple of stenographers. He was tearing up little pieces of paper, crumpling them up into balls, and throwing them into one corner of the room. Now, this was a way he had when things were going to his liking; but Charlie did not venture to speak to him about the item in *The Evening Post*. Moreover, a copy of that journal lay open on his desk.

"Shall I buy any more Allegheny, sir?" said Charlie.

"How much more have we got?"

"About eight thousand shares, so far—from 91 to five-eighths."

"Buy all you can up to 92 or so," said Tamms, cheerfully. Suddenly, a still full-bodied, though rather senile voice was heard in the main office, asking for Mr. Tamms. Charlie started, and even Tamms sprang to his feet. And Charlie fancied that that gentleman's face turned, if possible, a shade paler than its wont.

"What's this, Tamms?" cried the old gentleman, already angry, as the door flew open, without heeding Charlie's presence: "What's this about the Starbuck Terminal bonds?" And Charlie could see, through the open door, the clerks in the outer office huddling their shoulders over their ledgers, in evident consciousness of a coming breeze. Mr. Townley's face was crimson with excitement, as he panted in his stiff collar, his white hair making his face seem the redder, and his bald head beady with perspiration. Tamms had always a sort of patient, semi-patronizing tone in talking over business with his senior partner; but this time he tried, and tried in vain, to resume his usual manner.

"I am sorry to say," he began slowly, "that hitherto—the Terminal property—has not proved—a profitable enterprise."

"Stuff—and—nonsense!" interposed Mr. Townley, his sputtering enunciation in strange contrast with Tamms's clear-cut tones. "You yourself told me it promised most excellently."

"So I did, sir—last winter. I fear that I was mistaken," said Tamms, humbly.

"Mistaken, eh! Well, sir, and what do you propose to do about it?"

"I see nothing for it—but to fund the next coupon—and attempt a reorganization——"

"I do not mean as a director, sir; with that business you are familiar. But as a banker—as a New York merchant—as a member—damn it, sir, as a member of the house of Charles Townley & Son?" In his anger, the old gentleman had used the former name of the firm; and there was an ugly glitter in Tamms's eye, which he carefully kept from meeting old Mr. Townley's.

"As a member of the firm of Townley & Tamms," said he, "I see nothing to do but to look over our customers' margins and bear our own losses." Charlie made a motion to go.

"Stay there, Mr. Townley," ordered the old gentleman, "and learn once for all the traditions of the house of Charles Townley & Son. So, Mr. Tamms, a year after bringing out these bonds, with the ink hardly dry upon them, before the second coupon is cut, you propose that we who fathered them should stand by and see our clients and the public, who relied upon our recommendation and our name, deceived in both?"

"I don't see what else we can do, sir. We are not the Starbuck Oil Company." Tamms tried still to patronize; but Charlie marvelled that a man who seemed so large the day before with Deacon Remington should seem so small to-day before an angry old man with white hair who had outlived his business usefulness and sputtered when he spoke.

"I will show you, then. Mr. Townley, will you please take down this letter." Charlie moved his chair to a table and wrote, while Mr. Townley dictated:

"Messrs. Townley & Tamms—regret that unforeseen circumstances—have caused an embarrassment in the affairs of the Starbuck Oil Company—but have decided to guaranty the coupons on the Terminal Trust bonds—until the property has been put upon a paying basis.—From those who prefer—Messrs. Townley & Tamms will take back the bonds sold by them

—paying the price originally paid therefor, with accrued interest."

"There, sir," said Mr. Townley to Charlie, "you will have five hundred copies of that circular dated to-day and printed immediately. And Mr. Tamms, you will kindly see that a copy is mailed to every one of our correspondents and clients—or our partnership may end at once."

"Certainly, sir," said Tamms, calmly. "I presume you know what an amount of ready money this action may require?"

"No, sir, I do not," said Mr. Townley.

"It may force us into liquidation," said Mr. Tamms.

"Fiddle-de-dee," said Mr. Townley, as he rose and left the office.

Tamms looked after him long and curiously, as an artist might look after a retreating cow which had just knocked over his easel and trampled on his study of pastoral life. Charlie looked at Tamms. The hour for him to be upon the Stock Exchange had long since passed; but he still sat there, and nothing was said for some time. Finally Tamms took a bit of paper, and began to roll it up into little balls.

"It is very unnecessary for Mr. Townley to take up such a quixotic attitude," said he. "That sort of thing is all very well in Shakespeare." And he threw his little balls of paper, with great accuracy, one into each of the three other corners of the room.

"What shall I do, sir, about the circular?"

"You must have it printed at once, and mailed, as

Mr. Townley directed. But Mr. Lauer will attend to that." (Lauer was the bookkeeper.) "This insane action of Townley's will require considerable ready money. You must go to the board at once, and sell some Allegheny Central." Tamms had endeavored to assume his slightly contemptuous air in speaking of his partner; but it seemed to Charlie that there was still a pallor in his sharp face that belied his jauntiness.

"How much shall I sell, sir?"

"All we've got," said Tamms, curtly. Charlie nodded, and jumped up to leave the room. When he got to the street-door a clerk came running after him. "Don't sell yourself—get Lawson, Rawson & Co. to do it," said Tamms, as he turned back. Charlie nodded again, and was off. Now, Lawson, Rawson & Co. were Deacon Remington's brokers; *ergo* Tamms did not want people to know he was selling; *ergo,* he was selling in good earnest. It looked bad. And he had thought Tamms such a clever fellow!

Charlie was very busy at the stock-board that afternoon. He bought a few hundred shares himself, but this had little avail in staying the price against the thousands with which Lawson, Rawson & Co. deluged the market. Charlie did not trouble himself much then with thinking; he had no positive capital in the firm of Townley & Tamms; but he had a feeling that it was a critical moment for them. He could not help a slight wonder that Tamms had yielded to his senior so easily; but then he reflected that a violent rupture at such a juncture meant to Tamms even more certain financial ruin than the firm incurred by making good the Terminal bonds. Despite Charlie's strategy, and the few hundreds he bought with much vociferation, the price sagged from 93 to 90 and a fraction; and there was a wild and struggling crowd of panting men about the iron standard that bore the sign of Allegheny Central. Now and then Charlie would elbow his way into the outskirts and make a feeble bid or two; but a good-natured friend volunteered advice that it was no use, and "the best thing he could do was to wait until the Deacon had got his lines well out, and then catch him short," advice which Charlie received with a smile. At all events, the Governor could not say he had not done things well; for even his friend had not suspected that it was he who was selling.

Dick Rawson was standing in the middle, red-faced and breathless, his voice already hoarse, like a stag at bay amid a pack of leaping hounds. Charlie looked at him and for a fraction of a second caught his eye. Then Charlie looked at the wall beneath the gallery. That wall is used for members' signals, and as he watched it, a wooden lid fell back, revealing a white placard with the number 449. Now, this was Charlie's number, and it meant that there was some one for him in the lobby; he went out at once, and the number sprang back out of sight with a click, worked by some clockwork mechanism. In the lobby Charlie found a messenger with a sealed note addressed to him. It was a hastily pencilled scrawl from Rawson, the very man who was standing in the focus of the excited throng, but of course had given no sign of any understanding there.

"I have sold 11,000. Shall I go on?
R."

Charlie thought a minute; much of their stock, he knew, had been pledged at about 80, and to drive the stock below this point would cause a call for further margin. And, unless Charlie was very much mistaken, the firm of Townley & Tamms had just then no more securities to pledge. He wrote on the back of Rawson's note:

"Sell all you can down to 85.
C. T."

The boy went back upon the floor of the Exchange. Charlie did not deem it wise to follow him; but in a few minutes a renewed roar from the Allegheny Central crowd told him that his order was being executed.

He went back to the office, where he found Mr. Tamms still sitting in his private room, much as he had left him. A certain unusual idleness, a subtile air of expectation pervaded the clerks in the office, which Charlie did not fail to note. Tamms looked up at him, as he entered, but made no remark.

"We have sold over ten thousand," said Charlie.

"What's the price now?" asked Tamms.

"It broke 90," said Charlie, laconically.

"We shall know exactly in a few minutes," added Tamms, calmly. "See, I have already got a proof of Mr. Townley's proclamation." And Tamms tossed the paper to Charlie, giving the word *Proclamation* an accent that was slightly contemptuous. "You will keep the correspondence clerk to see that they are all duly mailed to-night."

Charlie went out to get his lunch, as he had had no time to eat since breakfast; and when he hurried back at a quarter after three, Rawson was there with his account. They had sold 16,400 shares at from 93 to 85¼—an average of nearly 89. "I shall not be in all day to-morrow," said Tamms to Charlie. "You will see to getting in the stock that is out as collateral, and its prompt delivery."

"I had arranged to go on my vacation to-day," said Charlie. "May I go to-morrow night?"

"Certainly—after that is done." And Tamms left the office, to all appearance unshaken by the events of the day. Charlie went to his lodgings and dressed, and then dined at his club alone.

Though he had no money stake in the firm, its success or downfall would mean much to him. With its failure went all his future, all his business prospects. And Charlie went over in his mind, for the twentieth time, the extent to which they had been injured. First, there was over four million dollars of the Terminal bonds which they had sold and Mr. Townley ordered to be made good. At the best, the loss on these could hardly be under a million. Then Charlie knew, though possibly old Mr. Townley did not, that they had a very heavy holding in Starbuck Oil stock. Although Tamms had let out to him at Ocean Grove that they did not actually hold a majority, as people had supposed, they certainly held a large amount, probably as much as Mrs. Gower herself, if the Deacon had held the balance of power. But if the Terminal mortgage was foreclosed, it would possibly wipe out all the stock, and this was all dead loss. And the Allegheny Central stood them in at 85 or so, so they had not cleared a sum worth mentioning on that. And he ought to have telegraphed Mrs. Gower, after all.

For once in his life, Charlie passed a sleepless night; a thing less common to his kind than to John Haviland, for instance, he being also a healthy animal, but with a conscience. In the morning he had his trunk packed and sent to the station; and after finishing up for the day at the office, he got to the Grand Central Depot at four o'clock. But here he took the train, not for Newport, but for Lenox. Now, Mamie Livingstone was still at Great Barrington.

He opened an evening penny paper, and the first Wall Street item that attracted his attentive eye ran as follows:

"It is reported that a certain prominent banking-house, largely identified with Allegheny Central, has been hard hit by the recent developments in Starbuck Oil."

And in another part of the same paper:

"It is now believed that yesterday's selling in Allegheny was not from Deacon Remington, but long stock sold by insiders for reasons of their own."

Charlie was not surprised that their tactics were discovered. He knew that such devices as they had used might serve the purpose for the moment, but could not deceive the hundred keen-eyed men that constitute "the Street" for twenty-four hours together.

He alighted at Lenox in the cool of the evening, and went to the hotel. The country air was grateful to him, and he slept soundly. The next day he idled at the Lenox Club, waiting for his horse and dog-cart, which had been shipped the day before. In the evening they arrived, and he transferred his head-quarters to the inn at Stockbridge. The following afternoon, his cart and harness well cleaned, his horse carefully groomed, and his groom riding behind in full livery, he drove over to Great Barrington and called upon Miss Holyoke—and Miss Livingstone. That is, he asked for Miss Livingstone, and left a card for Gracie. Mamie came down, all excitement; it had been getting so dull in the country, and here was Charlie, like an angel dropped from heaven all for her! "I am staying at Stockbridge, you know," said Charlie, "and I have driven over to ask if you will not come for a little drive?"

Mamie turned her pretty eyes away and blushed a little; but she was thinking of Gracie, not of him. But after all, Gracie was little older than was she; it was not politic to admit her right of chaperonage too far. So they went, and had a long drive through the woods; and never, even to married ladies, had Charlie Townley made love so charmingly. And it must be admitted, though his male friends had no inkling of it, that Charlie could, upon occasion, make love very well. And when he left, it was quite settled that he was to come again—not the next day, of course, but the day after. Poor Mamie! Poor Chloe! She did not know that it was the Starbuck Oil Company that had forced Mr. Strephon's hand.

And on the following evening, Charlie Townley, sitting at the Lenox Club, took up his *Evening Post* with some trepidation. He fully expected to see that the house of Townley & Tamms had suspended payments.

ALLEGHENY CENTRAL.

At a meeting of the Allegheny Central Railroad Company held this morning, the following resolution and vote, introduced by Mr. Phineas L. Tamms, were unanimously adopted:

*Whereas*, Under the terms of the late proposed consolidation of this company with the Silas Starbuck Oil Company, certain bonds of the latter company were authorized by vote of both boards of directors, and have been duly issued, to provide for terminal facilities, wharves, etc. And although, during the process of construction, and in consequence of certain extraordinary expenses, the earnings of the Silas Starbuck Oil Company have proved temporarily insufficient to meet fixed charges, the directors of the Allegheny Central Company are convinced that the ultimate value and returns of such improvements will more than compensate for the outlay involved; therefore be it

*Resolved*, That inasmuch as the faith and credit of the Allegheny Central Railroad Company have been largely relied upon by the investing public in purchasing said bonds, though not in terms guarantied by said company, your directors deem it proper to definitely guaranty said bonds, principal and interest.

*Voted*, That the President and Treasurer of the Allegheny Central Railroad Company be authorized to affix the guaranty of said company, both for principal and interest, upon such bonds of the Starbuck Oil Company as shall be presented at their office for that purpose before the first day of October next.

By Jove! A great light burst upon Charlie, and the paper fell from his hands. He took it up again, and read, lower down in the same column:

At a meeting of the Silas Starbuck Oil Company held this afternoon, a new board of directors was elected. Phineas L. Tamms was elected President, and the board is the same, with the exception of Deacon Remington, who is replaced in the new board by Adolph Lauer. It is currently reported that the control of this property has now definitely passed into the hands of Messrs. Townley & Tamms.

"Great heavens!" gasped Charlie. Lauer was merely one of their clerks. It was Tamms himself who had been buying all the Deacon's Starbuck Oil stock quietly, unknown even to Charlie; and he had sold all their own Allegheny Central; and then met his senior partner's order by causing the latter corporation to guaranty the former. He had served both God and Mammon, captured the keen Deacon, pleased his partner, and made money at the same time. And Charlie turned to the quotations.

Allegheny Central was down at 73, and the Starbuck Oil had gone up to 140; and the bonds were well above par. And Tamms had secured the reputation of an honorable financier into the bargain!

Charlie began rapidly to calculate. Tamms must have now over ten thousand Starbuck Oil, upon which he had made at least thirty dollars a share; and he had finally got the control besides. He had sold much of their Allegheny Central at nearly the highest prices, averaging 90 or so, making perhaps $200,000 here. Add to this the $100,000 or more they had made originally upon the Terminal bonds, upon which the firm's endorsement was now unnecessary, and——

"The Governor is a devilish clever fellow," concluded Charlie. And as he thought of that drive with Mamie, he feared that he himself had been too precipitate.

## CHAPTER XXIV.

### MAMIE GOES TO THE SHOW.

GRACIE had looked forward with a yearning she would not even to herself allow to the summer and her coming to her father's home once more. There are times when rocks and woods and fields and streams speak to us with sympathy no human being seems to have; why is it, I wonder? When nature was an enemy and men were savages, they seemed unconscious of her and thought only of each other; now that men have all learned human sympathy, and altruism is the cry, some, and those perhaps the gentlest and the noblest of us all, must fly to nature for a refuge yet. But perhaps we have not yet learned human sympathy; or perhaps it is the divine that we should have instead. Perhaps our sympathy is too often one of common objects or of common lusts. Perhaps each one seeks his glory, rather that he may dazzle others with it than lend his light to them.

But Gracie was not complex, nor analytic; it is only the diseased who so apply the scalpel. If she ever was unhappy, she thought it willed from Heaven; or sought the cause in herself and not in other things. And at all events, she was not unhappy now, save as some lily may be sad for loneliness. Yet who would wish no lilies grew but such as serve in balls or churches? Some will tell you that all lilies are forced; not natural even there. But others of us may believe in lilies still.

And Mamie too had some of Gracie's happiness; some sense of things she had not felt before. They walked, and rode, and read together; and if Gracie dreamed, Mamie would think, more practically. But Mamie, too, had learned to love her cousin; still, perhaps, with some slight shade of patronage. Thus they had been together, until that day when Townley called and brought with him to Mamie the envied savor of the world again. She returned from her drive, full of triumph, to Gracie; and then Gracie had been forced into the thankless attitude of a duenna. Gracie could not have told why she did not quite like Charlie Townley; and Mamie had begun to pout once more. And Mamie had looked for Charlie the next day; but he did not come, nor yet the next day; and Mamie had blamed Gracie with being rude to him.

For Charlie, after reading the paper that night, had almost had his confidence in Tamms restored. He meant to marry some time, and to make his fortune by it; but he had a dread of wedlock, even gilded; as every sensible man must, he thought.

Then he had seen old Mr. Townley one day at Lenox. "I fear I did Mr. Tamms a great wrong that morning, Charlie," he had said. "He was too proud to defend himself; but I suspect he had all the arrangements made, even at that time, and felt deeply the injustice of my strictures." Charlie had thrust his tongue in his cheek at this, but had held his peace. He did not tell that Tamms had sold 12,000 Allegheny Central first. For Charlie had made a flying visit to the office; and there he saw enough to convince him that Tamms was already buying back his Allegheny Central stock again. And indeed it was obvious enough that he would have to do this in order to retain the control of the great property against the next election. One paper had called the guaranty a fraud.

"The Governor is certainly devilish smart," said Charlie to himself; "but I fear he's almost too smart to last out my time." And Charlie drove over to Great Barrington again. So his drive with Mamie was many times repeated; and what could Gracie do? for, as Mamie told her, laughing, she would yield to her in anything but this. For, of what her course in the world should be, Mamie considered herself much the better judge. And Gracie could not bring herself to write and bear tales to her aunt, who was growing old, while Mr. Livingstone was still less to be thought of. For men and women, for youths and children, for mobs and voters, there is a something absurd now about all the constituted authorities; and so we laugh, and the dance goes on.

Since the affair with Deacon Remington, Tamms had taken Charlie quite into his confidence; and on the first of September surprised him with conferring the firm's signature. But, though Charlie was now a partner, he had no capital; and his added dignity gave him little more than a closer knowledge of the firm's business—and a liability for the firm's debts. But this last responsibility did not disturb his slumbers; and he continued to be as attentive as ever to Miss Livingstone.

One day, late in the month, Charlie ran up to Great Barrington for a Sunday, and, to his surprise, found Mr. Derwent there. Now, what the deuce might this fellow be doing? thought he, and looked at him askance. Derwent filled up the entire parlor, as Charlie afterward put it to Mamie, and it was impossible for him to get a word with her. "I thought you had gone to British Columbia," said Charlie to him, at last, suggestively.

"Did you?" replied the other, simply.

"My afternoon was quite spoilt, and I had come up from New York on purpose," complained Charlie, the next day, to Mamie; and by this time the speech was really true. Courting is a pleasant sport while it lasts, and Miss Livingstone was a very pretty, bright young girl; and had it been merely flirting—but, as time went on, Townley began to take some interest in the chase for the game's sake, and not for sport only. And Charlie had come up for a special purpose, which was to get Miss Mamie to go with him to the first meet of the Bronx hounds, to be held at their kennels in the Sands country the following Tuesday.

The day before, they had a great scene in the office. Mr. Tamms had for several weeks been off in regions unknown to Wall Street, upon his own vacation, and had just returned. Hardly had he torn open and roughly disposed of his morning mail, when in came Deacon Remington. "I am informed that Mr. Tamms is returned," he announced. "I desire to see him."

"How do you do, Deacon Remington?" said Charlie, stepping forward. "I haven't seen you since Ocean Grove, I think," he added, politely.

"I desire to have an interview with Mr. Tamms." The Deacon continued to speak with precision, ignoring Charlie's courtesies as uncalled for and unbusinesslike.

"Mr. Tamms is in his private office, I think," said Charlie, blandly. And he inducted the earnest Deacon into that apartment, and closed the door upon him, with much the feeling that one has who shuts up a monkey in a parrot-cage. This done, Charlie resumed his desk and his occupation, which latter was nothing more arduous than the writing of a note to Mamie Livingstone. "Everybody will be there," he wrote; "and I hope——"

In a few minutes the door was opened, and Mr. Tamms came out. Mr. Townley," he said in flute-like tones; "will you kindly step in for a moment?"

"Certainly, sir," said Charlie. He went in, and the door was closed behind them. The pious Deacon was sitting upon the lounge on one corner, with folded wings, like a large blue-bottle.

"I wish you to tell Deacon Remington under what circumstances the house of Townley & Tamms were compelled to meet the deficit in the Starbuck Terminal bonds and avert foreclosure. Do you remember anything about it ?"

"Certainly, sir," said Charlie. He hesitated a moment, but was much too clever to seem to look to Tamms for the cue. "It was by order of Mr. Townley himself."

"Do you remember the day ?"

"It was the day after my return from Long Branch—three days after our drive to Ocean Grove."

"You see, Deacon ?" said Tamms, in the meek tones of a Christian unjustly wronged.

"Oh, yes, I see," said the Deacon.

"And am I right in stating that Mr. Townley's attitude was most peremptory ?" Charlie nodded. "That he went so far as to threaten a dissolution of partnership unless his orders were instantly complied with ?"

"He made me mail the circulars and send one out over the tape the same afternoon," said Charlie.

Again Tamms looked to Remington. There was a silence of some minutes, rather embarrassing to two of the company, at least.

"Well, well," said Remington, at last, "I may have done you wrong, Tamms. But now you've got my stock." And without the formalities of leave-taking, he rose and shuffled out of the shop.

Tamms watched him almost regretfully, and when he disappeared down the street, turned to Charlie.

"There, I fear, goes a man who will be a chronic bear upon the Allegheny Central," said he. Tamms had fallen into a way of making these semi-confidences to Charlie; and the latter was struck with the justice of this remark.

This scene was fresh in Charlie's mind to day when driving with Mamie through the calm, deep woods that clothe the Berkshire hills. Charlie was afraid of the Deacon; and sought Mamie's money's aid against him. Ah! Shakespeare's heroines had a simple time enough; what would they do in these days, when Shylock masks as Romeo, and Othello, turned soldier of fortune, seeks distinction at his mistress's mouth? I fear me even Portia would have found her match.

But Mamie would go to the meet—yes, she would. Where love, inclination, and social ambition coincide, what prudent counsels of a country girl like Gracie could resist them? She wrote that evening, thanking Mrs. Gower for her invitation, and only on the next day told Gracie what she had done. Gracie knew Mrs. Gower only slightly; though, had she known her a thousand years, she would not have known her well. The kennels were at the "Bogardus Farm," and after the meet there was to be a hunt dinner and a hunt ball. Mrs. Gower had many mansions, many places in which to lay her pretty head—and the heads of her guests—and now, it seems, she had a cottage near by, in which Mamie was to go. And the other guests, as Flossie wrote, were to be only Lord Birmingham, Kitty Farnum—and Mr. Wemyss.

For this meeting was indeed "select;" only of the very gayest, smartest few, those of whose prominence there could be no question in the race after pleasure, only those whose purses and whose persons kept the pace that fashion, for the time, demanded. And both the horses and the dogs were also of the choicest breed and blood, and were worth, each and all, his hundreds or his thousands; and the human beings, too, if of their blood we dare not say so much, were of breeding *à la mode*, and worth, I dare say, any sums you like. John Haviland was not here, nor Lionel Derwent, nor even poor Arthur yet—but only those who made, or seemed to make, the very lightest little game of life.

When newspapers describe all this, they speak a little of the ladies' dresses—but chiefly of the horses. For this fashionable life of ours, the life of so many of those with whom our lines have, thus far, been cast, seems founded, in its last analysis, upon the horse alone. That noble animal, in all his varied uses, under the saddle, in a four-in-hand, at Mrs. Gower's carriage traces—take him all in all, he stands for everything; he is almost the protagonist of Flossie Gower's little play. Sculptors, historians, students of social science, would, in ages yet to come, I am sure, term this the age of the Horse; they would, I say, if Mrs. Gower and her set shall even leave a wrack behind. But the wracks they leave behind are, alas! too often not their own. And to others, perhaps, to Jem Starbuck and the workers in the Allegheny country, as well as to the future historian, this age may rather seem the age of Coal.

So Mamie Livingstone went to the show, and the

show was very fine indeed. First there was a pack of fox-hounds—real fox-hounds—and then there was a pack of beagles, sixteen or more, with little curly tails; and the gentlemen and ladies rode some miles behind them, on a scented track, and jumped several fences. And Charlie looked very smart in his pink coat, and took the leaps most daringly; and thereupon Mamie did admire him very much, and therefore begin to think seriously of him for a husband.

And the dinner was exquisitely cooked, and quite bright and gay; and the men had all red coats and the women all white throats; and when the ladies left the table the fun was even faster. For when the stories were all told, and they could not talk of the ladies, both because many of the husbands were there and because the subject was a bore at best—and the best of it is surely tête-à-tête—and when even horses had been talked about enough, they went into the ball-room, did these merry dogs, and danced with these fine ladies; only some of them chose to walk in the lawns and over the turf steeple-chase course, where there was shrubbery, and hurdles, and much helping over of carefully preserved stone walls.

Have you had a good time, reader? Here we have been a hundred miles on the outside of a coach, and quite three weeks in the open air, and, I am sure, have had dinners and balls galore. Take your last deep breath of all these joys, for all even of our lines, may not fall in such pleasant places. What—we shall not say we are tired of it—we who have been with the fortunate few? Why, who can make more, who could make more, of life than they? Is it not a pleasant play?

Well, a secret, then: Van Kull and Wemyss, too, are bored, and even Tony Duval finds it slow. For Flossie Gower I speak not; she has a great, still fed, self-pride, and when that, too, grows stale—she is too clever to let it bore her—she will leave it first; and Birmingham is saved by his British atmosphere and healthy, dormant brain.

All this is why Charlie Townley—no, Charlie fears rather that he may not always be rich enough to keep it up, and is making up to poor Mamie, in consequence. But that is why, or all these things are why —for those who make of earnest life a play needs must make it stronger as the play goes on—Van Kull walked still with Mrs Hay, that night; and even Birmingham made overtures to Kitty Farnum; and Charlie did propose to Mamie Livingstone; and Caryl Wemyss propo—told Mrs. Gower that he loved her.

## CHAPTER XXV.

### KITTY FARNUM TAKES THE PRIZE.

JOHN HAVILAND was in town that summer. Many things kept him there; he had his own business, and he had his schools, and he had his workmen's clubs. And just now he had, more than all, the new young men's club he was founding on the Bowery. He would usually dine at his own club; and there the men he most commonly met were Derwent and Lucie Gower. There seemed to be a certain bond of sympathy between these men. Gower also was kept in town by his business; for Gower had his duties in life, and performed them punctiliously, too. Derwent—well, Derwent was kept there by much the same reasons that kept John at home; the reader may know them later. Furthermore, these men, not being pleasure-seekers, were all three unhappy—for the moment, only, let us hope.

Haviland lived most of the time on his little sloop, which he kept moored at Bay Ridge, and he took little cruises in her when the wind served. Derwent was apt to be with him on these; he was an enthusiast in everything, and just now was much interested in John's work in New York. Then there was politics; the primaries were already beginning, and John was at work over these; a most fascinating subject for Derwent, who was fond of saying that the most noticeable industries in all "property-democracies" had been plied by those who made a trade of patriotism; but John was not a trader. It was Derwent who called ours an age of coal; but "machine civilization" was his favorite term for the nineteenth century, and just now his notion was that property was the pasturage that gave life to the monster that he fought.

Certainly, it had been an evil year for those who thought and hoped. That showed itself even in the primaries, where now the local leaders found it hard to keep their rank and file content. Still less could John get on, with his abstract talk of pure government and simple laws. Sovereign voters were showing a strange tendency to go in directly for abstract benefits, or what they conceived to be such. Even city workers were discontented; and there was said to be much misery in the mining districts. The coal magnates—Tamms, Duval, and Remington—finding that that ichor of our civilization was growing too plentiful, had laid their heads together and were "diminishing the output;" that is, they forbade that more than a certain number of tons should be mined per week. Thus did they not only cut off that draught of life from the general social fabric, but about one-third of the cupbearers thereof were thrown out of work. Upon this, many of the rest had struck. Their places in the mines had promptly been filled by other human energy in the shape of so many head of human beings, male and female, shipped from Poland; while the strikers and even some of the Poles, who had escaped and could read and write, were making trouble. But these themes are too heavy for our slight pen; except such outcome of it as even all the world might see—and Mrs. Flossie Gower may feel.

And, if politics had thus all gone askew, John was just a shade discouraged with his social work as well. Many a talk did he and Derwent have about it, lying becalmed off the sullen Jersey coast, smoking their midnight cigars beneath the sky. "They will come to the club fast enough," he would say, "and read a newspaper or two, and smoke a pipe—when they have not money enough to pay for drinks at the bar-room. They will listen to what we tell them, politely enough. But what I find is the hardest thing to cope with is a sort of scoffing humor: as if we were all muffs, and they knew it, and only put up with it so long as it suited their convenience.

"A curious thing this jeering habit in your democracy," muttered Derwent. "They have caught the trick of Voltaire's cynicism and turned it upwards. They are incredulous of excellence and of benevolence in high places—even of yours, old fellow, I am afraid," he added. "I never could see how there could be class-hatred in America; but class-hatred there certainly is."

"I talk to these boys of books and pictures, and the joys of art, and the delights of nature; and I fear, if they do not cry 'Oh, chestnuts' at me, or some other current slang, it is out of mere good-nature and because they like me. Their delight in nature is limited to the nearest base-ball field, the newspapers they take up are generally those printed on pink paper, and as for books—I doubt if many of them ever opened one, except he knew it was obscene."

"All literature has had but two sources—religious hymns and merry stories," said Derwent, gravely. "These boys must naturally begin with that one which is left them."

"Ah, they are such finished positivists! As for fearing the Roman Church, it is but an old wives' tale to them."

"How much did our friends at *La Lisière* care for this higher side of life?" said Derwent. "It is true they substitute wine for whiskey, and straight-limbed horses for bow-legged bull-pups, and steeple-chases for sparring, and French novels for the pink newspaper. I fancy our two sets of friends would understand one another, Tony Duval and Birmingham and your boys, much better than you do after all. As for Mr. Van Kull, he would be a hero with either lot, and Caryl Wemyss a muff."

"There are plenty of rich people who are not like Mrs. Gower's set."

"True, but they do not advertise themselves, they do not make a show, they do not 'lead society'—suggestive phrase. And probably you are the first rich man of that class whom your Bowery friends have ever seen. No wonder that they set you down for a muff!"

"Of course a poor boy covets his neighbor's goods, if he sees that his goods are the only thing the neighbor values," sighed John.

Thus did these two hold converse, and often Lucie Gower with them. Indeed Lucie Gower had got quite interested in John's plans, and if he did not feel that his personal assistance would be of much value, he helped John out with money, which was almost as much to the point. The simple fellow was not happy, and he did not quite know why; surely his wife, the admired leader of all their world, was all that he desired? At times he would seem on the point of confiding with John, and would turn his eyes to him with the troubled look of some not healthy animal; a look, alas! which John saw no way to answer.

But if John made little progress with his missionary work, James Starbuck made greatly more with his. The discontent on the line of the Allegheny Central Railroad and in the coal mines was certainly spreading; and Starbuck, in his capacity of travelling inspector, had much opportunity to see this and to work upon it. Now and then he would enter Haviland's club-room; he had had himself inscribed as a member thereof; and each time it was noticeable that he would take many of the young men away to some secret meeting of his own. John at first had welcomed him as an ally; he was much better educated than most of the young men, and his influence was certainly for sobriety, at least. But of late he had begun to doubt.

Meantime Tamms, the man who ruled the Allegheny Central, was continually at the office; for he was not without anxiety about all this. His clever manœuvres of the previous summer had had one result of doubtful benefit; it had left him saddled with all the Starbuck Oil Works stock, and nearly all the Allegheny Central. A time of extreme prosperity had been expected by him that year; he had just made one great monopoly of all the neighboring coal interests; but the one thing even clever Tamms could not see and provide against was a general revolt among the men and women whose lives, as he thought, he had bought and paid for. Mrs. Tamms and the daughters had come back from Europe, loaded with rich laces and new gowns, and paying a pretty figure therefor at the custom-house; but without any offers of marriage as yet, or at least without sufficiently brilliant ones.

Charlie, too, was at the office frequently, and when he was there, looked into things pretty closely; though Arthur was still revelling in the new delights of Newport. Old Mr. Townley would come in regularly once a month, and cut the coupons off the bonds of his trusts. Thence he would drive up to his club —he was the oldest member now—and wag his white head sagely among his friends, financiers *emeriti* like himself, and tell them what a treasure he had in his clever young man Tamms.

Gracie came back to her aunt's house early in October; but she came back alone. Mamie had been quite taken up by Mrs. Gower; why it should be esteemed an honor by young girls to be taken up by

Mrs. Gower, I leave unsaid; but such it was. She translated them to that higher sphere which she had so completely made her own. Before such promotion a maiden was simply a pretty girl, nothing more; after it she became "the thing," for married men to flirt with, for young men to pay attention to, and perhaps, finally, for one of them to marry. So Mamie Livingstone was staying with her at *La Lisière*.

It is needless to say that Charlie Townley was there too. If Flossie was somewhat sceptical of other worlds, she was quick to recognize an eternal fitness of things in this. And what more fit than that fashion should wed wealth, and a young man who had so well proved his taste in spending money should be given a pretty helpmeet and with her the wherewithal to shine? Mrs. Gower had a good-natured custom of pensioning off, in this pleasant manner, her old adorers; for all her loves, so far, had been platonic affairs of fashion and make-believe, like the Bronx hounds' fox-hunting. For Flossie had never been in love in her life; I question if she could be; though hoping always much to be the cause that love should be in others.

Charlie, then, found a strong ally in his old friend, and we may be sure he pushed his advantage to the utmost. Caryl Wemyss was happy too to have him there; for Charlie's pursuit was obvious, and the pack of tongues will often follow only one such scent at a time. And though ready enough to startle the world when the proper time came, Wemyss did not wish to diminish the effect of his *coup* by anticipation. Moreover he had not quite made up his mind.

As for old Mr. and Mrs. Livingstone, they only knew that Mamie was off enjoying herself; which our parents now have learned to be also part of pre-established harmony. Gracie was their comfort now; they were fonder of her than of their own daughter, I think. But Gracie was more troubled. She had taken pretty little Mamie to her heart. Down-stairs, with the old people, she was a sweet presence, like still sunlight after rain; she read to them, and talked, and smiled, and helped. But up-stairs, I wonder, in the temple of her maiden's chamber? What shall we do for Gracie, I beseech you, reader? We can find all their happinesses, in this world, for Charlie, for Flossie Gower and Mr. Tamms, and even, through his vanity, for Wemyss—but how for her? And Gracie was—she was very lovely and contented, and she had the sunniest of smiles; she was one for some of us to love perhaps—but she was not exactly happy, you see. But what can we do? We cannot go with her to her own room, when she is alone; we may not dare to console her; we may not venture in, but stand awe-struck, hand upon the door. I wonder what happens there, when the light figure is bent down, and the face forgets to smile, and the dark eyes look out, unrestrained by other's presence, on the four mute walls?

Why did Haviland—yes, and Derwent too—go to the house so often? When Mamie came home, Charlie Townley came often, too; and Gracie, beginning her winter work, would have left them all to her, but that they rather sought herself. And, as if by some strange chemistry, she began to feel that these two had some understanding with her, of things both human and divine.

See, there she is, standing in the shadow; John is talking to her. At a distance sits Derwent, pulling his tawny long moustache, his blue eyes fixed simply on her like a young child's. Here is Mamie Livingstone, prettier, some would say, than Gracie, with her nameless touch of style, and girlish distinction; she ripples and flashes like a summer brook, as Charlie bends over her, so that the rosebud in his coat is just beneath her eyes, and he says something to her about it.

But Mamie was not the only girl who gave trouble to her friends that autumn. In another street—the Fifty-Somethingeth—sits the Beauty, Kitty Farnum, lounging back lazily in her chair, her perfect arms clasped behind her head, a sort of democratic Cleopatra, looking, with her silent idle scorn, at her mother, who is chiding her. Her mother is carefully dressed, well-educated, worldly enough in all conscience sake; and yet there is something about her, about her or about her voice, that makes the haughty beauty sicken with a consciousness of difference between them. Kitty has the pride of a coronet, if not the taste for one.

"I heard you positively discouraged him at Lenox." The mother is speaking of Lord Birmingham; and the daughter is thinking that, when a girl, her mother must have been admired of "gentlemen friends" and have worn gold ornaments about her neck. For Kitty has that intense appreciation of small differences of social habit that a clever child inherits when parents are acutely conscious of their lack of social position. If the factory and railroads and exchanges be the all-in-all of life, these things are trifles; but our economists who ignore them forget how much of life is left besides mere work, how great a part in life is played by self-esteem. Your baron of the middle ages scorned them, for he had his horse and battle-axe and coat-of-mail; and, perhaps, had you given these to his hind, the churl might have made as good a baron, and the baron would have been like any other soldier, in his eating and his thinking and his lying down. But to-day you put these two together, and they speak two words, and each knows—and much more their wives and daughters—that they "move in different spheres." But why then, in this democracy, does the one sphere, in successive stages as you ascend, hate, envy, imitate, and seek to enter the other? Alas! if they were better men, even as our mediæval baron was the better man than his churl, the folly of the imitation would be gone. But *amour-propre* still rules humanity, although democracy apportion out its goods, and when *amour-propre* shall turn from show of affluence to proof of excellence, we shall see great things. And love it may be yet that makes the world go round; but, alas! in so many marriages, both sides love themselves.

"It was reported even in the *Herald*, that it was to be a match," said Mrs. Farnum, plaintively. "And now, he has gone off on his yacht, and they will say that he has jilted you."

"Mother, I will marry whom I like—and when I like," said Kitty.

"But tell me, my darling—you do not like anyone else?" said Mrs. Farnum, coaxingly.

"My dear mother——"

"I do wish you would say 'mamma,' and not insist on calling me mother." And she thought hastily over the men she knew her child had seen that summer. "I hope it is not Van Kull—or that young Holyoke," she added, in increasing terror.

Kitty turned her back and intimated so plainly a dismissal that the obedient mother felt constrained to go.

"It *is* young Holyoke," she thought, with a sigh that was meant to soften her obdurate daughter's heart.

She poured her troubles in her tired husband's ear that night: "Kate shall marry whom she likes," said that unimaginative person. "I guess her half million will be worth any beggarly marquis of them all. You weren't a countess, when I married you." And Mrs. Farnum had to cry in silence.

Poor humanity! How much trouble do you give yourselves. As for Kitty Farnum, she had been asked in marriage by the Earl already; and had refused him twice.

## CHAPTER XXVI.

### FLOSSIE ENJOYS HERSELF.

FLOSSIE GOWER lay idly upon her couch; it was her reception-day. She was waiting for the monotonous round of callers; and, while she waited, she gave herself to reminiscences. It was not usual for her to ply her memory so hard; but to-day, thinking of her whole life, and planning her campaign to Russia, all the events of her career passed in review before her. Her dainty morning dress curled away from the throat, and rippled gracefully, in a cascade of laces, over to the ground; simple and pure as any Endymion might clothe his dream in. The neck was white as ever; but the face had a wearied look the world had never seen, a pout of unheroic discontent, like any other woman's who was old and out of humor. And yet our heroine was telling to herself her triumphs, like beads.

She had early learned that she was rich, and thus had quickly found that riches were, alone, unsatisfying. No pedant moralist was more sure of this than she. But there they parted; while the moralist might prate of other worlds, or the love of humanity, Flossie was a positivist. No unknown world should drag her,

Saturn-like, from her chosen orbit, and bid her leave her balls, her troops of male admirers, for nunneries or the domestic fireside. Unknowables might be disregarded: she knew no other world than this; and as for the love of humanity, she sought it for herself.

Of course we men do not understand the keen delight that Flossie took in swaying from his balance every man she met. We are not pleased when a pretty woman shows her sensibility to us. It may even rather shock us; we do not expect that sort of thing; moreover, if obvious to us, it is perhaps seen by others and that cheapens the conquest.

But it is a woman's *carrière* to work her will and worth through men. And what else is her whole training, her education, the lessons we read to her of history? You may talk, and raise statues, in your female colleges, of Princess Idas and Corinnes; but it is Helen, Cleopatra, Heloise, who have left their woman's mark upon the world; and they are women enough, yet, these Vassar girls, to know it.

Still, it was some years before Flossie took her natural course and found in men's admiration her own highest reward. She had seen so much of men, her brother and his friends, in her early youth, that perhaps she had a little contempt for an animal so easily tamed, so soon domesticated. Whether she had yet found the king of the forest in her Boston Paris, we must leave to the reader. He was the only lion she had.

Perhaps the earlier battles and campaigns, the Italys and Marengos, were the best, after all. Yet they were so easy! Poor Lucie had been such easy prey, even to a Nantucket neophyte! And to conquer the world of New York scarce justified a Corsican lieutenant's triumph. To trample on the patrician matron, and dazzle the jewels from Cornelia herself, was hardly harder. Then she even, in her wealthy way, had tried to serve the Lord; but found that fruitless, too. A fashionable ritual was all she had retained.

Then she had led, and they had followed. Thorough ditch, thorough briar, from fad to folly. Was she not the high priestess of that circle *debonair*, known as well in Boston or in Philadelphia as in New York, as the "married women's set?" They pretended to be in love with one another's husbands, and they dazzled young girls; and led their Pauls away from such Virginias as were "coming out."

But all this was not the tithe of her triumph. Some had tumbled in the ditches, or been torn and spotted in the briars. Surely the glory of these was hers also? She set the pace; and some had failed, and some had fled, and some had forged, and some had fallen through. But she had always stayed at the head, indifferent, frivolous, successful. Then was she not a patroness of art and literature? She dabbled in politics, too, and went to Washington, and corrupted simple Congressmen, and made herself a model to their wives.

Mrs. Gower was at home, this afternoon; and she rose and swept her robes to the adjoining dressing-room for another gown; in this one she was visible only to her maids, her maker, and her husband. It was five or ten minutes when she came back; her pout was gone, and in its place a smile—her *pas de fascination* as it were. She graciously beamed upon the two young girls who had come to make their dinner-call upon her, and was graciously pleased even to apologize for keeping them waiting. And their hearts were won by her at once—they were the very poor descendants of one of the very oldest pre-revolutionary families—and they talked enthusiastically about her, going home, and wondered if it could really be true what the world said about her and that Mr. Wemyss from Boston. They were stylishly dressed and poor, and waiting to be married too.

Then came in Mrs. James De Witt, *née* Duval, just made a matron and fresh from a wedding-journey which had proved somewhat slow to her; Strephon and Chloe did not go on wedding journeys, I suppose; it was Helen and Paris began the fashion. Then Mrs. Malgam came in; and Flossie had her usual velvet battle with her dear enemy and rival friend. Mrs. Gower envied her her stupid youth, and silly round cheeks. Shall I go and leave the field with her? she thought. But the field would be hers, anyhow, in a few years.

Then there came in two prying matrons, of those whom Flossie had defeated in the world's esteem, so many years ago. They had lived to see their fiats disregarded, and their reception-rooms depleted, and their daughters put out and their sons dazzled, all by this little Flossie Starbuck; and they loved her accordingly. Would their hour of triumph never come again? Flossie wondered why they came to-day;

they had not been to see her, save in the most symbolical of paste-board calls, since three months after her marriage. But they had never, since that first triumphant season, dared to question her divine right, by wit and beauty and style, to rule. Could it be that they really meant to bury the hatchet and surrender unconditionally? Or did they scent, like envious ravens, her coming overthrow? She was indifferently polite to them; but made little effort to conceal that she was bored.

Dear me, will a man never come? Mrs. Gower rose, when they had gone, and pressed her feverish brow against the mirror. How marked the wrinkles were beneath the eyes! Men's voices were heard at last, and Flossie turned her back to the window. It was only a silly fellow, an artist, whom Mrs. Gower had made, and who now presumed upon it; and with him a dancing boy. The boy was nice enough at germans; and was at least a gentleman, but the other was only a swell, which even Flossie Gower realized to be a different thing. Genius soars above birth, so Van Smeer disowned his mother; but he preferred to be known as a gentleman rather than as an artist, and only painted the portraits of his fair friends carelessly, à la Congreve, and by way of flirtation, as it were.

It was fun for Flossie to snub this man, and see his color change. Mrs. Wilton Hay had come in, the woman to whom Flossie had suspected Van Smeer of transferring his incense. "I have been thinking for some time of setting up an establishment in England," said he to Mrs. Hay, who was going back. "My friend Lord Footlight is by way of having a sort of historical pageant in his theatre at his place in Surrey, and is very keen to have me come." To which Mrs. Hay made no reply, but Mrs. Gower did. "Do, Mr. Van Smeer," she said; "I should think her native air would do your poor mother so much good."

Van Smeer turned livid and ugly, but had to turn and smile to Kitty Farnum, who entered then, for Kitty was said to be that season's card. "Who was his mother?" whispered Mrs. Hay. "An English ballet-girl," said Flossie in reply, and Van Smeer knew she did, and had to leave her unavenged. But I know not what he said to Mrs. Hay, when those two left together.

Mahlon Blewitt came in. He represented yet another period in Mrs. Gower's life, and she had been his Beatrice. But this Dante had been born in Western Ohio, and she had taught him a profound disbelief in all divine comedies, the Inferno even with the rest. He had come from his father's vast wheat-fields and the infinite prairies, to New York, full of dreams of Shelley and of Chatterton; and Mrs. Gower had taken him up. Then he had gone back from her to his dreams. But he had really fancied him in love with her, and somehow her presence had remained with him and made his dreams absurd. Now he was a man of fashion, and turned his white ties more carefully than the sonnets he still peddled in large quantities to all the magazines; and he cynically talked about his country's decadence like any Caryl Wemyss, whom he chiefly envied, and of whose verses he wrote bitter reviews upon the sly. Had he really loved his clever patroness, the Inferno at least might have been left him to do; but he knew now that he had not loved her—only his dreams had seemed a poorer thing since Flossie Gower had shared them. The Polish minister came in; he knew his Flossie well and liked her much; he had seen women something like her in continental courts, but known none so bright, so good-natured, or half so free from danger. With him was young Harvey Washburn, a civil-service-reformer who had been sent to Congress to reform the world, and whom Von Hillersdorf was forming for it. Flossie would have liked to go to Washington, and have political power, and vulgarize that too; but there the mighty middle class control, who did not understand her; by the time they do, perhaps, the myriads who make no play of life will have their say, and break her, with other butterflies. Poor Flossie! she does amount to much, after all, in all America; and is angrily conscious of it.

And now comes in our hero, Arthur Holyoke; no one, even Von Hillersdorf, is more perfect a man of the world than he. Well he places his bow and smile, his outspoken compliment here, his whispered word of adoration there; his coat is as well cut as Jimmy De Witt's, who has also come, some time later than his bride. But no one of these is earnest, thinks Flossie, and is bored again, and glad when they all go, and Mr. Killian Van Kull appears. Here at last is her peer, one who can understand her. Van Kull is a frank libertine; and she likes him for it; he does not play with foils; he is a *viveur*, like the puissant Guy Livingstone who was the hero that her youth adored. Mamie Livingstone, by the way, has come in too, and gone out with Charlie Townley. Charlie has come to present to Flossie his partner's lady, Mrs. Tamms, and her marriageable daughters; and Mrs. Gower will have a new pleasure to-morrow, when she meets and cuts them, driving in the Park.

Killian stays some time; there is a dark devil in his eye to-day, and Mrs. Gower thinks his pale face never looked so handsome. When Mr. Wemyss is announced, he rises with a slight smile, and he too goes away.

Mrs. Gower is rude to Wemyss; she throws herself upon a sofa, and has the migraine; he assumes his devotional manner and makes bold to take her hand. She draws it away impatiently.

"Have you a headache?" says he. "I hoped you would let me go to drive with you."

The carriage is ordered; the pony carriage that Mrs. Gower drives herself. He gets into it, and she after him and takes the reins. It is her whim to have no footman behind them; and Caryl does not dare remonstrate, though he thinks of it. He supposes she is going to the Park; but she turns down Thirty-fourth Street and drives toward the East River. They come to the ferry; and she sends Wemyss out to get the ticket. "Wherever are you going?" says he, returning.

"Why? Do you think I am going to elope with

you?" She says it with a slight contemptuous smile; and he is silent.

They come to the Long Island shore; and she rattles up the hill and drives familiarly through some narrow, squalid streets, where the air is not pleasant to breathe and the dank entries of the close brick houses swarm with half-naked children.

Ahead of them now is the group of high chimneys and great tanks of rusty iron; the scorching sky is a veil of brick-red smoke, chemical, unnatural in color. The stench of oil is almost overpowering; but Flossie drives rapidly into the gate as if it were her own park avenue at *La Lisière*.

"Why have you come in here?" says Caryl Wemyss at last, looking, for the once, surprised. Mrs. Gower has dropped the reins, and seems suddenly listless.

"It was my favorite playground when I was a girl," she answers, finally. "It was a whim of mine to see the place again. Perhaps you did not know that here we made our money?"

Wemyss struggles with some speech about his indifference to the birthplace of the rose he wears; but Flossie is not hearing him; her eyes wander over the arid, unsightly factory-yard, the blue pyramids of barrels, and up to the tramways high in the air, and the masts of the iron ships.

"Come," she says; "give the reins to that man there."

Wemyss does as he is bid, and leaves the man with a silver dollar, wondering; and, wondering no less himself, he follows Flossie through the iron maze she seems to know so well.

They go up the foul ladder to the summit of the great storage tank, Wemyss caring for his fine overcoat, and almost sickened with the heavy smell of the crude petroleum, while Flossie's delicate nostrils dilate as she breathes it in once more. She guides him to the "tail-house," where the first run of naphtha has just begun, mobile, metallic, with its evil shine. Flossie looks at it closely, and notes, with an adept's eye, the hour of the run. A few hours more and it will be standard, water-white, as she has made herself; but she with gold, not tested yet with fire. Then she takes him to the spraying-house, where the tested oil lies lazily, girdled by the sun with brilliant rings, fair to look upon as any sylvan spring. This finest oil shall burn in quiet household lamps; it is the naphtha, surface oil, that flies to gas and fire.

Mrs. Gower was obstinately silent, going home, while Mr. Wemyss still wondered. They dined together and went to the play; and it was after midnight when he got to his rooms.

He had his valet pull his boots off and bring his smoking-jacket; and then, dismissing him, began to cut the pages of the last French novel.

"She is capable of anything," he said to himself, before he had read the first page of his book.

"She is a devil," he added, under his breath, somewhat flattered, somewhat frightened at the thought.

## CHAPTER XXVII.

### JEM STARBUCK AMUSES HIMSELF.

AMES STARBUCK'S breach with his sister had been a permanent one. He probably had as little affection in his nature as any man you could well find; but what he had was centred in pretty Jenny, and he was both grieved and annoyed by this. He said to himself that his love was given to his brethren, and his work the cause of labor; and certainly he had no love for his master, the great double monopoly of a corporation that employed him, and his maker he deemed a cleverly contrived bogy of the rich. Perhaps it was more his hate of these than even love of his fellow-laborers that really ruled his actions; he recognized no difference among men but riches, and put on these the burden of all their miseries.

One hot morning in the autumn he returned from his periodic journey over the Allegheny Central Railroad. There had been trouble that week on the line of the road; trouble with a strike among the coal miners, and Starbuck had had much ado to keep their own men in order. It was a Saturday, and his work was over for the week. James was never idle from preference; but he saw no work to which he could turn his hand that day. He visited the bar-room in the lower Bowery which formed his club, and found that even this was silent and deserted. One fellow only he met—a silly, drinking workman named Simpson—and he asked him to go to the races. "Everybody has gone," said Simpson, "and I've got the tip on Ballet-girl." And James remembered that all the penny papers had been crammed for days with talk and bets and naming favorites for the great sweepstakes. He cared little for such things himself, and had a sort of contemptuous wonder at the interest they aroused among his acquaintance; but after some beer, to which Simpson insisted on treating him, they took their tickets by the railway, and paid their dollars at the gate; dollars which, as Starbuck reflected, were more rare to Simpson than to him.

The day had grown intensely hot; not a breath was stirring on the track, and the air, impregnated with dust, seemed lifeless, overbreathed. But the grand stand was packed with humanity; poor people from his own neighborhood, dingy men, fat mothers of families, gasping for breath, young men with their girls, in soiled white dresses and gay ribbons, many wearing the colors of their favorite jockey. He could see that they were all intensely eager about the race; often they had even little betting-books, or cards upon which they marked the winners. James had never been at a race before, and was amazed at all the crowd, at the money they spent for this, at the amount of betting, at the interest they showed in all the horses. Above them, in the private boxes, was a similar crowd, but more finely dressed; Starbuck recognized some of the people he had seen driving in the Park; for he was fond of frequenting such places and having the rich men's wives pointed out to him. There even was his employer, Mr. Tamms, and his wife and daughters in crisp bright dresses, with snowy throats that made one cool to look at; and there in the shade was Mrs. Gower, whom he also knew by sight. They, too, seemed to be betting; but with less excitement than the common people (as he called them, to himself) below.

"Come to the paddock," said his friend; and they walked out there and saw the horses unclothed and the trial paces of the jockeys. "Isn't she a daisy?" said Simpson, pointing to a slender mare as Ballet-girl; and Starbuck looked at her. Just then her jockey dropped his whip, which Simpson obsequiously picked up and handed to him. If this numberless crowd were the working classes, they were little better than "their betters," said Starbuck to himself, grimly.

The bell rang for the first race; and Simpson hurried him back to the lawn. A false start, a cloud of dust, and they were off, amid the wild cries of the multitude. He watched the little knot of gay colors bobbing around the track. How little they meant to him, and how much to all the throng around him! Starbuck turned and watched the mass of people with all the cynicism of a Caryl Wemyss. Close by him was a rather pretty, pale-faced girl; she was evidently very poor; a black jersey was all she wore and a lilac-twigged cotton skirt; but she rose to her feet, and shouted and clapped her gloveless hands.

Between the races nothing would do but they must have some more beer; and they went behind the grand stand where the pool-booths were, and men, and women too, were drinking it. At the booths was a great press of disreputable men, crying hoarsely and waving rolls of dingy bank-bills at the gamblers. James saw that his friend had had too much to drink already; and he insisted on putting another "fiver" on his favorite. Above them in the stalls James could see the ladies drinking iced champagne and fanning themselves after the excitement of the race. He walked out upon the lawn again, where the well-dressed gentlemen were also making up their books; and went along to the sacred place reserved for private carriages. Here they had hampers; and young men in fawn-colored coats were leaning over the shoulders of pretty young women, having flirtations with them, which he, perhaps, interpreted too simply. "Really," said one pretty face's owner, "this is more like Longchamps than I had supposed possible!"

"We are improving, Mrs. Malgam," said the man. "New York will no longer be provincial, one of these days. And it is getting like Longchamps in more respects than one," he added. "Have you seen that pretty woman just ahead of us with the cream-colored ponies?"

"Dear me, how interesting!" cried the lady, levelling her opera-glasses in the direction indicated; and James Starbuck followed her look with his eyes, as he stood beside the carriage. "It seems just like being abroad to see such people! She *is* handsome—and she's awfully well dressed," added the lady, candidly. "I never can get my woman to cut a dress for me like that. Who is she, Mr. Van Kull?"

"You had better ask Mr. Townley," said the other.

"Ask Lucie Gower, you mean," said a gentleman who had not yet spoken.

"You know very well that that is not true of poor Lucie," answered the first; "and my cousin would not thank you."

"Well, they call her Mrs. Beaumont, that's all I know," said the other, sulkily; but James did not hear the end of the altercation, for he pressed forward among the drags and carriages to the person indicated. As he did so, one of her cream-colored ponies reared and turned, and was about to crowd him against a dog-cart that was standing next in the row. Starbuck grasped the bridle and gave its mouth a savage wrench. "So it's you, is it?" said he, facing his sister. "Mrs. Beaumont!"

Jenny gave a half-suppressed scream, as the pony still reared and plunged; and a gentleman who was beside her grasped the reins. "Who is it?" said he.

"I do not know," said Jenny, looking full at James. "Some drunken fellow, I suppose."

Starbuck started, as if he had been struck. Then he turned away, dropping the pony's bridle. He walked back to the lawn, where he found Simpson, much the worse for liquor. The great race had been run, while Starbuck was not looking; and the favorite had lost. Simpson was quarrelsome and angry; and ended by begging James for the loan of a dollar, which he gave, and hurried back to the city. As he passed up Broadway, he looked curiously at the bulletin-boards before the newspaper-offices. A dense crowd was standing about each one; but Starbuck gathered the purport of the news from such messages as were passed out from the centre of the crowd. The strike had ended in a riot. He stopped at his rooms but for a moment, to get a small hand-bag; then he took a cab to the Jersey City ferry; here he boarded the Pennsylvania train.

Starbuck had a pass, and he rode in the parlor car; but his sleep was troubled, and his dreams seemed full of strange noise and glare. He woke up once and found a reason for the latter; the train was running by a long row of flaming coke-furnaces, which lit the whole valley with a sullen red. The dawn broke as they rolled through a long tunnel, choking with coal-gas, and came to Pittsburg. The forest of chimneys stood smokeless, now that a subtiler agent than the coal was found, and the ringing of bells was in the Sunday morning air, which now lay clear above the city; and the steep river hills were visible, and the red brick town, heaping up its apex in the bold mediæval castle that is its modern city hall.

James had little cause to dally here; but noticed, in the hour or two he had to wait, an unusual, unquiet expression on the faces of the people, who were swarming from the tenement doors into the street, like ants from some huge ant-hill. By mid-day he found a freight train that would take him to his destination. His journey lay up a river valley, its sloping mountains clothed in reds and yellows of autumn woodland. For many miles everything was silent with a Sunday stillness; then the crests of the hills were lost, and the blue sky shaded into yellowish brown, at the touch of a few tall iron towers. These were pouring forth black cinders, as they had for seven years past; for the iron smelter may never say, "it is good," and rest, upon the seventh day. James watched the carload of ore climbing up along the outside of the furnace, until the great tower's top was opened, as the tons of ore fell in; then the prisoned flame burst forth and the lower surface of the sulphurous brown cloud that filled the valley was dyed a vivid crimson with the pouring flame.

This river basin had been lovely once; but now its soil was coal-dust, and the soft swelling of the hillsides, all up and down the stream, was spotted with huge red tanks, of rusting brick-red iron, large as ancient forts, the storage fountains of the pipe-lines. And the whole country bristled with the abandoned scaffoldings of old oil-wells, like a scanty fur.

James talked with the brakeman and found that his accustomed engineer was disabled. Bill, he said, was a non-union man, and had been given many a hint; but he stuck it out and wouldn't join, and so the Union had deputed Ned O'Neal, the engineer of the local freight that ran just ahead, to choose the steepest down grade and "drop upon" Bill's time. O'Neal had "dropped" accordingly, lagging behind under pretext that his engine would not fire, and finally getting his long train of fifty coal-cars just at the bottom of a curving trestle. Bill had gone into him and scattered the last dozen coal-cars, doing some injury to his locomotive; but his head was badly cut open, and his brakeman had broken his neck. Starbuck was too well used to the tyranny of laboring men to pay much attention to this murder; and he asked about the riots. Yes, said the brakeman, he believed they had had quite a time at Steam City for several days past. A few men had been hurt, some of them Hungarians at the mines or such-like. But they had smashed up a terrible deal of rolling-stock.

It was night when Starbuck reached Steam City. The streets were jammed with people, but the town was very still. Only, just in front of the station, was a piece of vacant land that might have contained two or three acres; this was closely strewn with the wreck of cars, machinery, and engines; nothing but the trucks, wheels, and other iron work remaining, all twisted in a wild confusion of iron arms and limbs.

He found that most of the people were going in but one direction, so he followed them. It was a strange country; the soil was coal-dust, the very streams were still with oil, and through every crevice in the earth poured the gas, flaring with wild fire that flamed there night and day. The night was very dark; and at every street-corner waved these torches, never quenched, belching fire from the iron tubes stuck anywhere, carelessly, into the ground. A strange country, fitter place for northern runes than modern men; where Loki still lurks in the mountains and the smitten rock gives forth petroleum; and, where the spear or pickaxe strikes the earth, gush still the mythic rills of fire.

The crowd went on, to a wild and open hillside above the town. Here perhaps a dozen lengths of pipe were flaring with the natural gas, glowing ruddily and fitfully upon the upturned faces of some dozen thousand men; and at the highest point, below a flaming well of the gas that had been but lately and rudely piped (for the volume of the fire still shot up straight some hundred feet or so, pillaring, like a groined roof, its canopy of smoke), was a sort of rostrum. From this a man was speaking; but his words were hard to hear above the roaring of the burning well. Starbuck knew the man: he was a certain Moses Jablonawski, a Polish Jew.

The man was pale and narrow-chested, with a reddish beard; his strongest notes varied from a low hiss to a sort of thin shriek; this last he employed in climaxes, and managed barely to carry his words across the great multitude. But Starbuck knew well what he was saying; he preached simple anarchy, nihilism, resistance to any government or force, destruction of all industrial system, annihilation of all wealth and works. Starbuck had never, even in his secret meetings, gone wholly with the man—(openly, of course, he was a "boss" and on the side of the employers)—for secretly James had rather a greed for the wealth of others than a desire to do without the material things of civilization. But to-night there was something in the cold, logical, merciless reasoning of the Pole that went with his mood. Why dally with the pitch at all? Undoubtedly, if they too got their part of this corruption, they would be just as bad. His sister Jenny spoke to him. *Destroy, destroy,* was the burden of the orator's speech; *then ask what new thing there shall be, when all is gone. And if it be but suicide, society's suicide, better that than humanity in misery. The slave must break his chains before he ploughs and sows.* But the most part of the speech was a clever rousing of the passions, among his audience, of hate and envy. He brought their own woe home to them; and painted brilliantly the pleasures of the idle remnant. And always came the refrain, *Kill, kill, destroy, resist all office and authority*—till mankind be as the beasts of the forest once more, lawless, unrestrained; then may they build anew and better, freed from superstition of another world, from tainted lessons of the past of this, from silly lessons of a priest's self-sacrifice, from fashions of a feudal aristocracy. He showed them that their government was but a tyranny more formidable, more insidious, than the Czar's; that their rich masters were worse than kings; that commercial *bourgeois* (he used the word) were more blood-sucking than military dukes; and common schools and priests, policemen, laws, and soldiers, their implements of selfish wrong. All these must go; and labor, the primal curse, go with them too.

He stopped; and the crowd murmured; and another man got up. This speaker was tall and muscular, and his clear voice rang deeply to the farthest corners of the crowd. "Some of you know me," he said, "some of you have heard me speak before; and some Englishmen among you have heard of me in England. My name is Lionel Derwent." There was a shout or two at this; but most of the crowd remained expectant.

"You know why I have come; I heard that there was trouble here and I came down to see what little thing I could do to help you. You must know me as the son of a working-man who has leisure, and who tries to see the truth for working-men. You know, too, that I have no interest against you; every penny of property my father left I gave to the working-men's schools in England; and I support myself by writing for the papers.

"Now I must tell you that the man who spoke to you just now is wrong; and he is not only wrong, but he means to be wrong; in other words, he lies. He would have you behave like a child who has just been given a gold watch, and smash it because he does not know how to use it. You have all got your gold watches. You have got your roads and your mills and your schools and your votes. When he tells you to destroy the government, he tells you to undo what your hands have created. Bad as things may be, they are bad because you voters are not wise enough; but he would destroy all wisdom, do away with schools and votes, and then the first big general would be a czar over you again.

"I say you are not wise enough. If things are wrong, whose fault is it? It is you who make them.

Do you trust to the best men? Do you try to see who is wise and what is excellent? or do you give the power to him whom you justly hate—the rich monopolist, the selfish trader, who says he is a coarse, plain man like you, and then buys your sovereignty with the sweat of your own brows and a sop of the very mess of pottage you have sold your birthright for?

"If you care more for a glass of beer than your welfare, whose fault that selfish men have found the beer comes cheaper than your family's comfort in their dividends?

"Your foreign friend—who is no wise leader for American workmen, and if you choose him, you will choose wrong—your foreign friend has told you to destroy. Suppose you tore up these railroads and wrecked these mills and furnaces and flooded all the mines and burned the oil—you know what farmers' wages are; would you be better off? And if you all went out and wanted work in the fields, where would the wages go to? You say you would not want wages, but would take the land; very good, there is the land now: will any of you like to change your work and earnings for a freehold farmer's life? 'No, we want the mills and railroads, but we do not want the rich,' you say. And if we wiped away the rich, who would build your railroads? Can you do it alone, and feed and pay yourselves? But if the rich must do it, what shall be their reward? They give you money—what will you pay them in? Money, or money's worth, and human bodies, are the only values that the world has ever known. Will you pay them in your bodies, in your slavery? If no, why, then, object that they have money?

"Because they have more than we, you say. Well, that may be mended. But if people are to use money to help you build your railroads, they must have the money to start with.

"Because they have more money than we have, you say again. And now be honest. Will you promise me one thing: that you will try not to think the world all wrong until it has no justice? They say there is no justice in the country of our friend here, and that is why he had to fly to us. If you can say there is no justice here; when you can honestly say, 'I have not got what I deserve'—then we will take it, though we wade through seas of blood, and I go with you. But tell me honestly, now—do you think you want money so much as some of the rich? Do you think it so needful to you? Do you think, each one of you, your know-how is so valuable? Do you think to-day, if you had a million apiece, you would use the money on the whole so well? You all know Coal-Oil Patsy—he got five millions, and he kept a bad circus, and a bad hotel, and a bad base-ball nine, and bad women, and took to drinking himself blind, and bribed himself a seat in Congress, and killed his wife or broke her heart, and at last he lost his money, and now he gets a dollar and a quarter a day, when he is sober enough—and he is worth no more—and what cent of his money ever did you any good? It is now all gone, and he built no single furnace, nor mill, nor railroad, nor worked a mine, nor gave any one of you a day's work while his money lasted. And one thing more: do you think you are better, or as fit to spend this money that your railroad or your coal mine makes —I do not mean, whether you may be so in a short time—but fairly now, as you stand, to-day, are you kinder, wiser, nobler; have you higher tastes, more learning, better knowledge of all the things that take money to buy? For remember, beer and beef and clothes and tobacco and rum are cheap enough—you know you get all of them you need to-day—it is fine learning, and clean manners, and great pictures, and new sciences, and poets, and high music, that come expensive. Even are you *quite* as good? Are your boys *quite* as well-bred and sober and respectful, and your little girls *quite* as generous and gentle? I do not say that all these things are so for ever—that you may not all become so—and believe me, the first young man or woman that comes along and says, 'Look here, I am fit to be a gentleman,' and the world does not admit him such; the first old man who has knowledge to make and spend money, and has not got it—and I will let him say, like our friend here, 'Away with learning and effort and order and wisdom and their universal works, and let us burn and kill! for behold, I have not my deserts.'"

The great mass of men had begun to hear Derwent speak with some attention; but the crowd thinned rapidly. Probably the greater part of it did not understand English at all; and toward the end several Huns and Poles collected little groups about them and began themselves to speak in the corners. But as the

Englishman closed, James Starbuck took the place; he was known to be one of the masters in sympathy with them, and the multitude pressed eagerly back.

Starbuck looked slowly around the great multitude; and you might have heard the murmur of a child, so silent was their expectation. Then he began; and his words dropped hissing, one by one, like drops of molten iron falling into water.

"What has this fine gentleman to do down here, with us rough workmen?" he began. "Do you think he would let one of you marry his sister?" Starbuck uttered each word staccato, by itself, thinking of his sister Jenny; and his frame seemed to quiver with malice; and he paused again, as if to recover his control. "I saw him riding many times last winter, in a carriage with footmen, with servants in livery, and a lady wearing diamonds, whose dress would buy a house for you and me. She is a fashionable belle, in the newspapers, and they say she is no better than she should be; but she would not touch our wives and daughters with the glove upon her hand.

"This aristocrat may have lost his money—as many of them do, by gambling, as well as poor old Coal-Oil Patsy—and he may have other ways of getting it, for all I know. Perhaps he was paid for his speech to-night. But are you such flats as to think he really cares for the likes of us?" The crowd already had begun to murmur angrily.

"The rich are better than we, he has the cheek to tell you. Yes, their dresses are better, and their food is finer, and they have learned how to lie and swindle with a soft tongue. They drink champagne instead of beer, and bet bigger money on their horses, and smoke cigars, and take their girls to ride in fine turnouts with a span of horses; but they don't mean honestly by their girls, and they turn them out upon the streets at last. And they don't have to work in the dirt, and they can take a hot bath every day, and their wives and daughters can keep their bodies clean and their faces fair, and so they go to the theatre and show themselves in dresses you'd be ashamed to see your wife in.

"But in all the rest, he's gassin' you. I think my girls could wear their diamonds as well as them, and flirt and show their dresses; and I could drive my span, and take my fancy drinks, and bribe the judges and the lawyers. Do you suppose if they couldn't steal from us, they could earn even so much as Coal-Oil Patsy? And as for books and pictures, they leave all that to the long-haired fellers at the colleges; they don't care a damn for art an' all that stuff any more'n we do.

"Do you suppose if any boy o' yourn studied to be a gentleman, and was as good, and as clever, and as gifted with the gab as our fine friend here, and went to him, he'd take him to his clubs and balls and parties? He'd say, 'Your hands are coarse and rough, and you don't talk enough like a dude'—and what he'd really mean all the time would be, 'You ain't got money enough.' I tell you all this talk is guff, and it just comes down to the money. All we want is money, and they've got it.

"Then he says we aren't smart enough. Of course we aren't smart enough. This world has been run for the smart fellers about long enough, and it's about time it was run for the honest men. It's the rich fellers on top that are the smart ones, and we are the fools who let 'em make all the money. It's they who are the judges and make the laws and run the legislatures, and then they have the cheek to come to us and say, 'Oh, lord, don't break the law!' And they bring you men over by the shipload, and give you seventy cents a day, and rent one room of their houses to your families at their own price, and herd your girls and boys together naked in the coal-mines, and then say, 'See how much cleaner we are! how much more virtuous we are!' And if you strike, you starve, and they know it; and if in your despair you give a kick or two to their damned machinery, they cry like cowards as they are, 'Oh, lord, that's my property—don't break the law!' And the law is theirs, too, not ours, nor God Almighty's whom they talk so much about.

"I tell you, friends, you can never touch these people but through their pockets. The law's a fraud, and when they don't find it suit, they laugh at it. And they don't care a damn for you or your wives or children or your souls or your bodies or the lives of your boys or the virtue of your daughters—but only for what they can make out of you. And they talk about the freedom of the country, and the Declaration of Independence, and ballots and that; and all the time they ape their swell English friends and marry their girls off to rotten foreign princes and would have a king here if they could—except that it's easier to throw the dust in our eyes under what they call a republic.

"And now I say, don't you care a damn for their laws, either. And if they hire their Pinkerton spies who are paid to shoot you down, you shoot them too. They won't care much for that; but then when you burn a big works, and blow up a mine or two, they'll see their money going and squeal fast enough. That's all I've got to say."

Derwent had listened to his speech intently, none the less so that threatening glances were cast at him from time to time. As he finished, a score or more of orators leaped to the platform; and many of them began to speak at once. Starbuck, having done his work, disappeared; the crowd was beginning to thin; the speakers spoke in Polish, Bohemian, Hungarian, Sicilian, each in the dialect of his own audience. Many were waving their hands violently and making threatening gestures in the direction of the city, which lurked, black and sullen, below them in the valley, shrouded in the thick smoke itself had made, bright-pointed here and there with many torches; and now and again from the bowels of the thing would burst a blaze of white-hot metal, like the opening of the monster's fiery eye, ending in a wide red glare and a hissing shower of sparks; and all was dark again.

Hardly any men of the English race were by this time left upon the ground. Derwent noticed it, as he stood watching, in one corner of the throng; and thought how un-American a scene it was. At last the anarchist who had first begun stood up again, as if to close the meeting. This time his voice seemed stronger or more sibilant; his speech was but a string of curses, of tales of crime, full of a savage's lust of ruin. *Let it end! Let them suffer, too; let them die, as we have died. If they mean to starve us now, let these mills and machines, these tools of wrong, these mines, these gaols of wretchedness, let them all burn or blast—what care we—we who are to be burned or hanged ourselves? Let their towns be gutted, and their homes be razed and their factories be burned—aye, let them burn, burn, burn, as this shall burn, from now on, day and night, winter and summer, for all time!*

And as the orator closed, with a group of men he threw himself upon the structure of the piping of the flaming well. The wooden tower swayed and rocked and fell; and with a roar like the ocean the gas, freed from its casing, flooded the sky with its flare of fire. A great mass of pebbles and timbers rose with the first outburst, and fell flaming on the shouting crowd below; then, igniting close to the earth, and even below its surface, running rapidly around the rock, leaping and tossing in liquid tongues, the red rills seemed to spring from every crevice in the earth, until the place that had been the rostrum was sunken in a lake of flame.

The Pole had kept his arm extended, as one who invokes a spell, until the shock of the explosion had gone by, and all the flaming timbers fell; then, when the fire was steady, reddening the valley even to the distant mountain-tops, he swept his arm in a gesture not without some dignity toward the silent city. With a hoarse cry the multitude seemed to take his meaning; and the sea of swarthy faces, red-sashed men and olive-cheeked women, with their motley dresses, and their odd diversity of foreign cries, swept downward to the city's rolling mills.

Of all the crowd who spoke that night not one American except James Starbuck; of all the thoughts in those ten thousand heads, scarce one the fathers of the republic could have owned with honor; of all these men indeed, not one who understood the principles which gave his country birth.—Derwent was reflecting. Where were the true Americans? Where were the descendants of the colonies, and Virginia and Old New England? What had been Starbuck's training, that he talked like that?

But, you will remember, it was long since Jem Starbuck had left that old New England village, dying out amidst its sturdy hills; and his old uncle Samuel Wolcott had hanged himself, a long year since, to the rafter from the barn in his hillside homestead.

## CHAPTER XXVIII.

### ARTHUR HAS A LITTLE DINNER.

ARTHUR was thinking of getting up a little dinner for some of his most worthy friends and most valuable acquaintances, and he was sitting in the reading room of his favorite club, trying to make up his list. There was a reception at the Livingstones that afternoon, and he proposed going; but this deuce of a list took much more time than one would suppose possible. He threw impatiently into the waste-paper basket the third tentative sketch which had proved impossible, and looked at his watch. The cards said half-past three—"to meet Miss Holyoke"—it was indeed the first time Gracie was to appear out of her deep mourning.

Arthur looked at his watch. It was after three already. He had thought of going early, before the people came; however, he would make one attempt more, and meantime ring and order the cab.

John Haviland—he must come of course—he was the man he really esteemed most, of all the men he knew. But Birmingham did not like Haviland—and Arthur could not possibly do without the earl—well, so much the worse for his lordship; they could be put at opposite ends of the table. So Haviland went in. Then there was Van Kull and Charlie Townley; there had been some trouble, about a woman, between these two men, and they were not upon the best of terms. But then Arthur particularly wanted Van Kull; his presence at a stag-party was sure to give it just the cachet that it needed, and Charlie was by no means so popular, among the men. After all, he could not be forever deferring to his friends; he would tell Charlie who was coming, and if he didn't like it, he could stay away. Besides, the dinner was but an impromptu affair, gotten up for that very evening; at least, the invitations were to be sent out then, though Arthur had schemed about it for several days; and they might not half of them be disengaged. He had spoken to Birmingham already; and he had promised to come. Caryl Wemyss—there was another man. Him, at least, he would cut; for he disliked him thoroughly. But, after all, Wemyss was a great card; he affected to look down on young men, and it would be quite a social triumph for him to get him. (It is difficult perhaps for us, who have seen this celebrated personage from the inside, to realize what a figure-head he had made himself in that portion of American society which has aspirations beyond the ocean.) Yet it would give him the keenest pleasure to leave this man out for once, more so than to put in all the others; for he knew that Wemyss would like to go. Which was the greatest pleasure—ambition or revenge?

A servant came up just here, and whispered that Mr. Holyoke's cab was ready. "Tell him to wait," said Arthur, impatiently; and he admitted Mr. Wemyss, with a sigh, to his list. Who next? There was Lucie Gower, of course; every one liked Lucie; and Arthur wrote the name, this time with a sigh of relief. Then there was Lionel Derwent. He himself liked him very much.—But confound it, no; Van Kull and Birmingham would leave the room if that self-assertive, carelessly-dressed radical were of the party. Who else was there? Mr. Tamms? Arthur was anxious enough to get on in his business, and had even thought of his angular employer at first. But it really would not do; that was a trifle too much of the shop; he could ask him alone some time, to Coney Island. The list would do as it was: the earl, Wemyss, Van Kull, Gower, Townley and Haviland.

He looked at his watch again; it was after four, and little Gussie Mortimer, that dried-up old beau, would be sure to be there by this time; he always went first, to get his fine work in with the very youngest girls, while the coast was clear. There was no use seeing Gracie with Gussie Mortimer. He might as well write the notes and get them off; some of the men he could see at the Livingstones, and Birmingham he was sure of, as that gentleman had lately been accepting his hospitality at the Hill-and-Dale Club, and he had asked him yesterday.

But Jimmy De Witt came in just then, and began to talk; it was nice to be clapped on the shoulder by him, for he was very rich, in the right of his wife, and given to entertaining. An enviable fellow, popular, a great athlete, with a rich and pretty wife, who did not look much to his comings in and goings out, having far too good a time herself for that. It will be seen that Arthur's ideas had changed a little from his poetry days; but what would you have? He had been studying *les moyens de parvenir* since then. New York life is not a lyric, nor yet an epic, or we had not called this book a satire. Before he knew it, Arthur had asked him to dinner also, and Tony Duval; and then remembered that the latter always cut John Haviland. But everything seemed to go wrong that afternoon; the very de'il was in it. Derwent came in too, and asked him if he was not going to the Livingstones. Arthur answered irritably; and felt glad he had not invited him. He should go, he said, if he got time. So, that we may not miss the kettledrum ourselves, perhaps we had better accompany Derwent.

For Gracie has long been wondering why Arthur has not come; she has looked forward to her "coming out" chiefly that she might see our hero every day once more. Derwent goes to her at once. "I have just left a friend of yours lamenting that he cannot get here sooner," says he. "Holyoke was positively savage that he was kept so long down town." It was a white lie, I know; yet few men would have been at the pains to tell it. And Gracie smiles once more; and the burly, blond-bearded man stays by her, like some comforting, protecting power. But he seems destined to annoy his friends that afternoon; for Charlie Townley finds him near by, too, and with quite other feelings. Charlie was there early enough, you may be sure; and he is sitting with pretty Mamie Livingstone on a sofa just behind them. And Birmingham, I fear, is cursing Derwent too; such a knack have fanatics of making themselves disagreeable! For every time he makes a pretty compliment to Miss Farnum—and pretty compliments are slow and heavy things for our peer of the realm to struggle with—it seems as if his beautiful companion caught Derwent's eye. And the beauty is, even to the Briton's eye, a bit unconscious of his fine speeches; and looks about her as if she too were looking for some other swain. Only Mrs. Gower and Wemyss seem to have escaped; but they are sitting by a certain screen in the tea-room and fancy themselves unseen; so they are, indeed, save by the eyes of some old dowagers—the same who had called upon her the day of the drive—barbed by a touch of malice to a keener sight than even "that damned adventurer's," as Birmingham calls him. But Pussie De Witt is there, in a gorgeous dress her novel matronhood permits her, perfectly happy yet; and Kill Van Kull, her partner, manages to get his amusement out of all the world and everywheres.

Then Derwent takes his seat by Mamie, calmly turning Charlie's flank. So the Wall Street knight has to retreat; and Derwent flirts most desperately, so that her little head—heart—what shall I say? is tickled. And it is very late when Arthur comes, and he finds that Gracie has gone up-stairs with a headache; so that he is angrier than ever.

But the dinner that night is a great success. Everybody came—except Van Kull, which is, indeed, a little of a disappointment—and the wines and cooking are most excellent. A great success, that is, until Wemyss, most unfortunately, began to talk of American families. Some one said something about Kitty Farnum, and what a fine woman she was, and what a pity it was that her people was so ordinary. "Pooh!" says his lordship, "all your Yankee families are just alike."

"Without impugning Birmingham's knowledge of American families," says Wemyss, thinking of his own, "I think I may submit that there are differences. Take Mrs. Gower, for instance, Mrs. Levison-Gower, I mean—I think that is a family name not unknown in England, and blood shows itself in every line of her face, and, in every motion of her figure, breeding." Wemyss never forgets his polished periods, even in the heat of argument. "Or take," he goes on, "Miss Holyoke, whom we saw to-day, she is perhaps even a better example of what I mean. She has not perhaps much style; she is countrified, if you like—but she comes of the best old Massachusetts stock, and I submit there is no older blood in the England of to-day than hers."

"Oh, come, now, I say," says his lordship, "you don't mean to set up that little filly against us? That's the sort of thing our governesses are in England."

It is a little hard for Arthur to sit by and hear this; but he remembers that Birmingham is the guest of the evening and keeps silent. But Haviland takes it up. "If that is true, Lord Birmingham, I congratulate you upon your *governess's* breeding; and am only sorry that its lessons are so soon forgotten."

"I think, sir; you should remember the lady is a cousin of our host," adds Lucie Gower, pluckily.

"Damn it, man," cries Birmingham, "we all think so in England. Do you suppose the prince cares a curse for your shop-keeping distinctions? As much as I do for Jess the farrier's daughter and Nell the draper's wife in my county town. He only takes up one Yankee woman after another because they're easier than the women that he's used to. That's why your Buffalo Bills get to the Queen's levees as well as your poker Schencks—we might as well marry a Chicago pork man's pretty daughter as any Yankee Boston professor's—if she's got the money and the looks."

"And damn it, sir," cries little Lucie Gower, "I tell you that if you had spoken but just now of my wife as you did of poor Miss Holyoke, I'd have shied this bottle at your head."

Gower looks fierce, as he stands up, grasping his decanter; and Charlie Townley interposes to pour oil on troubled waters. "Sit down, Lucie," says he, "I've no doubt all our ancestors were no better than they should be; Lord Birmingham's own included." With which American reflection, and something in the ludicrousness of Gower's gentle nickname, the altercation passes for the time. Birmingham, being a bit of a coward, is brought to apologize; "and perhaps," adds Charlie, "Lord B. has just been touched upon a tender point." All laugh at this, save Birmingham, who blushes red and angrily. But John has said nothing, and is twirling his mustache grimly.

Meantime the wine circulates again; and the earl, who has already taken too much, takes a little more.

And every man has had some little irritation on that unfortunate day; poor Arthur, who expected so much from his little dinner! For Arthur has been thinking now of Gracie, and there is some uneasy feeling on his mind he does not seek to analyze. Though, indeed, it was by her wish that they had never been engaged.

No small talk seems to be quite ready; and Birmingham goes on. "Of course, it's all very well for you fellows to talk," says he, as if he meant to be amicable, "and I'm sorry that I said what I did. But you must all know well enough that it's ridiculous for Americans to talk of family. Why, the country was settled by the very scum and refuse of Old England; and all your ancestors were either thieves, or slaves, or prostitutes and domestic servants shipped out here by the carload——"

He stammers a moment; for John Haviland, eying him calmly, as one might eye some servant seeking for a place, rises, folds his napkin with great deliberation, and stalks out of the room. Gower follows him, assuring the Englishman first, with great particularity, that "he is a confounded blackguard and knows where he may find him." With which grandiloquent speech, a little out of date perhaps, the other five are left to continue their instructive conversation. Arthur is a little pale, but Charlie Townley, when they have fairly left the room, breaks into a roar of laughter, and Tony Duval seems to think it all good fun; his grandfather, a French barber, had married a Paris grisette, and both had come to America to make their fortunes.

"That's like 'em all," says the bellicose Briton, "they court our company, just like the snobs at home, and then are vexed if we don't treat them as our equals. And all the fuss about a Kitty Farnum! I mean to take her back with me, but damme if I've yet decided to marry her first!"

"You will oblige me first by taking your name off this club; or as I put you down, I'll save you the trouble by doing that myself. Perhaps I had better pay your bill for you too, lest you should forget it, as you did that hundred I lent you last year. And I will write to Mrs. Farnum and the ladies to whom I have introduced you, and apologize to them for the disgrace of bringing you," says Arthur. "Waiter, you need give this gentleman no more wine; he has had too much already." Arthur speaks in a loud tone, so that all the other men in the dining-room have heard; and then he too stalks away. "Oh, dammit, no, don't do that," begins Birmingham, in answer to the last of Arthur's threats but one; but our hero is already beyond his hearing.

Charlie is still laughing, but now he finds his breath again. "Never mind, old fellow, you were drunk," he says, consolingly. "It'll be all right, to-morrow."

Birmingham is red and puffing like a turkey-cock: and at the same time struggling with some clumsy speeches of repentance.

"Upon my word," says Wemyss, who has been most uncomfortable throughout this scene, "there has been no such time since the declaration of independence."

"The fact is," adds Charlie, soothingly, "you touched them both on a tender point; that fellow Haviland I suspect of being a rejected suitor for Kitty F. herself; and Arthur, I know, has had a soft spot for his cousin since he was a calf."

But by this time Birmingham is going maudlin; his drunkenness has come on him so quick that Wemyss and Townley have much ado to get him home to bed. He is full of fulsome expressions of regret; and ends with blubbering that he is sorry for what he did.

The next morning, he woke up late, and with a headache, in his room at the hotel that he had found it pleasant (and economical) to abandon for so long; and came down-stairs to find a portmanteau containing all his clothes that he had left at the Hill-and-Dale. With it, but without a letter, were his receipted bills from both the clubs.

Birmingham was very repentant. Late in the afternoon he took a walk with Wemyss, and entered timidly the Piccadilly Club, where Townley—good-naturedly—had put him down again. He passed two or three ladies driving on Fifth Avenue who bowed to him no less cordially than before; and in the club some men came up and spoke to him. He began to fancy that the thing was being hushed up; it is so pleasant to hush up disagreeable things, and we Americans do like to be on good terms with every one, lest some one say we are not good fellows. But the earl was mortally ashamed of the evening's occurrences; and finally he mustered up courage, with many brandy-and-sodas, to sit down and compose to Arthur a letter of repentant, almost grovelling apology.

Having done this, he felt that he had done all America could well demand. Judge then of his indignation, when, on the morrow, the letter was returned to him unopened.

It was the first time his lordship had ever had a letter sent back to him unopened; and he curses Arthur for a cad up to this day. But what he most feared was that some one should bear tales of his behavior to Miss Farnum. For he had thrice asked her to marry him, already.

## CHAPTER XXIX.

### CAPTAIN DERWENT SEALS HIS FATE.

HE autumn winds began; winds that in the country bring red leaves, and ripening nuts, and smells of cider, and the crisp white frost; and in the city come with clouds of pungent dust of streets, and sticks and straws, and make one's daily walk and ride a nuisance, not a pleasure. But all the world, or all the world that Arthur saw, was busied with its dresses and with its future entertainments, and with rejoicings over future marriages, and, now and here, perhaps, regrets, and longer days for women, and sterner work for men. For the beauty of our modern view of life is that it bids no man be content who stays in that position where our simple fathers used to say a wise providence had placed him. Not even our primers have this lesson now; but tell us, with A who is the architect of his own fortunes, how we all may rise in life. We are brought to make light of lessons, too—all lessons, from the first and second down—and the small boy has formed the taste of the nation and dictates its likings not only on the fourth of July; let us have our fun, and jest at all the school-marms and the moral tales. For the school-room's mimic can make faces long years before the first scholar understands.

Terrible indeed must have been the elders of a generation ago, that we kick our heels so high at having gotten loose from them.

So the race of life began again; and Charlie Townley on the home stretch, but laboring heavily. Old Mr. Townley came to the office seldomer than ever, this year; but Tamms was there, as regular as the clockwork beat upon a bomb of dynamite. His wiry red mustache was bitten close above his upper lip, and his discreet eyelids more inflamed than ever. And Charlie knew that all their Allegheny Central stock was still held in the office; and the strike seemed no nearer to a settlement than ever. "These labor troubles have played the devil with the market," he would say to Charlie; "and public confidence is entirely lost." Tamms depended much on public confidence. And Deacon Remington's brokers would go into the board and sell their ten thousand shares, day after day, as punctually as doom. "They must have borrowed lots of stocks," suggested the younger and the smarter Townley. "Can't we squeeze them?" But wary Tamms would shake his head. A "corner" was a risky boomerang—suchlike manœuvres he was too old a bird to try.

The firm had acquired a new customer that fall; no less a personage than Lionel Derwent. This unaccountable person sold or bought his hundred shares a day, and spent half his time in the office, and pored over the ticker like any other speculator. "So much for your reformers of the world," said young Townley to Arthur; and Arthur would have thought it strange, but that he was so rapidly learning the lesson of the world; and its first lesson is, as he fancied, that all men are alike; a lesson you will hear nowhere so frequently inculcated as in Washington and Wall Street, though we have humbly expressed our own opinion upon this theme before.

Tamms said that Mr. Derwent was a damned nuisance; but he made himself most agreeable to old Mr. Townley, and would hold the old gentleman in converse by the hour whenever he happened to meet him in the office. Derwent seemed still to take great interest in Arthur too; but Charlie found him even a greater bore than Tamms. For he was also a continual visitor at the Livingstones; and Charlie worried over it. "Where a man's treasure is, there shall his heart be also."

Charlie was growing very nervous about the state of things down town; and it would be a little too bad to have the prize snatched from him in the moment of fruition. He had had a devilish good time in his life for the last ten years; since in fact he had got out of leading strings; and then he had looked about him with a judicious eye, and carefully selected the rich girl who seemed, on the whole, the best adapted to make him comfortable; and he meant to continue to have a good time for many years to come, please the pigs. A conservative estimate (and Townley knew something of the state of the coffers) placed the Livingstone fortune at a million and a half; there was no entangling family, and both Mamie's parents were very old.

So he sent her flowers for every evening's amusement, whether it were concert, ball, or dinner; and called there twice a week; his flowers never came with a card, but always had a sort of trademark of their own. Good judges said that Charlie Townley was compromising himself. Not only this, but all the most recherché little parties that so experienced a fashionable could invent; just the sort of thing that made Mamie's young friends open their eyes, with envy; club dinners, and private dances at the country clubs, and seats upon the smartest coaches and in the most unquestioned opera-boxes; and these not mere "bud" parties, but with Mrs. Malgam, Pussie De Witt, or Mrs. Gower herself as guests. Thus Townley wooed her millions with his own scarce dollars and the aid of his acquaintance and his worldly wisdom. And Gracie found that Mamie was infatuated.

Something impelled her to make no secret of her troubles to John Haviland; and Haviland had taken Derwent into council. And that audacious gentleman had seriously proposed, first, kidnapping; taking him off for a cruise in a yacht; a month's delay, he said was all they needed. Then he suggested that they might get him publicly drunk. The enthusiast was no stickler for the commonplace, at best; Derwent was a man of Oriental methods, obvious and frank. But Townley had, unfortunately, no small vices; it would be quite impossible to get him drunk. And Derwent cursed "the bourgeois squeamishness for human life" that prevented as he said, "an honest duel, while making dull misery of all one's days, and vulgar trash of the nineteenth century's soul." And then Derwent hit upon a plan which surely no one but himself would have thought of; and all for Gracie's sake; and began to frequent Townley's office.

People began to wonder why Derwent stayed on in New York. It was true he was very attentive to Mamie Livingstone; but it was scarcely possible that the lionized Derwent had met his fate at last in a boarding-school miss. Mamie herself, however, began to think such was the case; and was duly flattered by it. Gracie had many a time told her that a lady need never allow a gentleman to propose to her whom she proposes rejecting;—but, dear me, that was all the zest of a girl's life—before she was married. She made one or too fitful efforts to discourage him, but the big man would not be discouraged. And really who could have the hardness of heart, even sober Gracie, to forbid a girl her very first offer? And such an interesting one too; Mamie was so anxious to see how he would do it. And she blushed with pleasure as he came to see her.

But all this was rage and desperation to our friend young Townley. He seriously thought of forcing the issue then and there; but he did not quite yet dare. Yet he certainly must do something soon; no one—not even the clairvoyant Derwent—knew better than Charlie Townley that he certainly must do something soon. The strikers down in Pennsylvania were said to be starving; but sooner or later starving men will make a hole in even Tamms's pockets.

Suppose they had a panic. They could not possibly carry the great railroad, and the margins, and the Starbuck Oil, through a serious trade disturbance. So long as the strikers contented themselves with trying to burn up railway iron and killing an obscure policeman or too—railway iron was cheap enough—in fact, they made it—and a policeman or two could be replaced. But a big, dramatic bit of rapine that would strike terror to the investing public, the comfortable bourgeois, the lambs who sat at home in their carpet-slippers and looked at chromos of old English farmyards—and Remington's big pile stood no longer ready to support them when things got bad; in fact, he suspected that that obsolete old Christian would like nothing better than to make the public run.

Still, Townley did not dare to ask her at her house. You are at a woman's mercy, there; she may ring the bell; she may even call her mother; you cannot choose your place, the stage-setting that most becomes you, arrange your lights, and select your own *dramatis personæ.* Charlie Townley was much like any other man, in the garish afternoon, and by the domestic fireside; in fact there was a certain quite intelligent look in Mamie's pretty eyes at times which Townley found it hard to face. Yet he was perfectly certain that he had fascinated her. How did he know? Well, he had kissed her. Townley's maxim was to kiss a woman first and win her afterwards; at the worst, you got but a rebuff for an audacity not in all eyes unadmirable; while, if you formally proposed, and were rejected, you had your value lowered in the eyes of all the world.

He resolved that it must be on his own ground and very late at night, and in the midst of a very gay assemblage. He got up a country party of his own, matronized by Mrs. Malgam; and had meant to settle matters while exhibiting this other pretty woman submissive at his feet. But Mrs. Malgam also had another string to her bow; and the other string was Derwent, whom Townley had to ask: "a damned clumsy Englishman," said he to her, "who has a cursed knack at getting in the wrong place at the wrong time."—"In the right time, you mean," laughed Mrs. Malgam; she knew Townley's game well enough; but did not conceive it possible that he could mean to marry yet. And this belief was indeed so general that it came to Mamie's ears; and she began to doubt it, too, and was for the doubt, ten times more infatuated with him than ever.

So Townley made up his mind that his only perfectly certain chance was the Duval ball; and this did not come off for some weeks yet.

For the whole Duval *gens* was about to celebrate its reception among the immortals and Miss Pussie's happy marriage, by giving a grand ball, the grandest ball that e'er was known, in our republican simplicity. Two thousand invitations had been sent out addressed to every one who did not care to go, and to nobody who did. Two smaller packets of tickets had been sent, one to Boston and one to Philadelphia, addressed to Mrs. Weston and Mrs. Rittenhouse respectively, to be distributed by these ladies, where they would do the most good, as they knew best;

and old Antoine Duval felt that he had safely bought his social distinction at last as he had bought his membership in clubs from obliged business friends and the legislation for his railroads from Congress and the Legislature of his native State.

Meantime, Townley's visits grow more frequent; but no more so than Derwent's; and poor Mamie is quite puzzled and troubled between the two. All her maiden's dreams are yet of Townley, and gilded with his social splendor; but she secretly bought a copy of Derwent's "Travels in the Desert" and read it on the sly. She was surprised to find the book was all about the East End of London; and a friend told her that if she had wanted his real adventures, she should have read "The Treasures of the King." Yet she is sure she does not care for him, and indeed will tell him so, if she shall ever have the chance.

She has the chance, and very soon—some three days before the great Duval ball. But it is hard for a maiden at such times to be very speedy with her tongue; particularly when the man is a very strong one, whom she is very much afraid of, and yet holds in some reverence; and who has a marvellous blue fire in his two deep eyes. Still, Mamie does refuse him; and he only seems to plead the more; as if the refusal were the one thing needed to put new heart into him. And he takes her trembling hand—there is a magnetism in his own brown and steady one that is not to be resisted—and begs at least for some respite—three months' consideration—a month's, at least—and there is something strangely thrilling in hearing a brave man talk to you of his love, his love, for you, just you, and not some outside person—and Mamie knows not how, but somehow, strangely, finds herself in tears. And then, as he draws still closer to her, the door opens and Gracie comes in.

She starts back, of course, but it is too late, and the man has sprung to his feet, and she is still sillily blushing and crying. What is it that makes Mr. Derwent's face turn, as he stands there, so strangely white? His voice is strong enough after a second, though, and he speaks almost instantly.

"I beg you, do not go, Miss Holyoke. You have seen quite too much to have any doubt; nor need there be embarrassment about so plain a thing. I know that—that your kind heart loves your cous—loves Miss Livingstone—more than all the world, and you will surely tell her what is best. As—as you must have fancied, I have asked her to marry me. Unhappily, I have not seemed worthy to her; and I only beg her now for some delay." Yet there was a curious dead level about Derwent's voice, as if he dare not trust himself on more than one key; and Gracie's quiet eyes turn on his with some wonder. There is a silence broken only by Mamie's sobbing. She had no idea such fun would prove so little mirthful, for she knew very well that she did not care for Lionel Derwent, who was old enough to be her father, and yet, as it seemed, he really loved her.

Derwent cut the matter short at last. "I must spare you any more to-day, Miss Livingstone. Forgive me, Miss Holyoke. I will call for your answer in a week, Miss Livingstone—surely, you will grant me that delay?" And he strode out of the room, hat and cane in hand, valiantly, and yet his eyes did not meet Gracie's; a month's delay, he was sure, would save her cousin from Townley; and he had sacrificed himself to gain this month's delay. For now he might never tell his love for Gracie.

As he entered the hall the servant opened the front door and let Charlie Townley in. Derwent nodded slightly. "H' are you," said the other, as they passed.

## CHAPTER XXX.

### ARTHUR IS MADE HAPPY.

JOHN HAVILAND, too, was working very hard that fall. He was not perhaps so happy even as Charles Townley, if this is any reason for hard work. And have I not said that we all work in New York? We work to drive away that bugbear of young Americans—discontent; much as Flossie Gower and her set work to drive away that other bugbear of Americans who have, surely, no cause for discontent—ennui.

But it was for neither of these two great things that John had ever worked; nor did he now work quite as usual. He strode down and up his town, breasting the December snows, and would have said that he was just as usual; and have half believed it, but for that strange choking that took him, by times, deep down in the throat. And yet, through his moist eyes, the earth looked fairer, and his life a deeper thing.

How dare I speak of John's life, day by day? How he goes to his office, and reads his review, and writes his speech, and looks to his other labors, and walks home alone and late? Such humdrum coloring, and so same throughout; it would be a deadly thing to read about; and as for living—is it their horror of such a life as his that set Kill Van Kull and Townley to life's pleasures and Flossie Gower and Caryl Wemyss to seek life's vanities? Surely; and the reader too has justified them; for is he—or she, more likely—not tired already of all this moralizing?

But she must suffer me one moment more.

For to John himself, his life had never been either sad or dull; nor was he sad now, despite his heart was wrung. The word *sadness* would not well suit the Sidneys and the Falklands, nor even such of us who know that life is a thing that we must either throw away or sacrifice, not cherish and enjoy; for "he who loves life overmuch shall die the dog's death, utterly." Is it sad, when some fair corner-stone is mortised to the temple? A Sidney's life is always used.

Yet had John one deeper sorrow, admitted hardly to himself. And this I hardly dare to say, lest it be scouted. For this thing was nothing other than an absence of belief in God. Not disbelief, but nonbelief; and it was a cause not of sadness, but of sorrow; quite a different thing, believe me; for the latter thing is manly.

This mattered not one iota to his action. Whatever lack of sight his mind might make him see; of one thing he was sure; that somewhere, everywhere, in the universe there was conflict. And is not that enough? Does the subaltern who finds himself he knows not where, nor with what general, in command of his little squad of troops some foggy day or night; the narrow saddened field, so full of dead and dying, is all he sees; no emperor, nor king, nor fort, nor even flag, but only some enemy he sees, and this, alas! more clearly; does he cry for leadership, or play at hazards with the man beside him, or lay him down to death? What does he,—with his sense of battle in the world about, and the distant cannon sounds, and smoke that hides? He stays where he is, and fights.

*Servus servorum Dei*—perhaps, is all the title such a man may claim; yet Popes of Rome, acknowledged as vice-gerents of Heaven, have worn it proudly. Servant of the servants of God. The battle sky is canopied with smoke; yet on the brows of some near leaders is the shine of heaven; and these he follows. There are not yet so many that the one need be ashamed; but shall take his orders humbly from his poet or priest. And some fair souls still seem to see directly, as do women often. Servants of God are these; as such, twice blest. And Gracie Holyoke was one of them.

Haviland adored her. This was his sorrow; yet a sorrow he would not have been without. He fancied she was pledged to Arthur: he almost knew that Arthur had her heart. That was why he saw so much of Arthur, from the very first; this fair-haired, blue-eyed fellow, who stood so near him in the ranks. John had seen another friend, another young man like him, fail and fall; a man who succeeded in the world, and failed with life; a suicide, that Henry Vane whom "Baby" Malgam has forgotten. But Arthur had a truer guide; and John had hoped for his and Gracie's happiness.

So John was sorrowful; and he was troubled too

with things of honor. Is honor, then, a false light too, when so many men must stand by it alone? I trow not; not wholly so, at least. So John had had this added trouble; whether he should tell Gracie of his love. And he had settled with himself, now, that he would; and in plain words; and had resolved that he would do so, too, at Mr. Duval's ball; such earnest things may balls be, after all. He had small hope, but only great resolve. Man has no right to hope, he read; no right to happiness, and hence to hope of happiness;—and consoled himself.

Novels should end well, they tell us; does then the novel of life end well? Life, that is so novel to each one, so old to fate. Let us hasten back to those with whom the novel may end well: to fortunate Caryl Wemyss, and favored Flossie, and worldly-wise Charlie and to Arthur Holyoke.

He had made his way. He had bettered his position. He was popular, and his life was full of pleasure. If he had not written a great poem, he had done things that the world would prize more highly. He saw his way, at least, to substantial success, as Charlie Townley had seen it before him; John Haviland still tried to be his friend, but Arthur liked Charlie better now. Was not Faust glad on that first morning, when he saw the world once more, and left the devil to his God to fight—*permitte divis cetera?*

Take this one bright December day for instance; he rises in his comfortable bachelor apartment; his head still full of dreams of bright eyes from the night before; for it is his fortune to be petted by women. He has a few hours so-called work, to be sure; but the work is among Millions, which it is pleasant to think may yet be his some day.

He left early in the afternoon and took his drive in his own pretty cart, glad to see and be seen by all he called his friends. Then he went to dine with a millionaire, Mrs. Malgam, and Mamie Livingstone; in the evening to the opera, and to the first great subscription ball. He was a manager of the last, and wears his honors with much grace; and he has the offer of a partnership in a rich young firm.

Late in the afternoon sat Gracie in her room. We have not seen so much of Gracie, lately, as I, for one, should like; she does not do much in these pages, perhaps. When women have the nobler lives they ask for now, our heroine shall perchance do more; now she merely lifts the men about her to their higher selves. She is a power wrought out most in other lives—Derwent's, Mamie's, Haviland's. I own I am unable to describe her; I cannot print the fragrance of a lily on these pages; those who have seen the lily do not need it. Perhaps, if Helen, Heloise, are the women that Flossie Gower, clever Flossie Gower, in these days of women's rights still envies most, I may have still some maiden readers —my courteous greeting go to them—who think the nobler Helens and the purer Cleopatras may yet not have too small a part in life, and dream their sweet heart-dreams of Una and Elaine.

In her bedroom, then (for our hand is on the doorknob and we must enter now)—sat Gracie, through this afternoon. Mamie has been in, from time to time, and had close talks with her; and she has promised Gracie she will keep her word with Derwent, and wait, although she is sure she cannot care for him. But now she is gone, to dress for Arthur's dinner, and Gracie sits alone.

The house is silent; and she knows the old people are down below, and she must go and read to them. But the vault of heaven has been unfathomably blue, that day; and she has been looking into it, over the crowded city walls. She knows that Arthur is not thinking of it, or of her. And now the air has faded to the lilac winter twilight, and all men are going, tired, to their homes. But she is idle; and idle hours she finds so hard to fill! She took a book she loved, and read; but gradually the dark came, and the book fell from her hand; and now her hands are on her face, and her soft eyes closed, and she is crying, silently.

## CHAPTER XXXI.

### THE FINANCIER'S DINNER.

THE new year has come; and all the world has been celebrating, with children's dances and with children's dinners and with a multiplicity of costly toys, the birth of Christ. Grown-up people who have been good-natured have assisted, and helped their boys play with candles and with evergreens as they helped them play with fire-crackers on the fourth of July, that other great feast or holy-day our calendar still keeps. Grown people who have not been good-natured have kept to their clubs, mostly, men to men; and the women have snatched the chance to get a week of resting and a little early sleep. For now the children's play is over; and the winter's balls are to begin in earnest, a serious business, as we have said.

On the evening of December thirty-first, young Townley was invited to dine with his partner, Mr. Phineas Tamms, in Brooklyn. He never liked these dinners; but yet he learned too much from them to stay away. A voyage to Brooklyn combined all the discomforts of a trip to Europe, without the excitement and rewards—as he said at his favorite Columbian Club, where he stopped to take a modest tonic on his way down town. "I wish I were going," said one of the circle, who dallied a little in stocks, "and had your chance of getting points." For these dinners of Tamms, the great street leader, were known as meetings where many schemes were laid, and information gleaned, as Tamms unbended after dinner, worth many thousands for each syllable, in gold.

"Yes," said old Mr. Townley, wagging his gray head sagely, "my partner is a very able young man—a very able young man indeed." He was taking nothing; but it was his usual hour to be at the club; and the New Year's time inclined the old gentleman to kindliness for all the world; so he had left his private and particular seat by the window and joined the group of younger fellows, to see how "his Boys" (as he called all young men he knew) were getting along. As such, he was liked by them; and treated with but the faintest tinge of patronage his age made necessary.

"What do you think of the market, Mr. Townley?" said one of them with a manner of much deference. "We have had a long spell of sag, and the public are not in it."

"Ha, ha," chuckled Mr. Townley, delightedly, rubbing his hands. "Townley & Son have seen a longer spell than this. The public will come in it fast enough when we pull the market through. Wait till after the holidays, my boys—I say no more; but wait till after the holidays. As I was saying to my old friend Livingstone, just now, a panic never comes on a long falling market. There was fifty-seven—

and thirty-eight—he did not remember thirty-eight—Charles Townley & Son held up the banks, not they us, in those days—" and the old man went off, chuckling, and joined his old friend Livingstone, the oldest member of the club, after himself, in the corner window that was sacred to them.

Jimmy De Witt looked after the retreating figure sadly. "What a pity the old man does not know anything," said he. "He would not lie about it, if he could."

Charlie left the club, and drew his fur overcoat tightly about his chest, as the biting wind swept, from river to river, through Twenty-third Street. He was not surprised his senior partner was not going to the dinner, and only wished he did not have to go himself. Day after to-morrow was the Duval ball; and he wished to keep himself fresh for that. Was he not going to put his fate to the test, and win or lose the girl he meant to marry? And New Year's day would be all work for him; for Tamms had bespoken his most private services; and he had some reason to look upon the balance-sheet with apprehension.

Nor was his peace of mind restored by Tamms's dinner. No ladies were allowed at Tamms's dinners, and only one well-tried and proven waiter. Tamms sat at the head of his table, and until the coffee was brought, said nothing; or if he did speak, talked of church matters or of the weather. But when the coffee and cigars appeared (for cigars and coffee were almost his only food, and he was never known to drink wine at a business dinner) Tamms's rusty iron jaw would open and the slow words drop out gingerly, one by one, over the stiff curtain of his beard, while all the knights of his round table craned their ears to hear them.

But Townley noticed some very curious things about this dinner. In the first place, the guests were all young men, and rich men; but not men of much experience or sagacity upon the street. Deacon Remington, who in times past had had his regular seat, was notably absent. And Tamms talked more freely than was his wont, and more steadily throughout the dinner, which last was far more rich than usual and was served by half a dozen hired waiters.

"What do you think of the market?" was again the question a beardless youth asked of Tamms anxiously, to the dismay of all about him. But the beardless youth had just come fresh from California with his father's fourteen millions, bent on becoming a power in the street; and had not learned his money-changer's etiquette as yet. But to the surprise of all the rest, Tamms answered quite naturally and fully. "I don't know much about the market," said he, cannily. "I guess perhaps there ain't much in the market, anyhow, of itself——"

"You think it a good sale?" broke in the beardless youth eagerly; while his neighbors kicked him under the table and the ones placed farthest from their host swore at him audibly.

"I ain't sayin' what I think it—at least, not jest now," said Tamms, with dignity. "I s'pose things is kind o' stagnant—unless some feller drops a stone into the pool."

The attention grew breathless; you might have heard a pin drop; though not, perhaps, the flutter of an angel's wing. "There's a good deal of money coming in on the first of January; and I don't know but what things might start up a little, if some stock got kind o' scarce." Tamms spoke these last words with greater precision, and in much better English than the former ones; and his young partner knew that in this accent he was always lying. But all the rest had treasured every syllable of the oracle's words, more carefully than any reporter's note-book could have set them down, while in appearance dallying with their cigarettes and iced champagne. "He means a corner," said every man to himself; "who's he gunning for?"—"He wants them to think he means to corner Allegheny," said young Townley to himself.

"Old man Remington has caused the present break," said a rich young stock-broker with an air of much importance.

"The deacon and I are kind o' out," said Tamms. "The fact is, I'm afraid the deacon may have been selling too many stocks."

"Remington has sold nothing but Allegheny," said every man to himself; and felt that they were well repaid their ferry-trips to Brooklyn. But after this, Mr. Tamms obstinately refused to talk any more stocks, but only Shakespeare and the music-glasses, that is, of Mr. Beecher and the Coney Island races.

Charlie outstayed them all, and then went home

alone. "It can't be done," he said to himself; "the Governor knows it and he's desperate. I don't believe that we can borrow fifty thousand more." He was sitting alone in the ladies' room of the ferry-boat, his fur collar pulled well up about his face, smoking one of his own cigars; for Tamms's were too strong. There was only one other passenger upon the boat; a drunken working man; and he was cursing Townley for a swell. "Confound him, they wouldn't let me smoke there, though it is late at night. But I ain't got no fine cigar, perhaps."

Tamms's fertility of invention was miraculous; but still it seemed to Townley that he was hard pressed now. Their profit on that last summer's operation had been large—on paper; but it was this devilish tightness of money that made things bad.

Suddenly, there was a peal of joyous bells, ringing loud all at once, chimes, church-bells, factories, and schools, from both sides of the river. Townley started nervously, and then remembered with a laugh that it was New Year's day. "What damned rot it is," said he; and then betook himself again to thinking. It seemed as if that merry music brought him new ideas; for he slapped his thigh, and said aloud, "By Jove, I have it."—"What's the swell a-chuckling over now?" said our friend Simpson, looking in the window from outside.

"The deacon must have sold about all the stock there is," Charlie went on to himself; "and if we can only carry ours, and those rich lambs go in to buy—the deacon can't deliver. Why, it's making them do the cornering for us—doesn't cost us a cent—and if we get a little short of money, we can even drop a few shares to them ourselves, and no one be the wiser. Provided only some devilish panic or strike or war of rates does not come in just now," he added, as the boat jarred heavily against the dock.

The bells were silent now, and Charlie, wrapping his fur about him, walked up the snowy and deserted street along the wharves. There was a foul dampness coming from the tired water that still splashed beneath the piles; but the city's faults were charitably covered up in snow. For once in his life, Townley had an instinct of economy, and took no carriage; a fact which Simpson, slouching along behind him, had noticed. There was no horse-car waiting, so he walked briskly up a narrow cross-street into the city, still smoking his cigar. "Damn him," thought Simpson, "I wonder how much he's got? I'd scrag him for a hundred." And he drew a long knife from its sheath, and hid it with his right hand, in his breast. Simpson has been unlucky lately, with his pools, even as has Mr. Tamms.

But Charlie is still thinking; of Mamie Livingstone and of the ball to-morrow night. The evening's talk has had one consequence, not wholly material, at least; it has won for little Mamie the cavalier she loves. Townley feels now that all his future hangs upon this slender thread: curse it, he may have waited too long. He has had a dozen chances to marry girls before this; Pussie Duval, herself, who gives the ball to-morrow night—

He is stopped by a man at the corner of the street. "Got a light, boss?"

The voice is rude and husky, and the man has been drinking. Charlie looks at him good-naturedly, and throws open his fur-lined coat; and as he does so, the man notices that he too looks pale and worried.

"Certainly," says Charlie. "Take a cigar, won't you—for the first of the year?" Charlie has a pleasant smile; and he meets the other's eye frankly. And Simpson takes his right hand from his breast.

He takes the cigar, shame-facedly; and shambles hurriedly off, not waiting for his light.

"Poor devil, I suppose he wants to smoke it in a warmer place than this," says Charlie; and pulls his furs close about him and hurries safely home.

# CHAPTER XXXII.

## THE DEACON'S VENGEANCE.

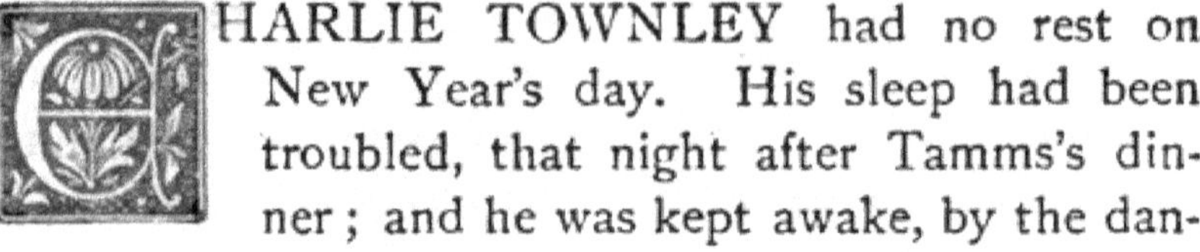

HARLIE TOWNLEY had no rest on New Year's day. His sleep had been troubled, that night after Tamms's dinner; and he was kept awake, by the danger that he saw, ignorant of the greater one unseen that he had escaped. The day was a holiday; "the Street" was as deserted, almost, as on Sunday; though the policeman on his rounds and the children, playing at snow-balling in the centre of the empty street, could see, above the half-drawn window-shades, troubled faces of men inside and clerks bending industriously over the great ledgers.

Townley was there all day, closeted with Mr. Tamms. He scarcely gave himself time for a bit of bread, at noon, when the chimes of Trinity at the head of the street were ringing again joyously. Thus he kept his holy day, counting his money in his counting-house, making up the balance of their year's labors, as is our modern way of keeping holy-days. And as the day wore on, it became evident, even to him, that the money, or rather those slips of paper printed or engraved which might bring in money, were distressingly scanty; while on the other hand, the footing of notes payable grew most portentously. He might, indeed, have thanked his holy-day for one thing—that many of their loans fell due upon the morrow, in consequence of it.

Charlie had never quite thoroughly known the business. Mr. Tamms and Mr. Townley both had their private iron boxes in the vault; and he had no means of knowing what might be in these. And Mr. Townley Senior had another iron box marked "Trusts." On the other hand there was also no means of his knowing how much they had borrowed on their private accounts.

Tamms had been very silent through the day; and his calmness gave Charlie some encouragement. Nevertheless, the total of liabilities was appalling: counting their own loans, and loans of the railroad, and of Starbuck Oil, it was over thirteen millions of dollars. True, to meet this, they had two-thirds the entire stock of Allegheny Central—all, in fact, that was not held by private investors or in permanent trusts, for they had not dared to sell a thousand shares since the past summer—and all the bonds and nearly half the stock of Starbuck Oil. But every share of both was pledged for their large debts; to sell even so little as a thousand shares would break the price and bring a call for further "margin." And they had no further margin to put up. Charlie was appalled. "Couldn't we get Remington's brokers to sell some for us?" he hazarded, at last.

"What's the use? We'd have to buy it ourselves," answered Tamms. "It's been the old deacon, right through—damn him," he added. Charlie had never heard him swear before; and it struck him, all at once, that Tamms was growing careless with his mask.

"Never mind," said Tamms, as if he had read his thoughts, "let's go to dinner—then we'll feel more like tackling the assets. You'll have to go in and buy the whole market in the morning, anyhow."

This bold speech restored a little of Townley's courage; and they went and had a somewhat grim banquet, with plenty of champagne, however, at the Astor House. Then they went back to Wall Street in the evening; and worked together until midnight. And Mr. Tamms showed Townley a list of securities that almost gave him strength to face the morrow. "These," said he, showing the paper, "are my own; and these other," showing a still longer list, "are Mr. Townley's."

"Had I better see him?"

"What's the use of bothering the old man? He won't be down to-morrow." Now Charlie had never heard Tamms call Mr. Townley "the old man" before.

"How much shall I buy?"

"Buy Allegheny and Starbuck Oil until you're black in the face. I can get two millions on this stuff easy. And those young fellows who were at my dinner will be buying too, I guess. I'll catch old Remington, by God, and this time I'll bleed him white." And Tamms's bleared eyes glared, and his beard bristled, and his straight red mustache shut down over his thin lips like a wire trap. He was not a pleasant sight, as he said these words. "If you get frightened, send around for me," he concluded, more quietly; and they locked the offices and separated on the corner of the street.

That night Charlie did not sleep at all. He lay broad awake, thinking now of the business, now of Mamie Livingstone, his lady-love. He angrily wished that he had put his courtship to its climax sooner. A pretty mood he was now to woo in—at the ball to-morrow night! Sleep was impossible; and he got up and smoked cigars and paced the room impatiently.

In the morning, however, his hopes were higher. After all, they might probably weather this squall, if only for a few weeks; and on that evening, by all that was holy, he would win the hand of pretty little Mamie—and her millions. Then Tamms might split his wicked head for all he cared. Mr. Tamms had not got to the office when Charlie arrived; but he went off to the board, and began his bidding boldly.

But that last night had come the news of the great Allegheny Central strike, no longer to be suppressed by the telegraph or the company, born of that riotous meeting which our friend Derwent had so vainly tried to check and James Starbuck had fomented, coming from the races and his sister's pretty pony-carriage that emulated Mrs. Gower's own. The stock had dropped a fraction actually before his own first bid was heard; and he knew that the message had flashed all over the country, "opening weak." There was a very maelstrom about the Allegheny Central sign—

he found it easy to keep in the centre of the whirl, however, and bought it manfully. But soon he found the reason of this; he was the only broker that was buying. Some of the young men that had been at Tamms's dinner he saw, upon the outskirts of the crowd, and tried to wink at them encouragingly; but evidently the news of the strike, or some other warning, had frightened them, for they held aloof. He could hardly pretend to keep account of the stock that he was buying, though he jotted as rapidly as he could on his bit of paper. A telegram was thrust into his hand; he read it hurriedly; it was from Tamms—"Keep it up—strikers reported starving."—"Confound 'em, they can't starve before to-morrow, though," thought he; but he went on taking all stock they offered; and it seemed as if all the world was offering stock.

It was a terrible hour. He looked furtively at the clock, the while he kept on bidding. Some minutes of the "call" still remained. A messenger forced his way through the crowd, with a note from the office. It was from their banking-clerk: "Money ten per cent. Fechheimer has called for margin." Curse the rate of money; what cared he what it cost if they had only got it? Why in heaven didn't Lauer tell him that? And he wiped the sweat from his brow and went on bidding.

And now there was a sudden eddy in the crowd, and it opened inward and he saw Deacon Remington himself. Townley's face fell, despite him; he was not yet old enough to be quite a perfect gambler; and there was a sort of awe-struck hush, as the ranks of the Greeks might have hushed before Troy when Achilles took the field.

"Five thousand at seventy-five," said old Remington, turning a wad of tobacco in his cheek.

"Take it," said Charlie, coolly. Now seventy-five was nearly two whole points below the last quoted sale; which had been a little lot of two hundred shares sold by—alas, shall we say it? Of such, however, is the friendship of Wall Street—his old friend Arthur Holyoke. Charlie was reckless now, and had nailed his colors to the mast; a pretty sure sign, by the way, that a man is beaten.

But the artful Tamms had still one more trick in his bag. In the momentary hush that followed this first discharge of heavy guns, Charlie got another telegram. It was dated Brooklyn, like the first. "Allegheny Central—special stockholders meeting for dividend—books close to-morrow." Tamms would have compressed the gospel of eternal life into ten words.

Then a clever idea struck young Townley. If they had no money, neither had Remington and his crowd any stock. "Post this telegram," he said to his clerk who had brought it. And then:

"I want ten thousand more of Allegheny Central—*cash.*"

Now "cash" meant that the stock must be delivered that day, as the books closed on the morrow.

There was another pause. He could hear the younger brokers among his adversaries anxiously inquiring the loaning rate on Allegheny Central. Now Charlie knew very well there was none to loan.

"I'll give seventy-six for ten thousand, cash." And this time there was a sort of wolf-like howl; but no other response.

"Seventy-seven?—Seventy-eight?—EIGHTY?"

The baffled deacon turned his quid again. "Seventy—at the opening," said he at last. But Charlie laughed scornfully.

"I want it now, please, deacon." And here some of those rich young men who had been at the dinner, seeing a turn in the tide of battle, ranged themselves on Townley's side. The price was run up with astounding rapidity. "Eighty—one—two—three—five—" the deacon looked on impotently. Not for one moment did he believe—nor, perhaps, many others there—that the house of Townley & Tamms could meet this contract. But the rules of trade forbade inquiring into that, so long as they had met their obligations.

"NINETY," said Charlie, in ill-concealed triumph. And the hammer fell, and the morning board was over; and there was a sort of cheer from the money-seeking multitude. Throughout the length and breadth of the greatest trading nation in the world it would be known in a few minutes that Allegheny had closed at ninety, bid. All danger of further calls for margin on that day at least was removed; and Charlie went back in triumph to the office.

And even yet, though it is three years since—and three years is a generation on Wall Street—this great battle is remembered; and the audacity of young

Charlie Townley and how he stood up before the great bear leader is told, as Romans told how Horatio held the bridge; told by brokers about their firesides, if they have firesides, to their children, when they have any. And Charlie's memory was kept bright; and his deeds of prowess not forgotten. For it was many a long month before he appeared upon the floor again.

He went back flushed with victory, like a warrior to his camp. Now he could look forward with due pleasure to the ball that evening. Once more he had leisure for thoughts of ladies fair and love. And as Paris, weary of the battle, might have looked forward to his Helen, so he looked forward to his tender interview with Mamie Livingstone that night. If Tamms had only got the money for their notes falling due that day, they might go on with safety for some months at least.

Now that he had time to think, it struck him as curious that both his telegrams had been dated Brooklyn. He quickened his step; and arriving at the office, his first inquiries were for his active partner. "Mr. Tamms has not been in to-day," said Mr. Lauer.

This was very strange. He telegraphed at once for Tamms at Brooklyn, telling him of the glorious victory they had won; and took his needed lunch while waiting for the answer. Then he went and ordered his flowers to be sent to Mamie. But when he got back, there was no answer yet.

He began to grow nervous. It was nearly two

o'clock; and he must be going back to the board. Leaving word at the office that he was to be sent for immediately when Mr. Tamms came back, he took the keys to their boxes and went to the vaults himself.

He found one certificate only in the box—for one thousand shares of Starbuck Oil. Well, this was better than nothing. But where was all the list of bonds and stocks that Tamms had shown him on the night before? In the elder partner's private boxes, he supposed. And these he could not get till Tamms's return. Could he be ill, by any chance? It was not like Tamms to be ill at such a time. His mind was greater than his body, too, and held the laws of nature in control.

In despair, he tried the lock of Tamms's private box. To his astonishment it opened at the touch. With an intense relief, he saw it was full of papers. Far-sighted Tamms had foreseen this, too.

But the relief was short-lived. The papers were nothing but insurance policies, contracts of no money value, leases of real estate, and a deed of a pew in Tamms's church. Could Tamms have taken the other papers with him to raise the money on himself? In his despair he tried old Mr. Townley's box. This also was not locked. But, to his horror, he found that it was quite empty. Empty? His head swam, and the open box seemed to yawn before his eyes like some black pit. He even dragged down Mr. Townley's box marked Trusts. That was empty too.

Charlie ran back to the office, streaming with a cold sweat of terror. His last hope—that Tamms would be there—proved equally vain. That ingenious person had not been heard from since the morning.

At three o'clock, the doors of Townley & Tamms, successors to Charles Townley & Son, which had not been closed in a business day before since sixty-eight years, were shut. And a notice, posted on the outer iron rail of the office, in Mr. Adolph Lauer's neat writing, informed their creditors that the old firm were "temporarily unable to meet their obligations."

But the "ticker" went on relentlessly through the afternoon; and the scared clerks, reading it, abandoning all other business, brought Charlie news, from time to time, of the great panic that was in the board; how Allegheny Central went to fifty; how even Starbuck Oil could find no purchasers. And while many a quiet home throughout the land was as yet undisturbed, little recking that the great railroad on which they had lived so long was at last insolvent, Charlie Townley sate doggedly in his barred office, hoping vainly for Mr. Tamms, or puzzling, equally vainly, how to meet the million that they owed that day, with his thousand shares of Starbuck Oil.

From time to time, he would lay down the hopeless task to think of the ball, that evening. Now he could not dare to go. Even he could not venture to ask a woman's hand on the day that all the world knew he was ruined. Ruined—aye, and fraudulently. Where were Mr. Townley's trusts that he so long had kept so well? In Tamms's pocket, perhaps, flying with these, too, to Canada. There was a swarm of reporters pressing at the door; vociferating for a member of the firm. The noise at last attracted his attention; and he went out and told them, with as calm a face as he could wear, that Mr. Tamms was absent; but on the morrow when he returned, all would be made good. But Charlie knew well that Phineas Tamms would never return to the house of Townley & Tamms. He sent a despatch for Mr. Townley, however, and waited; and worked over the weary figures, once more, till after midnight.

And this was how he spent the evening, while poor Mamie was watching for him, vainly, at the ball.

## CHAPTER XXXIII.

### THE DUVAL BALL.

THE evening of the great ball has come, at last; all the preparations have been made to the very last touch; the thousand orchids have arrived, that are to fade away their costly blooms in this one evening's pleasure; brought from forests of the Amazon, where, perhaps they saw no brighter colors and heard no louder chattering of bird or biped than they will to-night. And the fifty imported footmen have arrived also and cased their faultless calves in white silk stockings; and old Antoine is sitting in his private "library," smoking, with his ashcup upon the billiard-table that is the chief furniture of that apartment; and his daughter Mrs. De Witt, still sleeping in her dressing-room, or trying to; but her sleep is troubled with her gorgeous dreams.

But what are we to do? For it is only eight o'clock; just after dinner-time, and we cannot think of going yet. We have four long hours before us; where shall we go to spend the evening? We cannot call upon our friends; no one of them will be at home to-night. Gracie, to be sure, might be in; for her dress is but a simple one, and takes but little time of her one maid, who then hurries away to be an extra aid to Mamie; and Gracie will dress her hair herself, and she is now reading to her aunt and uncle. In a few moments she will go up to help Mamie, who is terribly excited, with cheeks all flushed already, and eyes of a feverish brightness. Mamie has such good reason, though, that we can hardly wonder: she has made up her mind that she will take the first opportunity to see Mr. Derwent, and give him his dismissal. Thus may she keep her word, and still be free to say—what shall she say, when she goes off with Mr. Townley, late in the evening, no doubt, to some fragrant nook, just beyond the range of voices, but murmurous with distant music and curtained with rare flowers? What the impulse of the moment bids her, no doubt;—she might refuse him—but it would be so nice to have the greatest ball of the century marked by one such scene. She means to be the leading "bud" at the ball, besides; and cannot spare all of those epochal moments, even for her lover.

John Haviland, too, is in; but he is sitting in his study with a pipe, and hard at work; at least, he is trying to be hard at work, that he may keep his mind at rest. He is on some political subject, writing an argument to serve with them who make laws for us at Albany; but it seems as hard to get them to take their functions seriously as it was with any Charles Stuart; moreover, the subject is a dry one, concerning only the ultimate welfare of indefinite numbers, and there is a small number, lobbyists, who are sure to meet him there with arguments *ad homines* and numbers much more definite. So his mind still turns from these abstractions to the girl he loves and whom he thinks that he shall lose forever, this same night. Nevertheless it is right that he shall do it; for he has lost all hope of Arthur, now.

But to Arthur himself, this is a red-letter day. Not only that he looks forward with some of Mamie's eagerness to the great ball, where he is to lead the cotillon—such homage is already paid his eminence and begins so soon to bore—he has more solid cause for his content than that. This day—this second of January—he has severed his subordinate connection with the house of Townley & Tamms, and gone in, as junior partner, with the new firm of Duval & De Witt, who, now that he has capital, naturally wishes to make more. Poor Arthur has little capital, and he has some debts; but he is allowed to put in what he has, and his experience, and may draw five thousand a year as a maximum, from the firm. On this, for the present, he can live quite comfortably; seeking, meanwhile, the other fruits of success, that in due time he may enjoy them, as his own.

It was pleasant to walk by the old shop, which he had entered almost as an office-boy, and see Charlie Townley, his former mentor, sitting there alone; looking a bit troubled, too, as Arthur thought. He had stopped in and smoked a cigar with him the day before; Tamms was not there, and Charlie had seemed distrait, and complained of having had to work all that New Year's day upon the balance-sheet.

It is nine o'clock now, but we have two or three hours yet to wait. If we have seen all the friends we care about who are invited, suppose we look in on some of our acquaintance who are not? There is James Starbuck, for instance; he is to be found in the little back apartment on Sixth Avenue, where he pretends that his sister still lives, though she does not, and he has not seen her since that day at the race. The name Rose Marie is yet on the door; and James has written many a letter, beseeching, imploring, perhaps. He does not like to supplicate; nor, perhaps, does Jenny like to be sermonized; and her pretty head is now full of envy that she can never go to the great Duval ball, which she has been reading of so much in the papers. And many another pretty girl has read of it in the papers, too, by many a comfortable fireside; though Wemyss perhaps would call it a middle-class one; and learned there were "high people" in this country, too. But James and his friends have been discussing it; and it seems to them an impudent taunt of the monopolist, flaunted in the face of suffering labor; so illogical are they. It happens that this festivity comes just about the end of the first century of actual American independence; and it is very certain, at least, that there have not been so many dollars spent on any jamboree—as Simpson calls it—of all that time before. But surely, the harvest of a century should be greater than a one year's crop in some new and oppressed colony? And the Duval fortune, made from a nation's hair-oil and cosmetics, and multiplied, when welded to the mace of capital, in a hundred corporations, has but grown in proportion.

But Starbuck is but telling them that these inert millions represent a greater tyranny than my lord duke of York's; and that the experiment of a republic has been tried for just a hundred years and failed. Starbuck is very bitter to-night and inclined to look upon things from their darkest side.

"Why," says he, "they have gone back like whipped curs to the very outward forms of the tyranny they broke away from."—(Starbuck has been educating himself lately, hoping that he might be fit company for his sister; and he spoke at all times much better English than does Mr. Tamms.) "It is as if they said, 'Yes, we have had our fling, and we broke away from lords and bishops and aristocracies and lords of the soil; and we were all wrong, and now we want again our powdered flunkies and our my lord this and that, and our coats-of-arms, and our daughters want to marry foreign princes, and our wives would like to be fast women of the court again, and our boys hunt foxes and have their poaching laws; and we ourselves would like to rule at Washington? Why, a man who owns a railroad is really a bigger, stronger lord than any feudal baron!"

"That's all very pretty; but we'd like to see a little less talk from you, an'm suthin' done," said Simpson, who had been drinking almost more than usual.

"Shut your mouth," said James. "You'll see something done before you're much older. For one,

I'm opposed to scarin' people much, before we're ready to really act and smash everything at once."

"That's damned fine talk, but you ain't boss, you know," sneered Simpson.

"Boss or not, I don't know as I've got any more stomach for one kind of a mastery than another—whether they call 'emselves reds and internationalists, or employers of labor! What do you suppose the G. M. G. wants anyhow? Fireworks—nothin' but fireworks."

"Well, but what's the use o' goin' so far?" said another man, pacifically. "We can take a job where we like—we've liberty, anyhow."

"Liberty!" cried James. "So's a horse his oats. They've got the mines, an' the mills, an' they fix the wages, an' we've got to live in the company's tenements, an' pay the company's rents, an' get up to the whistle, an' wash our daughters' faces when we're bid; and if we don't like it, the company'll import a lot of dirt-eating foreigners, but we've got to pay our rent, just the same. And all that these fellers, who ain't no better than we are, can have a good time and drink champagne at breakfast. I've had enough of republics and democracies; an' I tell you we don't want any kind of 'ocracy but just nothin' at all!"

"H—l!" snarled Simpson, who had listened with impatience to Starbuck's speech. "They ain't no different from what we are; you were a boss yourself until a few weeks ago, and then you sang a different tune." (It was true that Starbuck had lately been discharged, for his complicity in the mining strike.)

"You'd like ter be a swell, like the rest of 'em, and your sister's just the same."

Starbuck compressed his pale lips, and his mouth worked violently. "Don't you talk of my sister," said he.

"Naw," said Simpson, "we ain't to talk of your fine sister; and yet we all know that you're livin' here on what she makes outside—Eh?"

For Starbuck had thrown himself upon him with an open knife; and driven the blade well into his side. Simpson fell, and the others, clasping Starbuck by the body, sought to drag him away; but his right arm still was disengaged, clenching the open blade, and with it he was sawing viciously at Simpson's wrist.

Starbuck was the weakest man of all; but when he was at last torn away, the other's cries had ceased, and he was lying huddled in the pool of blood, with a hiccough in his pallid throat.

Starbuck stood looking at him, panting; while the others bent over him, and tried to lift him to the bed. "You'll swing for this night's work, Jem Starbuck," said one.

"I think not," said another. "The first dig didn't go very deep; and these flesh-wounds ain't no account. Get away from here, Jem, before the cops get wind of it."

And they pushed James Starbuck roughly, but with hands still friendly, out into the winter's night.

But it is after eleven o'clock; and now we must hurry, if we would be in time for the ball.

## CHAPTER XXXIV.

### THE DUVAL BALL, CONCLUDED.

HE carriage had been in waiting some half an hour; the coachman, who could not leave his horses, was swearing upon the box, while the footman sought the shelter of the area door; the deep snow which had begun the afternoon still lay heaped in chance places, while the rain, descending in straight lines, made scattered pools of slush and water, visible when they happened to reflect the wet shining of the corner lamp-post, at other times a perilous pit for horses' steps and men's.

But Flossie sat still in the rose light of her own and inmost room: her husband was away, and her quilted *sortie de bal* lay ready on the lounge beside her. Not softer it than her white shoulders; and even in the face their owner looked marvellously young for her age.

She rose and drew the satin cloak around her; it was of the very faintest, palest, wood-bud green, making strange harmony with her ashen hair; and she walked to the window and looked out into the inhospitable night. Then—and without the final glance at the mirror that all women are said to give—she rang the bell, and followed by her maid went down the stairs alone. The indoor servants, with huge umbrellas, helped her to the carriage—so silly was it, as Flossie had always told her husband, for the house to have no *porte-cochère*—and the carriage lurched off, through the heaps of yet white snow, careening and sinking in the pools of rain.

But Mrs. Gower's company is dull to-night; we may leave the ball with her, but we will not go. Her eyes are jaded with such sights; let us escort some brighter ones, and gayer spirits, and hearts more fresh to all impression. Such an one was Mamie's; and prettily encased it was, in her glove-like waist that seemed without a wrinkle and made of whitest kid, over which her shoulders peeped more snowy, and from which streamed a frothy train of rippling—illusion, do they call it? Gracie had been down some time, with the old people, when she rippled like the springtime, down the stairs, with her arch eyes dancing and her cheeks encarnadine. Gracie's beauty, to be sure, was greater still; only somehow, you did not look at it at first; it was but part of her, like the sky of some fair country.

Mr. and Mrs. Livingstone looked down on Mamie, though, with the happy pride of being parents to such a poem; they were much too old to go to balls, and so some married cousin had been found to matronize them. Miss Brevier alone noted Mamie's heightened color and evident excitement; but thought it due to her first ball alone; and the old people kissed her and complimented her, and gave her obsolete advice, and sent her off so proudly—to the choice, as some might say, of two adventurers.

Gracie and Mamie came down and took their first timid look at the ball from a sort of ante-room, that was one of the ball-rooms and was yet so near the dressing-room as to grant a hesitating woman *locus pœnitentiæ*, and not commit her finally to the floor. That first glance at the ball-room; tell me whom you see in it, and whom you don't see, and I can tell you, gipsy-like, much of those bodies whose orbits bode entanglement to yours. Thus it chanced that Gracie saw Haviland and Arthur; and both saw Mrs. Gower; and Mamie noted that she did not see either Charlie Townley or Mr. Derwent. I fancy that none of our three heroines will tell us much about the party, to-night—at least, we shall learn rather what people said than how they looked and what they wore—but I may tell the reader confidentially that were it not for this, we had not come. For may he not read, in to-morrow's papers, all about the flowers, and the servants, and the music, and the wines—aye, and the people who came, and how they looked, and all that may be known about the women's dresses?

Both fell to indifferent cavaliers, at first; that is, Mamie to John Haviland, with whom she had no sympathy, and Gracie to Mr. Kill Van Kull, who, being a gentleman, though a wicked one, had the grace most reverently to like her.

John stood with Mamie in the first or outer room,

wishing to be with her, yet knowing not exactly what to say. He could not feed this young butterfly on thought; and yet she was too bright for common-places; and then, he knew her yet so slightly! And indeed she had not fluttered through a season yet; and butterflies take knowing best in autumn. So Mamie thought him dull; and, all the time, that was in his mind which had made her start to hear. John's interest was but vicarious, yet, through Gracie's—and he was well assured that Charlie would not come. But we old fellows of a dozen winters, who talk to girls at their first ball—what chance have our stale cynicisms with the pretty ear by our side, when its pretty eyes companions are looking for that young fellow with the incipient mustache, who means shortly to tell her (when our Heaviness has only left her)—that she is the only person in all his long life long that he has really ever loved. Throwing over at once his nurse and his governess, as we may, with our caustic wit, remark; and we go to Mrs. Gower; she will not repulse us; she will understand us, and make our seasoned hearts beat fast again.

So, after John has danced once with Mamie, she happens to feel tired before a certain dark corner; and there Lionel Derwent is standing alone, torturing his tawny mustache. He has to speak to her; and then it happens that these two drop aside from the whirling circle—and Haviland is left alone upon its brink. He watches it for a minute, as Dante did Francesca's. It is a smaller circle; it is not "mute of any light," nor does Minos stand there "*orribilmente*," and grin—unless fat old Tony Duval may do duty for the same, with his unctuous swarthy face, like some head-waiter on the boulevard—but how much "*più dolor*"—or less *dolor*—it girdles than the outer world, is John then wondering. And there he saw "*Semiramìs, di cui si legge*—" many things, no doubt, and triumphant young Mrs. De Witt, Anadyomene; and Lady X., and the Countess of Z., and "*Cleopatràs lussuriosa*," and Mrs. Flossie Gower; "*Elena vidi—e 'l grande Achille—Paris, Tristano, e più di mille*—" and borne before, most light in all the waltz, Miss Farnum with Van Kull. She caught his eye one moment, as she floated by, and his own fell.

But Derwent gave Miss Livingstone his arm, and went—or suffered himself to be led by her—to a place of fragrant flowers and broad shadowy leaves. It was quite what Mamie had imagined; and yet she blushed to feel how pale she was, and then felt all the color leave again as her heart beat; and then blushed again to feel it beat so near his strong arm. The poets have told you how a maiden's color comes and goes—now you understand the process, quite in the modern manner.

She had no idea the feeling she would have would be like this, and almost felt the inclination to tears again; but the inspiring strains of a waltz that came through the heavy curtains helped her out just then, as does a fiddle to a tragedy-scene in a New York theatre. So she gave him his dismissal with much courage; and was relieved to find that Derwent neither fumed nor fainted.

Meantime John Haviland, growing tired of the "*schiera piena*" in the ball-room, had left his place and wandered from the room, before Miss Farnum in her turn came round again. Was it lack of tact that made him enter the conservatory—where so short a time before Miss Livingstone and Lionel had gone? Derwent looked up at once and saw him; but Mamie gave a little start that showed her freshness at this sort of thing. "I hope I don't interrupt an important conversation" said Haviland.

"Not at all; we were talking of trifles," answered Derwent, placidly. "Let's go down to supper." Now for a man who has just had his heart broken to evince a desire for supper, was a thing so new to all Mamie's novel-reading experience that she answered with some angry humor that she was not hungry. "Mr. Haviland can get me an ice, if he likes," she added. Just then, Gracie Holyoke came in; and it was poor John's heart's turn to beat. "I will sit here with Grac—with Miss Holyoke," added Mamie; and John must needs go get the ice, while Lionel Derwent stayed behind. He talked to Gracie, though; while Mamie was wild to tell her she had so well fulfilled her promise. So she passed the time by looking about the adjacent ball-room for Charlie Townley. Strange to say, she had not yet seen him anywhere. Well, there was time enough; she rather liked to have the whole ball gone through with, first. Perhaps she was foolish to get engaged, at her very first ball. She would give him his dismissal too; that would make two in one evening! It was outrageous in him to leave her to herself all through the evening, even at supper-time, that most favored time of all! Nay, I fear me, master Charles would have had but an easy victory, had he made assault just then.

But Charlie she did not see in any of the rooms; and some male individual in a white waistcoat and catseye stud, who took her through the rooms and down to supper, even told her that he had not come.

Impossible! Had he not sent her those most particular and private flowers that she wore, with meaning glances when he asked her of her dress and time? Had he not as good as told her, once before, when he had kissed her—Poor Mamie blushed with shame, while her heart pulsed quick with fear, and her eyes glistened with anger—Come, Charlie, come quick; and garner in your lovely conquest, ere it be too late! —But no Charlie comes through all that ball; and Mamie dances feverishly with anybody, and flirts aimlessly with Howland Starbuck, and is clever, witty, bright-eyed, radiant, irresistible—and then goes to Mrs. F——, the chaperone, with stories of a headache, and asking when she is going home.

When John comes back to the little room with the ice, Mamie who sent him for it has gone, and Gracie Holyoke and Derwent too. So he sate him down, disconsolate, amid the bed of orchids, screened by quite a jungle of banana palms; so poor, so clumsy a pretence of happiness did all this seem to him! The strains of the shallow music came to him from the distant ball-room; it was the waltz-tune that was the rage that winter,—

"Oh, lo-ove for a week—(*tum, tum; rum, tim, tum!*)
"A year, a day, (*tum tum; rum, tum, tum!*)
"But alas for the lo-ove that bi-i-deth alway! (*tum, tum; rum, tim, tum!*)

John tried to deafen his ears to the music, which went on despite him, like the pettiness of life. He had had but one full look at Gracie Holyoke that night; and that had told him nothing.

A stifling hot-house scent was in the little room, and John had started up to leave it when there was a rustling in the door-way and Kitty Farnum stood before him alone.

She had been selected to take part in the spectacle of the evening, the much-envied fancy-dress minuet, after supper, that was to open the cotillon; and she wore the rich red brocades of a Louis Quinze court-dress, her dense hair powdered white, and from this mass of blazing color rose haughtily the regal neck and head, and the proud shoulders, and beneath the white masses of her hair her eyes burned deeply, like two violet stars. A sort of hush of admiration had attended her wherever she went that evening; and Haviland had heard men call her the beauty of the ball.

Miss Farnum stood silent for a moment, playing with a scarlet orchid that was most conspicuous of all among them; a noble figure, the very picture of a duchess; and Haviland, who had risen at her entrance, facing her more humbly, and yet like a gentleman, too.

"Mr. Haviland—my life must be settled to-night, one way or another: *I* am weary of it. You once were kind enough to take some interest in me—am I right in supposing that I had a friend in you?"

"Yes," said John. There was an infinite respect and pity in his tone; he fancied that he knew what had happened.

"Lord Birmingham has just asked me to become his wife. Am I right in thinking that you—do not wish to be my husband?"

"Yes," said John, again. "But oh, Miss Farnum—when we talked of this upon the coaching-party, you did not——"

Miss Farnum shook her head slightly, as if to wave aside her own case from the question.

"That you do care for Miss Holyoke?"

"Yes," said he, without hesitating; but more softly still.

"You have chosen nobly, Mr. Haviland." She said it simply and a little sadly; and then turned to go.

John grasped her hand and detained it for but one second in his own. "I shall never win her," said he. "And oh, Miss Farnum——"

"No word more," said the other; and then, gayly, "I have better hopes. Look at me—and see—and see how easy it is to win a woman!" And with a ripple of light laughter, she was gone.

John sank back to his seat, his head, already a little gray, resting on his hand. Kitty Farnum's was the nature he had admired most of almost any he had ever seen: her soul was individual, cast in that heroic mould that almost seems forgotten in these days of good nature, of average adaptability. And yet not one single air of inspiration, nor one ray of sympathy nor sunlight that came from higher than the city's dust had fallen on the lot of this rich flower. Of all humanity, from her vulgar mother to the silly partners of her dances, he alone had said one word of truth to her; and in reward she had given him her heart! She, capable of being any heroine of all the full world's history; and not one red-cross knight was there to see and save her, nor any man with soul of strength enough to mate with hers; but only this titled barbarian, who saw the outside of her person and was pleased.

But the waltz-music still came through the fragrant fall of flowers that screened this eremite from the loud-laughing world; and the night was getting on. He felt now as if under pledge to lay his heart that night at Gracie's feet; and went in search of her.

He found her, sitting with Mamie Livingstone, who was out of humor and who would not dance; she was silent, with flushed face and dewy eyes, looking like some pouting, pretty maid of Greuze. They spoke together for some minutes; and then wise Lionel Derwent came up and took Miss Mamie off.

John led Gracie to the deep embrasure of a window; below them, on the polished floor, the famous minuet was forming; and all the world looked on expectant. John looked grimly on: he never thought to have said such words in a ball-room. His very hopelessness gave him courage to speak his deepest heart; and it was without a change of manner when he spoke—at last.

She had been speaking sorrowfully of Mamie; you know the strange confidence that was between these two. "I fear that she is disappointed that Mr. Townley has not come. Tell me frankly, Mr. Haviland—do you think there is anything really wrong about him? Do you think that he could make Mamie happy? She will be so alone in the world, I am afraid, before very long."

What could John say? There is a law that even the meanest men abide, to speak no harm of each other to the other sex. He hesitated. "I think you need have no fear of Mr. Townley, now," he said, at last. Derwent had told him of the day in Wall Street.

Gracie turned her dear eyes full on his; and then the barriers of his heart broke down. "But I must speak selfishly, Miss Holyoke. I love you with all my heart—for all my life."

The words had come so naturally, that they had passed among the spoken words of memory, and ceased—before Gracie started and the color left her cheeks. She had not dreamed of this; she had not kept, herself, the lesson she had given Mamie; and then she blamed herself for having been too much wrapped up in her own heart history. "O Mr. Haviland," she said; "forgive me; I never thought of this."

She was crying; John's voice was husky, and he did not trust himself to speak, but looked across the brilliant room. The minuet was being danced; and just in front was Kitty Farnum, looking as if radiant with the triumph of the night. She was walking the minuet with Arthur Holyoke; who was brilliant in a velvet court-dress, with a sparkling sword; and opposite was Birmingham, dancing with Mrs. De Witt, but with eyes for her alone. The other figures in the dance were Mrs. Malgam, Mrs. Levison-Gower, Killian Van Kull and Caryl Wemyss.

John turned his eyes to hers again. "You care for Arthur?"

Many women would have thought he had no right to ask the question; but Gracie's was too true a life for this.

"Yes," she said, clearly.

"Forgive me," answered John, humbly. And Gracie knew that he was still her friend; and Arthur's too.

And so, no more was said between them; and when the minuet was finished, Gracie and poor Mamie went home together and Lionel Derwent went away with John. Mamie tore the flower from her breast, and threw herself upon her bed in a burst of tears; and Gracie sat with her till the streaks of dawn appeared.

. . . . . . .

But Flossie and Kitty Farnum still danced on, untired; and all men were divided which of these had been the queen of the famous ball. Already had the business of the work-day world begun when Flossie took her leave, and went back to the dressing-room, and put on her satin cloak, and came down the grand staircase, looking strangely brilliant, younger than ever, people said, with her blazing diamonds and not one ribbon out of place about her perfect dress. She went down the carpeted pavilion, Caryl Wemyss putting the ermine *sortie de bal* with careful touch about her shoulders.

No one but a policeman and a little crowd of street boys saw them go, as she got quickly into Caryl Wemyss's carriage and drove off.

## CHAPTER XXXV.

### SORTIE DU BAL.

HE rain, that had come after the snow, had ceased in its turn, blown clear, like some light curtain, by a blast of northwest wind. Mr. Wemyss, as he entered the carriage, had ventured to lift her hand once to his lips; and then they both sat silent, Flossie looking thoughtfully out of the carriage window, her companion on the front seat looking at her.

It was already freezing; for the horses dragged them heavily through the crackling snow; and Flossie could see that the pools of water in the street were already needle-pointed with the forming ice. As they passed the cross-streets, she noticed a ruddy reflection on the face of these. "Can that be dawn already?" She let down the window; and, looking out, saw all the east a lowering, lurid red.

"I do not think so," said Mr. Wemyss. "'Tis hardly six o'clock. It must be some great fire at Brooklyn, or at Williamsburgh."

They stopped at Mrs. Gower's house; and requesting, or rather, ordering, Mr. Wemyss to stay in the carriage, she ran lightly up the steps and let herself in. All the servants had gone to bed, by Mrs. Gower's orders; save Justine, her maid, who was sitting waiting, with one candle, in the hall.

"Is everything ready, Justine?"

"Oui, madame," said the maid; who had been told that her mistress was about to make a sudden trip to Boston, and had discreetly asked no unnecessary questions; her perquisites had been very handsome lately.

Flossie went up to her room, the maid attending her; and laid aside her ball-dress and her diamonds. Then she had a woman's humor; and notwithstanding that Mr. Wemyss was waiting cold outside, she threw the satin cloak once more over her bare shoulders and wandered, with a lighted candle, all through the house. She went into the great ball-room which seemed gaunt and bare; then into the dark dining-room with its carved oak wood and its array of armor and of silver plate; then into the parlors where she had held her first reception—how well she remembered it, and her triumph over the great ladies Van Kull and the fine ladies Brevier!—and last to the little suite of rooms which she had occupied when first she came back from her wedding-journey. Poor Lucie! She wondered if he would really mind much.

When she got back to the great apartment she occupied now, the gray dawn was stealing in through the huge windows and the cold of the change of weather was already in the house. She shivered; and hastened to get dressed. Justine was all ready with a quiet travelling-dress, into which she quickly slipped her girlish figure. She had a moment's scruple whether she should take away the diamonds—a *rivière* that Lucie Gower had given her when they were married. But Flossie Gower had far too logical a mind to strain at gnats when she was swallowing a camel; she hastily thrust them in her bosom, and giving the solitary candle to Justine, bade her lead the way down the stairs. This time she wasted no parting looks; after all, the house was hers, though she would leave it to Lucie for a while, for form's sake.

It was already quite light in the street, and Mr. Wemyss was huddled in one corner of the carriage and chattering with cold. He made no reproach, however; and this time he got in beside her, and Justine took the front seat.

"Where are we going?" said Mrs. Gower to him.

"I thought perhaps you would come—I have a little breakfast ready in my rooms—the train does not go till eight." He spoke, for the first time we have heard him, with some shadow of embarrassment. "I thought it would be less public," he explained.

"As you like," said Flossie, indifferently. What did it matter? Her bonnet must yet be thrown over higher wind-mills than was this.

They drove across the town in silence. Flossie, at least, had done many things in her life and not known the sickly shadow of repentance yet; what Mr. Wemyss's thoughts were I cannot say. Justine alone, indeed, was repenting—that she had not known of this before she left the house, and acted on that knowledge. "*Que de choses j'aurais pu prendre avec!*" she thought.

"When do we sail?" asked Flossie, languidly.

"To-morrow noon," answered Mr. Wemyss. "The Boston steamer is much the best for us; particularly at this season of the year. They go almost empty, and are not crowded with commercial travellers."

Mrs. Gower's lip curled slightly: whether at Mr. Wemyss's refined exclusiveness or for some other reason, we dare not say. And the carriage stopped before his lodgings.

Mr. Wemyss got out, and helped his Europa to alight. "You may come up, Justine," said Flossie to the maid, who had retained her seat demurely.

Mr. Wemyss led the way to his rooms and Flossie looked about her curiously. The apartment was full of old china, books, and rare bronzes that showed its owner's cultivated tastes; a sort of studio led off from the dining-room, and in it were many samples of Mr. Wemyss's art; most prominent among them a large portrait of Flossie Gower herself, painted from memory, and not over good as a likeness. Flossie remarked upon it; and Mr. Wemyss made some speech about not needing the shrine now that the divinity was there. And as he said it, Justine not having gone into the studio with them, he made bold to clasp her in his arms. Flossie repelled him; and with some muttered words about getting a cup of coffee for her, he left the room; not quite so gracefully as usual.

Flossie walked to the window and looked out. The room was very high; and the whole cityful of brick roofs and spires and factory chimneys lay brooding in their own foul breath of smoke. Flossie had a momentary feeling that the climax of her life had fallen beneath her expectation, like the rest.—Far off, on either side, a clearer stratum of air marked the course of the two rivers; and to the eastward were some saffron streaks of winter morning. These faded to the left, in an ominous brown cloud of smoke, beneath which still, in the distance, licked some silent tongues of fire.

"It must have been a terrible fire," said Wemyss's voice behind her carelessly. "But the breakfast is ready, such as it is; will you not come, dearest?"

Flossie went back with him, and found a table spread with coffee, cold partridges, and grapes. Justine remained there, for propriety's sake. In a few minutes they were ready; and going down, she found another carriage waiting. Wemyss gave his orders, and they drove to the railroad station. It looked curiously common-place and familiar; it might have been the most respectable of quiet journeys! Flossie abhorred respectability.

Mr. Wemyss had a compartment ready in the car, with all imaginable ordinary luxuries of travel; he even got a bundle of the morning papers, which Flossie did not read. She was tired of the sight of an American newspaper, and never wished to look at one again.

Wemyss looked a little furtively about the platforms and then walked through the train; and came back and told her there was no one that they knew on board. Flossie would not have cared much if there had been.

A boy came through, crying the last new novels. Flossie shook her head. What were such insipid stories to the drama of her life? Mr. Wemyss carefully closed the door, and began to make himself agreeable, much as he might have done at a party, except that he talked more tenderly. Would the train never start? She yawned a little. For a moment, she half wished it had been Kill Van Kull.

At last a bell sounded, and the train rumbled slowly out of the station.

# CHAPTER XXXVI.

## THE NIGHT AT THE WORKS.

HEN Jem Starbuck, that evening, had been thrust out by his friends, and the door he heard slammed and bolted behind him, he found himself upon Sixth Avenue, at midnight of a night so inclement that even that thoroughfare was almost deserted. The trains of the elevated railway went thundering over his head, but the floor of the street was checkered with the drifts of wet snow and the pools of water, in which the mirrored gaslights glimmered a warning to the unwary step.

The rain had at this time stopped; it was the hour's lull before the downrush of the clearing northwester; and the flooded gutters still ran riotously and poured into the sewer-gates with a roaring that was audible a block or more away.

Starbuck walked some streets without conscious object. His heart beat violently with the struggle still, and he felt sick and faint with the passion of his anger. Remorse he had none; but he was ashamed at having gone so far; at having held himself in no better control. Yet why had Simpson dared to talk to him? "Damn the fool, I wish I'd killed him," thought James.

He spoke the words aloud; and, as he did so, came to a street corner; the crossing was exceptionally deep with melted snow, and on the other corner stood a policeman. Starbuck became conscious that he still held the bloody knife; there was a sewer-opening below him, and he threw it in. The rush of water was so great that it was gulped down without a sound, disappearing instantly in the turbid vortex. James looked after it a moment, moodily; he had little fear that he was in any danger for his deed of that night; beyond doubt, the fellow was not mortally wounded; and he would not dare to complain on his own account, and none of their friends would ever peach.

He hesitated some moments; then, with the decisive step of a man who has made up his mind, he turned and crossed Sixth Avenue. There was a barroom over the way, brilliant with a red electric light; he entered it, and called for a twenty-five cent cigar and a glass of whiskey. He was unused to drinking spirits; and the sharp liquor made him shudder as he swallowed it; but not with cold or fear. The intellectual predominated over the physical in his nature: such organisms are cowardly before immediate physical pain or contest, but shrink at nothing else. But one of his affectations had been to smoke cigars instead of pipes; his was a nature nervous as any scholar's; and he lit the black havana and went out again, taking his way along Thirty-second Street.

Fifth Avenue was less deserted than Sixth; it was full of carriages going to and from the ball. It was about the hour when Flossie broke off her reverie in her boudoir and, ringing for her carriage, walked to her window and looked out. James Starbuck may have seen the rose light that streamed from her window; in fact, he did, and marked the brilliancy of this and all the great houses on the Avenue, with an imprecation on them for it; but he did not know Flossie Gower's house, nor much of her, save that she almost owned the oil works over at Williamsburgh. But he stopped a moment, and looked up and down the fine street; it was going to be colder, and he foresaw that the weather would be terrible before dawn, though the ladies, well cottoned in their carriages, would give no thought to it. But the business he was on was not so safe for him at any other time; and he buttoned his overcoat about him and walked rapidly down the side street, just as Mrs. Gower's carriage drove up at her front door.

He soon got beyond the respectable streets, the level even rows of brown-stone houses standing shoulder to shoulder like well-drilled servants in a livery; the shops began, and the iron-balconied tenements, and the noise and sense of much humanity. The many sins of the pavement were charitably hidden in the snow; but even then there was a smell about the neighborhood that would have nauseated Mrs. Gower; and even in the middle of the night there was noise of living, and an undertone of working steam, throbbing still, among the sleeping places of its human fellow-laborers. Nor were they all asleep; here and there a lighted window, and what we needs must term a sound of revelry, showed that some of these, too, like their Fifth Avenue superiors, were wakeful to the pleasures of the night.

But the elevated trains had ceased running, as Starbuck crossed Third Avenue: the toiling places of the human workmen, at least, were stilled, and these were not needed to take them to and from their benches in the social galley. Mankind—except indeed the policemen or other watchers who had to see that mankind did no mischief while it rested—was not at work.

Starbuck threaded his way through the streets along the river. The forges, to be sure, were glowing brightly; for Iron gives his servants no rest; Vulcan is a lord who knows no Sabbath; he compels, unlike kindly Ceres, from eve till dewy morn, from seed to harvest. Starbuck came to the wharves, heaped up with coal mountains, built over with iron prisons for the gas; he looked about him, cautiously, for he was physically a coward and afraid of footpads, of the lawless gangs of roughs that infest the wharves. He had struck across the city too directly, instead of walking up Fifth Avenue, as he should have done, where he felt safe. He started once or twice in alarm, and his heart took to palpitating again, as he saw a dark figure among the wharves; but it would be only a policeman or a watchman, and he breathed more freely; and at last he reached the ferry in safety.

He took a seat in one corner of the ladies' cabin, pulling his coat-collar up over his face. The boat was not full; but there were a number of people still out, returning from supper after the theatres. The warm weather they had had was breaking up the ice in the Sound; and the paddles of the steamer went crashing and grinding through the broken floes. Several times the wheels stopped, as if the pilot saw a field of ice too large to be crushed through. At last, the clanking of the chains told Starbuck they had reached the dock upon the Brooklyn side.

He waited until all the other passengers had gone ashore. The night had grown much colder; and the freezing snow and water crackled beneath his feet. On this side the river, however, the streets were darker, and quite deserted; and not one lighted window broke the high brick housewalls that closed about him on either side.

The effect of the unaccustomed dram of spirit had quite left him by this time; he threw open his coat for a moment, to light another cigar; and then buttoned it tight about him, cursing the cold. He had walked some half a mile or so, without meeting a living being, and had got beyond the region of the tenements, and in the manufacturing district of the city. Already he noticed the strong smell of oil, borne backward through the city by the northwest wind. His way led downward to the wharves; and he stopped before the familiar iron gate. He peered through it; he knew it to be the watchman's station, or rather that of one watchman: there were two more down by the river side, whence the greatest danger was always apprehended. But he only saw the acres of tanks and stagings and pyramids of empty barrels, and beyond them, just visible, the high forest of masts tapering into the black sky, where, in the west, a few stars were already struggling out.

It was evident that the watchman, fearing, on such a night, no enemy but winter and rough weather, had sought some shelter; but Starbuck did not deem it wise to venture openly through the gate. He skirted the high fence around toward the river, where he knew there was a sort of swinging hatchway in the wooden wall; it was kept fastened only by an ordinary dropping latch inside, and this by inserting a length of wire in the crack, he easily lifted.

When he was fairly inside the yard, he sat down for a moment, smoking, and looked about him. The nearest lights were across the river or on the shipping in the stream; but the ground was white with snow, and the huge storage-tanks rose up about him, visible by their very blackness, like rocks at night in foaming water.

He got up, still smoking, but screening the cigar light in the hollow of his hand, and went toward the water. A double bank of the petroleum ships lay along the pier; but all was silent on board of them, the watch, if watch was kept while they were moored, having evidently followed the example of the watchman at the outer gate. Thus he made his way, slowly, to the end of the pier, losing his footing now and then in a snowdrift, or slipping suddenly into one of the great pits full of freezing water that had collected in the hollows of the ground. No vessels lay across the end of the pier, such mooring being forbidden; and it was unencumbered except by the great iron letters that stretched across it——THE SILAS STARBUCK OIL COMPANY. Starbuck leaned across the rod that supported the first letter S, and reflected. It was a curious fact that the identity of the name had never struck him particularly before; he knew nothing of old Silas Starbuck, nor who he was, nor whence he had come, nor even that Mrs. Levison-Gower had been his daughter. Carefully he walked around the end of the wharves; thousands of men were at work there by day; but at night a more lonely place it would be hard to find, and he met no one.

At last, it seemed as if the object of this unusual journey were satisfied; and he began to retrace his steps toward the town. As he passed the first piles of barrels, he stopped and looked at them again; then picking up a stick, he struck one or two of them a smart blow. They were empty, and it rang hollow. He pushed the stick among them and between them to the ground; the snow that had fallen upon them had melted, and the lowest tier were half submerged in a pool of water. Then he left them and went on to the receiving-house.

Opposite him, and a few hundred yards to the right, were the stills; lofty iron towers, under which a dull glow showed that the furnaces were still doing their work. When he had left Steam City, the strike was complete; but the oil still ran through the pipe-lines, and stokers had still been found to feed these refining fires. He turned sharp to the left; and the dull light was soon hidden behind the storage-tanks.

There was sure to be a watcher in the "tail-house," if the stills were at work, to mark the runs of oil; and Starbuck walked more slowly. But his steps were muffled in the drifts of snow; moreover, he was close by the blower, and the rapid whirling of the iron fans would drown all other noise. When he got to the steps that led to the door of the tail-house, there were fresh foot-prints in the snow; and he ascended cautiously until his head was at the level of the window and then looked in. The light inside came from a small tubular stove of ridged iron, white-hot; and by its comfortable warmth a man sat in an old armchair, his head upon his breast, asleep. Starbuck studied his features for a few seconds and then opened the door and entered.

"Who is it?" cried the man, starting up.

"It's only I, Ned," answered Starbuck. "Don't be so nervous."

"Oh, is that all," returned the other. "I was afraid it might be some feller come to do a mischief," he added, with a grin.

"I wanted to make sure it was your watch," said James. "You don't keep a good one—if anything happens to-night I shall have to report you."

"The h—l you will," laughed the other.

"I'm pretty sure I heard a boat land, down by the end of the pier."

"No?" said the other.

"I did indeed," added Starbuck. "I wish you'd go down and see. I got rumors of a plot in town, and came over to warn you."

"No?" said the other, again. "Did ye though? And suppose I'm kilt—I'm to come back and tell yer, I suppose? Why don't you come along yourself?"

"I want to take a turn by the spraying-house first," answered James. "I'll join you there in a minute—on the wharf, I mean." And as he spoke, Starbuck left the little cabin and went down the steps.

"It 'ud be awk'ard if any fellow were to happen in here while we're both gone, wouldn't it?" he called out; but Starbuck was already out of hearing, threading his way through the darkness to the spraying-house; the fountain not playing now, at night, when there was no sun to brighten it, and the great well of oil lying still and sleeping, warmed by the steam-pipes that were coiled, like warm-blooded serpents, in its depths.

The man called Ned watched him go, the grin that had accompanied his last remark quickly fading on his face; then, wrapping his overcoats around him, he, too, went out and walked away with rapid steps through the dark yard.

He left the door of the tail-house open behind him; and when, in a few minutes, James Starbuck returned, he found the place already cold. He shut the door to and sat down; the cigar in his mouth had gone out and he opened the door of the stove with an old iron rod to stir the fire and get a bit of live coal for a light. But he had no tongs; and indeed the live coal seemed unnecessary, as he pulled out quite a bundle of matches from his pocket. He let the glowing coals lie unheeded on the floor, and looked at his watch by the light of the open stove-door. It was three o'clock. And he cowered back in the chair, shivering.

It seemed so small a thing to do, after all! His lip curled with scorn as he thought of his simple-minded associates and how great a thing they made of it. It would fill perhaps a column in the morrow's paper—about as much space, perhaps, as might be allotted to the Duval ball. Yet such things scared the stupid public; and they encouraged his party, much as a boy is made proud by the loud report of his first toy-cannon. His own ideas went so far beyond, that he regarded it as little more than the bow-chaser some red rover fires across the bow of a fat merchantman, by way of preliminary parley. He was tired, too; and the earlier events of the night had been exciting.

However, he made an effort, and shook himself together. Time was going. He got up and went to the runs. There were the two glass-covered channels, side by side; and both were running oil. Outside the little shed they entered two long wooden boxes or troughs, supported on trestle-work, and running several hundred feet in a downward inclination to the receiving-tanks, whence they were in turn conducted to the spraying-house, a quarter of a mile away.

James Starbuck lifted up the iron rod he had used to poke the fire, and brought it down with a crushing blow over the glass-topped runnels. Then he struck a match across the stove, and standing in the doorway, leaned over and touched the blue flame to the edge of the running oil.

For some reason it did not catch; and he tried another match. This he fairly dropped into the oil; but with no better success, as the feeble flame was put out instantly. "Damn the thing," said he to himself; and lighting another match, he waited until the flame was fairly burning, and looked at the oil.

The little runnel he had touched, partly choked with broken bits of glass, was full of a thick dark liquid, yellowish in color, but blue with numerous big globules of water. It was almost the last run, too crude or too impure to take fire at a spark. He looked at the other; and in it he recognized the shining stream, and the strange metallic lustre of the naphtha's flow.

He took a small shovelful of red-hot coals from the little stove, and got well out the doorway with it, standing down as many steps as he could. For this was the light surface oil, taking fire at a spark, more quick and dangerous than the cruder average. And with a careful aim, he sent a handful of the burning coals into the now open trough.

Even with the care that he had used, the first blast of flame was greater than he had thought possible; and he was hurled by the outward rush of air, half-blinded, down the remaining steps of the ladder, and fell into the deep snow. He ran back a few steps and looked up. Already the shed was on fire, and the burning oil, running from it in the trough, was spurting into jets of flame upon the trestle-work. Though wet with rain, this structure, so long soaked with oil, was taking fire rapidly. But there had been little noise as yet, and no signs of an alarm. He ran back some distance, and took refuge beside a brick storehouse, behind a pile of empty barrels.

He looked at his watch; it was a quarter past the hour; and for once, whether from his running or some other reason, his heart beat quickly. He paid no attention to the flaming trestle, but looked in the direction of the spraying-house that he had left upon the stroke of three. For he had left in the spraying-house a fifteen-minute fuse.

And, as he stood there, watch in hand, the whole earth shook beneath him; and with a noise that was more terrible than loud the silence of the city's night was broken; and the iron roof of the spraying-house was hurled to heaven on a pillow of yellow fire. And Starbuck crouched behind his solid wall and screamed aloud.

It seemed many minutes before he heard the crash and rattle of the falling plates of iron. Then a flood of blazing oil poured forth, and ran in all directions, mixing with the pools of melted snow. Already the trestle was a roaring mass of flame; the woodwork about the receiving tanks caught one after the other; and Starbuck ran wildly to his distant gate in the fence and cowered there, behind a pile of wornout iron. He heard far off the shrieks of the sleeping watchmen, and then hoarse shouting from the city. Then, like some titanic minute-guns, the great tanks exploded, one after one, in majestic sequence; and the stars of the sky were veiled in fires of the nether world.

Then came the clang of bells in distant towers, and the shriller rattle of the fire-engines, and shouts of frightened men. In brief time he heard them crying at the outer gate, and saw them pouring into the yard, swarming over the high fence, thousand upon thousand of them; but the pouring oil now flowed steadily, in flaming streams, and cut them off as with a sword of fire from the enclosure; he could see them standing silent on the hither side, in motionless throngs, gazing with pallid faces at the world of fire.

He heard, too, the shouts of the Norwegian sailors in their ships along the wharves; the yellow flood flowed steadily toward them, its burning stream melting the snow and riding faster on the water's surface in great blazing pools. One fire-river had already reached the end of the wharf, and fell over it, in a cascade of flame, through the iron colossal letters to the icy river. The tide took it rapidly down among the ships; the first was now flaming, from the bowsprit up the foremast, licking the tar and oakum from the iron rod. He heard the groups of sailors, in a panic rush behind him where he sat; others stayed at their posts and worked like demons, with capstans and cables, to warp their vessels beyond the reach of danger. The city fire-boat had come; and the burning oil-ship was cut adrift and dropped down the river, the fire-engines of the steamer playing on it vainly; in a few seconds, with a loud explosion, it was shattered to the water's edge. The very river was blazing like a crater's mouth with patches of the burning oil; and now, last of all, the huge storage tanks, each holding its hundreds of tons, were scattered into seas of burning gas. No nook or cranny of the great yard but was lit with yellow light, intenser, vivider than the sun's; the sky above was like a molten plate of copper, touched with swarms of scarlet sparks; and only beyond the river, above the red-walled houses, were the cold pale streaks of dawn.

James went boldly out, mingling among the maddened crowd. His breath had returned; and a faint smile was on his lips as he took his way slowly back through the now thronged streets to the river. His quickened blood poured sluggishly again; and his mind was busy with thought. Do serpents pant in the heat of conflict; or does their blood turn warm when they have withdrawn the sting? He had, perhaps, a faint sense of gratified power; but the mere destruction of one piece of property was, after all, so small a thing!

While he was crossing the ferry he looked up the river at the flaming world that he had made; it was a fine spectacle, and he watched it as calmly, as dispassionately, as Flossie Gower had done, when, not knowing that it was her fortune that had gone, she saw it burn from Mr. Wemyss's window.

## CHAPTER XXXVII.

### THE OLDEST MEMBER.

THE following day, early in the afternoon, Lionel Derwent walked into the Columbian Club. It was a place that he did not usually frequent, though he had a stranger's membership; but we have already learned that Derwent was most usually to be found in most unusual places. No one was in the morning-room but old Mr. Livingstone; he was sitting in his accustomed armchair by the window, a chair in which he had a right of property between the hours of three and five in the afternoon that all the club respected. Mr. Livingstone did not notice Derwent when he entered; perhaps because he was growing very old and his sight and hearing were defective. His eyes were fixed upon an empty chair in front of him and he seemed to be lost in thought. Derwent took up a newspaper and sat down in another corner of the room.

We are fond of saying in New York that life there moves so rapidly that the morning paper is already stale at three. Hence, have we no Homers; who sing some ten years' action and take a lifetime for it. But to Derwent, the newspapers' deeds were stale even in the doing: humanity at three o'clock was like humanity at nine. Two young men entered, fresh and rosy, with camelias in their coats; they were of those who toil not, neither spin.

"Do you know, they say that Townley & Tamms have failed?"

"So I hear. Great ball, last night."

"Ugh—I'm sleepy yet."

Derwent looked back to his paper. Mr. Livingstone did not appear to have heard this colloquy, but was sitting idly as if dozing. In the financial column Derwent found, at last, a simple paragraph:

"Owing to the illness of Mr. Phineas Tamms and the temporary absence of the senior partner, the house of Townley & Tamms are reported as temporarily unable to meet their obligations. The rumor created much excitement at the close, and several thousand shares of Allegheny Central were sold for them under the rule. This is believed to account for the sudden weakness in that stock, which was particularly strong at the morning board. We are assured that the difficulty is but temporary; as the house is one of the strongest, as it is the oldest, on the street."

De Witt came in, and nodded a word to Mr. Livingstone, but the old man did not hear him; and Derwent turned over his newspaper to the account of the great fire. This he read with some interest. "There is a rumor that the fire was incendiary," it concluded; "the head watchman reports that he received a warning that some mischief was to be attempted; and shortly after midnight, getting word that a suspicious boat seemed to be attempting a landing at the river front, he left his post temporarily on a tour of observation; and it was during his absence that the fire broke out. Other than this there appears little ground for ascribing to the fire an incendiary origin; and no possible motive for such a crime can be suggested. The bulk of the property belongs to Mrs. T. Levison-Gower, well known as a leader of fashion in our most exclusive circles."

O sapient newspaper! Derwent turned to the first page, the bulk of which was filled by the great ball, where he read of the diamonds and the dresses, how Mrs. Wilton Hay wore a sleeveless satin and a rope of pearls; how Mrs. John Malgam had her corsage cut *en cœur*, and how well looked Mrs. Gower in a simple gown, cut *directoire*, and how well the footmen's calves in white silk stockings. But just then some young men entered from down town; and quite a group drew close about them.

"Is it all true about Townley?"

"Perfect smash, I hear——"

"No one knows where Tamms is——"

"Canada, they say——"

"Charlie Townley was there at the opening, but the fire finished him. A little Starbuck Oil was positively all they had." The last speaker was Arthur Holyoke.

"They say that even he left the State to-night. Poor Charlie, I'm sorry for him," said Killian Van Kull.

"There's a warrant out for Tamms already," said another. "Old Fechheimer got it."

"He pledged a lot of Fechheimer's bonds that he held in a syndicate, I was told," said Jack Malgam.

"Here are the evening papers," cried another, as a servant entered bearing a bundle of newspapers, which were quickly seized and devoured. For some minutes all was silence, save for an occasional ejaculation of surprise. Derwent continued to watch the club-room silently. Old Mr. Livingstone still sat in his chair, looking at the empty one over against him, which no one had taken.

"By Jove, it is worse than I thought," cried Malgam, with that certain pleasure bad news gives one when it is impressive and not personal. "Look here—the liabilities are said to amount to ten millions; the assets at present prices would not bring half that sum. The family of Mr. Phineas Tamms profess entire ignorance as to his whereabouts; but telegrams from reliable sources report his arrival at Montreal this morning."

"No other houses believed to be as yet involved in the failure." This latter news was read by De Witt with an air of some relief.

"I don't know about that," added another. "They held property for a great many people, to my certain knowledge."

"Tamms was to have been arrested to-night," Malgam read. "It is believed that a warrant has also been sworn out for Mr. Townley Junior.—I wonder where he is?"

It was noticeable that no one of them had yet mentioned old Mr. Townley's name. The company broke up into little groups, each discussing the great failure; which were added to from time to time as new men came in with their quota of news. Even the Duval ball had ceased to be talked about; so soon is one man's glory eclipsed by another man's disgrace. But Lionel Derwent marked that not one kindly word was said for Tamms.

There was a slight sensation at the door of the room, as young Beverly White entered; for White was Remington's partner, and had made much money in these last few days. Remington himself was not a member of the club; gossip had said that he could not get in, even though White had proposed him.

"Well, White, what news?" and the young men crowded round him.

"The news is that old Tamms has gone to smash, as I always said he would," said White; and he sank into an easy chair and called for some soda-water with an air of languid indifference.

"Pshaw! we knew that before——"

"Why did you ask me, then?" said White. "If people will speculate with other people's money——"

"Other people's money?"

"Yes—other people's money," drawled out the young man, sneeringly. "Old Townley got his boxes full, and then used it."

"Hush," said several, pointing to Mr. Livingstone in the window. "I guess it'll be some time before White gets his precious partner in here, after that remark," said another.

Mr. Livingstone, too, had taken a paper, and been

poring over it; but something in this last speech seemed to reach his ear, and he looked up.

"Let's ask the old boy," said Malgam, in an undertone. "He must know more than all of us."

"Have you heard this news, sir?" said Killian Van Kull. Mr. Livingstone nodded silently. "And is it as bad as they say?"

"Worse," said the old gentleman, his voice quavering.

"But you cannot suppose that Mr. Townley knew anything of it?"

"It makes little differenee whether he knew of it or not," answered the old man. There was a printed list of the club's members on the wall opposite him, and he was looking at it. Perhaps he was looking at the name of Charles Townley, whom he had played with as a boy.

"I knew that Tamms was a bad egg," said De Witt, "but that Mr. Townley——"

"Charles Townley, sir, is no better than a scoundrel," said Mr. Livingstone slowly. "He had all my wife's money, and nearly all of mine—but DAMME, sir, do you suppose I care for the money? If Charles Townley were sitting here with me again—I would give him— If Charlie Townley were sitting here, I—" The old man's voice grew weak, and he broke off in a sob.

The young men shifted about uneasily; and Derwent, in his corner, put up his newspaper before his face and tried to read.

Lucie Gower came in. He had just got home from

a shooting trip down South. "Is Mr. Townley here?" said he. "I stopped at Wall Street on my way up town; and they tell me that the officers have gone to arrest him."

"No," said someone. Then there was a long silence. Mr. Livingstone spoke again. "Charles Townley was the oldest member of this club. And I am the next; and was his oldest friend. And Charles Townley is a scoundrel." The old man rose; and the younger men thought he was going out, and made way for him at the door. But he walked over to the printed list of members that was opposite him upon the wall. "Charles Townley—1839," he muttered, as he found the place; and taking a pen that lay on the table beneath, he filled it with ink, and drew it, with a trembling hand, heavily across the name. Then he turned, and went to the door; while the younger men sat silent. There he stopped a moment. "We are gentlemen in this club. That is all." And they heard his uncertain step across the hall.

All the men sat and looked at one another; but no one cared to speak. After some minutes a group gathered around Gower, and conversed in undertones. "It was the only thing to do," said one. "He will never come here to see."

"We could not have expelled the poor old gentleman," said Van Kull.

"But is it really as bad as he says?"

"I have no doubt of it. Tamms has made a clean sweep. And the old gentleman must have given him access to his own trusts."

" Poor old fellow! But what will Charlie do?"

"Oh, Charlie will fall on his legs. Wasn't it plucky, the way he faced the market yesterday?"

"Damn Remington!"

"You forget he is my partner," said Beverly White.

"Then damn you, too," said Van Kull cavalierly. "But poor old Townley! I'm sorry——"

The speaker stopped, conscious of a sudden chill. For there was an opening in the crowd, and there stood Mr. Townley close behind him.

"Well, boys—bad times in the street, eh?" The old man's voice piped a shrill treble, and there was something almost childish in his laugh. "Ah, the house of Charles Townley & Son has seen worse times than this. I remember when my father—in thirty-nine——"

There was dead silence in the room. Gower went up and tried to lead the old man away from the group of strangers.

"Ah, Gower, glad to see you—— I've found a picture I think you'd like—you must come around to my house this evening—that is, if you've nothing else to do better than smoking with an old fellow like me. Eh! you young dogs! you young dogs! But why are you all so glum, my boys? Ah, you young fellows take things too earnest, nowadays."

"There's been a bad day in the stock-market," said Beverly White. "I hope, sir, the reports of Mr. Tamms's doings have been exaggerated?"

("Shut up, confound you," whispered Van Kull; but the other answered him with an ugly leer.)

"Mr. Tamms? ah, yes—clever fellow, Tamms. I like to help a young fellow along; he was in a tight place and I pulled him out. If you'd like a few hundred thousand I could let you have it—but they say Townley & Son have failed, you know. And Charlie told me something about my trusts—but that can't be, can it? I never lost a dollar on my trusts. All gone—everything gone! Where's Livingstone, my old friend Livingstone? His seat empty—why, he isn't ill? Tell me, my boy, where's Dick Livingstone?"

"He's gone, sir," said Gower.

"Gone? why gone? he always waits for me—there's nothing wrong with Livingstone, I hope? Why, he's a better man than I by most a year."

"He's lost much money, sir, they say—he said he couldn't wait."

"Lost? lost money? Oh, yes—all gone, gone—No, no—wait till my son Charlie gets down town—he's a bright boy; he'll carry on the old house, and show you boys a wrinkle, eh?"

No man there ventured to speak; for his son Charlie had died, some time back in the fifties.

Suddenly Mr. Townley began to laugh. "Aha, Dick Livingstone, we'll show the boys a turn or two—but where is he? Tamms—I know—my God—he's a rascal—it's gone, all gone."

The old man tottered toward his seat in the window. It was just before the list of members; and all were silent in suspense. Would he see his name, where Livingstone had crossed it off? But suddenly a firm hand was laid on the old man's elbow. "Come home with me, sir. I've got a carriage waiting." It was Lionel Derwent.

"Ah, Mr. Derwent—glad to see you." His wan face lighted up with pleasure; and he seemed to think he was talking again with Derwent in the office. "Yes, it's a good stock—always was a good stock since Townley & Son managed it. Come home, you say? Yes, I think—I'm not quite well. Good-by, my boys."

Derwent led his tottering steps to the door. He smiled vacantly, but leaned heavily on Derwent's arm. No longer prey for Tamms, nor fitting object for a sheriff's care, or other troubles of this world. They passed the silent group about the centre-table, which made way respectfully.

"Don't forget the picture, Gower," said he, as Derwent led him from the door.

## CHAPTER XXXVIII.

### THE END OF THE EPISODE.

HEN the train had fairly started, that morning, Flossie sank back into her seat with a certain sensation of relief. Almost immediately, they entered the long tunnel under the city; no conversation was possible, nor could she see Mr. Wemyss's face. She had the back seat herself; Justine sat with him, on the seat in front of her. As they came out of the tunnel and crossed the Harlem River, she looked at him. He met her eye nervously, and she could see that he was embarrassed by the presence of the maid.

"When do we sail?" said she. Flossie was quite indifferent to the maid. What cared she for the maid's opinion? And she ignored his glances beseeching that she might be told to go. But Justine herself asked Mrs. Gower demurely if she should not fetch a glass of water, and went of her own accord.

"The Parthia sails at six to-night," said Wemyss. "You will have ample time to rest in Boston, if you wish, dearest." The expression of affection sounded commonplace; and Wemyss felt that it did, self-consciously. "It is infinitely better we should go from

Boston," he went on; "the Parthia is slow, but that makes no difference; and there is certain to be no one in her we know, at this time of the year. I took the passage in fictitious names, of course."

"What did you do that for?"

"I thought you would prefer it," said he; and made bold to take her hand.

"It was very ridiculous and quite unnecessary," said Flossie, withdrawing it. "When I go to Europe, I am willing all the world should know."

Wemyss did not know just what to say; and fortunately the conductor made his first entry at that juncture. He attended to his business perfunctorily; and it struck Wemyss as curious that he did not note anything unusual about their trip. It seemed to him that all the world must see that he was going to England with her, and that she was not his wife.

The newspapers lay unread upon the seat. Mrs. Gower did not care to read them; and Wemyss gave his whole attention to her, as a matter of course. She was looking at the window, watching the familiar landscape fly by; and he began to think how they could pass through Boston with least certainty of being seen. He had had the passenger-list of the steamer telegraphed on the night before; and knew that no acquaintance would be on board; he felt it would be embarrassing to meet an acquaintance, until their position was regularized.

When the train had crossed the Harlem River, Wemyss felt as if the Rubicon were passed. But already the feeling of elation, the flattery to his *amour-propre*, began to pass away. There were certain difficulties, even in the Décadence; conventions yet remaining which annoyed him.

It had been tacitly agreed between them that when Gower got his divorce, Wemyss was to marry her. In the meantime, he was to escort her to England, where they both had many friends. And Wemyss reassured himself by thinking how these friends had treated similar cases; leniently, he was sure, with result of a not wholly unpleasant notoriety, and even, in the man's case, of a certain glamour. A little temporary retirement, of course, was fitting enough.

How long would that have to last? Six months? A year? They could go abroad—to the Mediterranean—up the Nile—that is, if he could persuade Mrs. Gower to do so. It would be terribly slow, being in England through the London season and not going out; for of course he could not honorably go out without her.—Not but that, of course, he would always be happy wherever he could be with her; as correcting himself, he hastened to think.—The train stopped at Bridgeport; and looking out, he saw a company of blue-coated, elderly men, rigged out with swords and divers sashes and parti-colored orders. It was some post of G. A. R. marching in procession, with a brass band; they did not march well, and yet seemed gravely impressed with the importance of the occasion. They took themselves seriously; and had not yet discovered the Décadence. Wemyss called Mrs. Gower's attention to them with some amusement; she looked at them listlessly, with her mind on other things. "Don't you want to go and smoke?" said she.

Mr. Wemyss had never felt so much need of a cigar in his life, but he felt bound to deny it. The train pulled out of the station; and he saw the bluecoats, now portly citizens, with weapons that seemed curiously out of place, marching cheerfully through the snow. Wemyss had not fought in the war. He wondered what he ought to do if Gower should challenge him. Wemyss was no physical coward, and he felt he ought to be true to the code of honor. But did not English ideas rather cast ridicule upon duels in such cases? And Wemyss dreaded ridicule more than anything else in the world; and was an Englishman above all things—particularly for the future. There was no question that the bourgeoisie of Boston would never condone his offence. Still, if Gower sent a challenge, he should certainly have to meet him.

"I wish you would go and smoke," said Flossie, impatiently. "I want to go to sleep."

"True—and forgive me, dear—I ought to have remembered you have been up all night, and your triumphs at the ball." He took her hand, and bent over it; and the trivial thought came into his head to wonder if Flossie had any doubts of her complexion; the thought annoyed him, coming at such a time; it was not like a Launcelot, hardly like Lauzun. But he walked away regretfully, and went to the smoking-room, where he did take the cigar he really needed; for he too had been up all night, and he, at least, was worn and weary. When he was gone, Flossie closed her eyes and went quietly to sleep.

There were two men in the smoking-room; but Wemyss looked in before he entered, and made up his mind that they were neither of them gentlemen. He sat down and lit his cigar without fear that they could recognize him. He looked at the two other occupants of the place, who were evidently on some business journey, and fancied to himself what they would say if they knew the object of his own. For all his indifference, Wemyss was more nervous after his *grand coup* than had been Jem Starbuck.

He reminded himself that he must think, like other heroes of great passion, of his lady fair. Last night, at the ball, he had really adored her; if, to-day, there was the faintest possible reaction, was it not natural after all? It takes a Dresden-china shepherd rather than a man of the world to be idyllic in a railroad car; he was sure that he admired her, that she fascinated him, that if he was not in love with her, he had never been in love. He had contemplated this step for years. He was ready to sacrifice his whole future for her.

Another man entered the car, a younger man; he looked at him almost inquisitively, and Wemyss felt sure that he had seen his face before. His cigar was nearly done; moreover his *savoir faire* reproached him with staying so long away from Flossie, and he left his place to the new-comer. But he found her still asleep; though she opened her eyes at his entrance. "Where are we?"

"New Haven." Flossie sighed.

"Don't let me disturb you," he added.

"Oh, I shall sleep no more." He sat down opposite, looking over at her tenderly; Justine sat up sphinx-like, and he was losing the constraint her presence at first had caused him. The fact that she took the situation so as of course even gave him a certain support. In this French maid's trained face he had much comfort. A new conductor came in to take their tickets; and they drew out again into the gray-white landscape of New England winter. Wemyss had made the journey many hundred times; and yet, as he sat there looking at Flossie, his one thought was a surprise that it did not seem more novel, even now. He tried, like Claude Melnotte, to think of Italy, and Como villas; but his imagination failed to go beyond their arrival in Boston and his arrangements for the voyage.

Meanwhile, Mrs. Gower's thoughts were larger and less troubled. She had no thought for the immediate future, at least. And as to the distant future—well, she, too, had made up her mind. They were both rich; and she had tried her woman's weapons on the world before. She by no means meant to give up her position in society; she purposed leading it with more celebrity than ever; and in Paris, London, not New York. They had no divorce in France; and no one she cared about would blame her for having exercised that envied American privilege. While in England—she could not go to court, of course; but what cared she for that? She had been presented once;

and the more fashionable London court, the circle to which all her social friends belonged, would not dream of caring what the status or position of an American had been. Her springs in Paris, her summers in London, her winters in Pau—ah, this last was the life she secretly looked forward to. She knew that she could be as full of conquests, brilliant, captivating, as any of her favorite Feuillet's heroines. She knew that she could still be there a *reine du monde.*

She smiled to herself as she thought how the news would fly around New York. She delighted to think that with Baby Malgam, her nearest friend and rival, a certain almost envious admiration would mingle with pretended triumph. Flossie had led them up to the very end; and then, when she was fairly bored with winning, she had dared the very steepest fence of all. But how the old madams would chuckle to themselves and the blue-blooded coterie she had laughed at so! She had driven a coach-and-four through all their stupid conventions, and led the fashion to its very end. And twenty years ago she had not been "in society."

She took up the newspaper, and read the long account of the ball. She had always liked to see her beauty and her dresses hymned in the daily prints; and two whole paragraphs were given to her to-day. "No one attracted so much admiration as Mrs. Levison-Gower"—Poor Lucie! She almost wished she had a different husband, though. Poor Lucie was likely to be simply sorry. She almost despised him again for this; if he had been a man like Kill Van Kull, for instance, it would have been an added excitement; and that faint reproach that came rather from her good nature than her conscience would have been gone entirely. She laid the paper down, and fell again into a reverie; not reading the news of that great fire which the ball had relegated to the second page. On such trivial chances do the actions of our lives depend.

She in turn looked over at Mr. Caryl Wemyss, sitting opposite; he met her eye with a glance of adoration that seemed affected to sharp-sighted Flossie. A well-bred polished person this; but hardly that Guy Livingstone of her youthful fancy. The journey was certainly tedious; they were not at Hartford yet, and she looked out the window and watched the rude fences of her native land fly by, in dwindling perspective. She half-divined his thoughts—he was still reflecting of de Musset and George Sand; of Byron and the Countess Guiccioli; or perhaps, more recently, of Lord Eskdale, his friend, and Mrs. White-Thompson. She, however, for long had had no romance in her composition; but only love of adventure, admiration, social primacy, for good or evil. She tried to banish her companion from her mind, and scheme of future triumphs. Yet she knew that his position was safer in the world than hers.

Already the gray day was growing dark; and the monotonous white wooden houses that they passed were beginning to be lit with evening lamps. The empty fields and wooded hills about them made her lonely; and she pictured to herself, with a shudder, their commonplace firesides. Heavens, how stupid a thing must life be to some! They passed an ugly manufacturing village with its dull, wide streets and garniture of unpainted wood; and her fancy seemed to paint to her all their obscurity of life, their ox-like submission, with really no more faith or virtue, as she thought, than she, only more hypocrisy and less courage. Yet she remembered just such a village, hereabout, in her awkward youth; and something of the view of life it taught came back to her, now; abandoned, as it had been, from her very girlhood.

So this was the climax, after all! And all her triumphs and all her cleverness had led to this? Some people would call it but a common elopement, and say that her position in respectable society was gone forever. She had not valued this, nor all these things, when she had got them; not even perhaps as any Jenny Starbuck valued her diamond ring; would she care for them more, now she had lost them? She fancied not. And she looked over the unpicturesque New-England landscape and pretended that she was a French duchess, travelling in some barbaric province. And then she looked at Mr. Wemyss once more, and again half wished that it had been Van Kull. She knew very well that there was no *grande passion* in her case.

When they got to Springfield, Wemyss got out; and came back in some trepidation. "I have seen Charlie Clarendon," said he; "but I don't think that he noticed me."

"And what does it matter whether he noticed you or not?" said Flossie, opening her eyes.

"Why, I thought—that you—that is, I wanted ——" He broke off in some confusion at Flossie's laugh; and nothing more was said between them, all his well-worded compliments meeting no response. "She snubs me as if I were her husband," thought he; and he wished the awkward journey well over, and they were safely on the steamer.

There was something pitilessly practical in the dull light of the winter afternoon; commonplace, dispiriting, and the twilight hour least suited of the twenty-four for daring deeds. The very way the newsboys cried the evening papers jarred on Wemyss's mood. Mrs. Gower had insisted on opening the door of their compartment, for air; and he could see his fellow-travellers. As Wemyss sat studying them, they seemed types too simple even to weave imaginations about; their natures could better be taken apart, like a piston from its rod, than painted, like a flower. He felt that his orbit transcended their imagination. Opposite him was a girl of twenty or more, but going back to school; attendant on her was a boy of nearer thirty, most obviously wishing to be contracted to her for matrimony, and most probably about to be. When his eyes returned from this roving they met Flossie's; hers were fixed on him, and remained so, though she did not speak, all the way to Worcester.

There she alighted for a little walk; and so they passed Charlie Clarendon, who recognized them and bowed. "Pray heaven he does not fasten to us in the train," thought Wemyss, devoutly. The young girl of twenty had also got out, and passed them, walking with her adorer, to whose arm she naïvely clung. When they got back to the car, Wemyss drew the sliding-door before their compartment, but Mrs. Gower again objected; and, as he feared, Clarendon was not the man to lose the chance of recommending himself to such a social shrine as Flossie Gower's. As the train drew out of the station, he stood before their door, smirking with delight and pulling his travelling cap like Hodge his forelock. But Wemyss had to curse him inaudibly; for Flossie looked up with a brighter glance than she had worn that day, and a certain gleam of her old audacity in her famous eyes.

"So glad to see you honoring Boston in the middle of the season," said Clarendon. "Ah—Mr. Gower with you?"

"No," said Flossie, "Mr. Wemyss is with me. Do you not know each other? Mr. Clarendon, Mr. ——"

"I have the *pleasure* of Mr. Clarendon's acquaintance," broke in Mr. Wemyss, dryly.

"Er— Gower too busy to get away, I suppose?"

"Not at all," said Flossie. "He did not know I was coming."

"Ah—quite so," said Clarendon. "I hope you mean to stop some time with us?"

"No," said Flossie. "I leave Boston to-morrow for——"

But here Wemyss took the word from her. "Mrs. Gower has only come on for the bachelors' ball, to-morrow night," said he. As he spoke, Flossie looked at him, amazed, as if about to speak; then pressed her lips together scornfully. Clarendon had been congratulating himself on his success so far; but now he seemed to meet with difficulties. For Mrs. Gower became obstinately silent; she turned her face to the window, though it was little better than a slaty square, and looked obstinately out of it. Wemyss made no offer to give up his seat, and answered mostly by unflattering interjections.

When Clarendon had gone, Mrs. Gower continued silent. He watched her for some minutes; then he ventured a remark. "That little Clarendon is the greatest gossip in Boston."

Flossie made no reply; and there was silence between them until the train reached Boston. Justine made a motion to go, as if to prepare herself for the arrival; but Mrs. Gower bade her stay. "We are here, dearest, at last," said Wemyss, taking her hand; but Mrs. Gower withdrew it without a word.

They alighted, and Wemyss looked about him; the electric light made the faces of a welcoming crowd terribly distinct; but he was inexpressibly relieved to find no familiar face among them.

He engaged the first carriage that he found, and put Flossie into it with the maid; and then went in search of her travelling trunks. The coachman put them on; and Wemyss began to tell him the hotel.

"I have already told him where to go," said Flossie. "I have decided to stay for the bachelors' ball." She shut the door; and before Wemyss could find his speech, the carriage had driven rapidly off and left him standing there, alone, in the Boston railway station.

# CHAPTER XXXIX.

## FLOSSIE DECLINES.

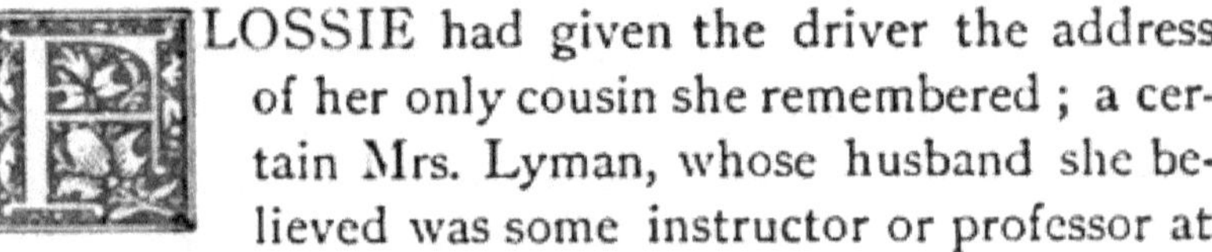

FLOSSIE had given the driver the address of her only cousin she remembered ; a certain Mrs. Lyman, whose husband she believed was some instructor or professor at some college, she could not remember where. They had sent her cards upon their wedding ; but Flossie had never been near them in her previous trips to Boston. She had an idea they might be poor ; and did not wish to trouble them ; and after all, what could there be between her life and theirs ?

So she had some qualms of social conscience when the carriage stopped at the little brick house ; the first time, perhaps, in twenty years, that she felt the slightest doubt as to her reception. But she was determined that she would go to no hotel, where Wemyss might find her.

But they proved hospitable people, and really glad to see her, if just the least bit surprised. Evidently they were much afraid of her, and still more of her maid ; but a room was found for Justine too ; and in the morning Mrs. Gower dismissed her, with her wages paid some time ahead. And gradually Flossie found that they doubted not so much their breeding as her own; they were by no means ashamed of the little house and its two maid-servants, but feared that Flossie might be. And they knew people high-placed enough in the world to be known, by name, even to her. "How different from New York!" she said to herself; perhaps she should have said, how different from that New York that she had made. They had several children, who all came to the breakfast-table; and Flossie noted, with much compassion, that Mrs. Lyman was her own nurse. She was persuaded to stay with them over the next day; their mode of life was a curious study to her. She did not envy it; possibly she even looked at it with horror, for she never lost her essential love for wealth; but she was quite clever enough to have for it a certain respect. Her favorite classifications seemed to fail; they were not "bourgeois," but even gentlefolk, such as she had read poor rectors' families were in England. And such as there are many in America, though she did not know it. Flossie went back to New York on the morning train the next day, the same way she had come. She read in the paper that Mr. Caryl Wemyss was a passenger in the Parthia for Europe. It was the best thing he could do.

She had given much thought to her coming meeting with her husband. Would he suspect anything, she wondered? She hoped not; and she turned about the paper to see what happened in New York. She had not read a newspaper for several days; her own news she had made, and she cared for no other.

A black headline caught her eye: *Failure of the Starbuck Oil Company.* Great heavens!

All her fortune was still in that; save only the house upon Fifth Avenue. She read it with avidity. The failure appeared to be complete; and from the account she gathered also the facts of the great fire. It was believed to be incendiary the paper said. How terrible that people could commit such crimes; what were the laws for, and the decalogue? The house of Townley & Tamms had also failed; it was believed the assets would not realize ten per cent. As most of the loss fell upon trusts held for rich private individuals, it was thought the failure would have no further disastrous consequences upon the street, the paper added grimly. Mr. Phineas Tamms was known to be in Montreal; young Mr. Townley was also a fugitive. The Allegheny Central was also heavily involved, but it was believed this property might recover. Warrants were out for the arrest of Mr. Townley, Senior.

Flossie put the paper down with horror. She found it impossible to believe that she was ruined; that she could really ever be poor.

And then the thought came to her, what a fortunate escape; Lucie still had money; but what would she have been, as his wife, undivorced perhaps, who had fled from him with Caryl Wemyss? She shuddered at the idea; well she knew how her world would have regarded her, poor, no longer able to dazzle her careless court into complaisance, no longer materially able to set the fashion she could lead so well. I cannot say she felt any remorse; women like Flossie Gower do not feel remorse; but she was at least devoutly thankful she had not made a worldly blunder.

How would Lucie take it? This was her one thought, now. He had been absent on his sporting trip; but was certain to be back the very day she left. How fortunate, after all, had been poor Wemyss's cowardice! She had all a woman's ignorance of business; and she felt, for the first time in her life, a need of leaning on her husband. Poverty was the one thing she dreaded, more than death, more even than old age; in dishonor she did not much believe. But she had never been frightened in her life before.

The journey passed much more quickly than her journey on; and arriving back at the great terminus, she had never thought to see again, she got nimbly into a carriage and drove quickly to her house. It was Lucie himself who met her at the door.

"I am so glad to see you again, Flo," said he; and she let him kiss her twice. "I have been so terribly anxious!"

"Tell me, Lucie—is it all gone?"

"All what gone?" said he; and he took her in his arms again. "You left no word where you had gone; and I have been almost crying!" And the honest fellow did let drop two big salt tears upon her little hand.

"I have been to Boston—staying with my cousin

—for a little rest. But do tell me—have we lost everything?"

"Lost? Oh, yes, I believe the Starbuck Oil has pretty well gone up," said he. "But what does it matter? I've got enough for two, you know. My dear, I haven't told you, but I've made some money lately! Isn't it a joke that I should make money? And I can't tell you how glad I am that I can give you something at last! Your income shall be just what it always was—I'll take care of that." Flossie gave a sigh of relief; and actually kissed him, all herself.

Poor Lucie! He had never been so happy in his life. Not even when they had first been married; for though he was a simple gentleman, his heart had grown, since then; and hearts do more of God's work than intellects, even now in the world. And that very day he went down and bought her diamonds, even finer than those he had given her upon their wedding-day.

Did Flossie change? I think not. It is only in novels that such natures change at nearly forty; it is only in novels, too, that the unrepentant are brought up with a round turn, and a moral pointed, in a flare of transformation-scene blue lights. But Flossie is still rich, and still she leads her set; she is still successful, and will doubtless be so to the very end. It is true some people say she is in her decadence. She seems to have resigned herself to her final place in life; and other younger members of her set, Baby Malgam, perhaps, or Mrs. Jimmy De Witt, are passing her. She will have no catastrophe; and though (perhaps) against all morals of romance, it must be said that she is making simple Lucie happier than he has ever been before.

She still had one great scare, however. It was some weeks or months after this, that the servant brought Lucie word a lady wished to see him. It was in the early afternoon; and he said that it must be for Mrs. Gower; but no, she insisted, the man told him, that it was for him. She was a veiled lady, the servant said, and he ran to his dressing-room and gave orders for her to be ushered to the parlor.

Going down, to his astonishment, he met Justine. He commonly took little note of his wife's maids; but this one he remembered because she had been with them so long. "You must wish to see Mrs. Gower," he said. "I'll go and find her."

But no, simpered the Frenchwoman, her business was with him.

"Has she not paid you your wages? she told me she had dismissed you—and for cause."

A black scowl disfigured the handsome face. "Madame has turned me out—like a dog. And I have had no time to get even the dresses that I left. And—" the maid looked at him curiously. "I do know somesings about Madame Monsieur would like to know—and Madame, she would give almost her beaux yeux not to have me tell."

Lucie's eyes opened wide; but in a moment their honest wonderment was changed to a look that Justine misinterpreted. "If Monsieur will make it worth my while—*je connais la générosité de Monsieur*—I can tell of Madame's voyage to Boston—sings zat he would like to know!"

She stopped; for Mr. Gower was struggling with many words. The soubrette looked cunningly at the gentleman; and he began with an indignant burst; but then he mastered himself. He took her by the wrist, and led her forcibly to Mrs. Gower's room. It must be confessed that Flossie's color changed when she saw the strange pair enter.

"Has this woman been fully paid?" said he to his wife.

"Of course," said Flossie. "I had to discharge her for insolence to me, and she went away vowing revenge."

"I thought so," said Lucie. "James, show this woman the door; and hark ye, Pauline, Fifine, whatever your name is, if you even ring this door-bell again, I'll have you arrested."

Ah, Miss Flossie, there are some advantages you had not understood, in marrying a gentleman, though not a clever one—are there not?

And this scene ended Flossie Gower's episode. She lived on, and still went to balls, and gave her dinners; some people even say that she fell in love with her husband. But this the author, at least, takes liberty to doubt; she liked him, in a way, for he made her own way his so good-naturedly. I do not even know if she be contented; but she certainly has more than her deserts. Perhaps she still hears, with half a sigh, of Kitty Farnum's—the Countess of Birmingham's—success in England; and casts a glance of envy at that lady's varied photographs in the shop windows, if she ever walks down Broadway. But then her whilom protégée had married a peer of the realm; and I am sure that she is glad she has not married Caryl Wemyss.

But Mrs. Gower leads no longer. She even has little influence for ill; or if she has, she does not choose to exert it. She is a model no longer; the débutantes have taken other patterns. I am not sure that Mrs. Haviland even has not greater influence—but this is anticipating. The young men no longer cluster round her carriage at the races; poor Arthur's was perhaps the last of all the lives she injured.

Let us turn to others, in whom, as may be hoped, the reader takes more interest. But first, we turn one glance at Mr. Wemyss. One glance will be enough. No one, of course, ever knew of his great adventure; he has sometimes wished to tell it, but never wholly dared. Moreover, his honor as a gentleman forbids. Clarendon has sometimes spoken of his queer meeting with him and Flossie Gower; people wonder idly, when they grow scandalous, what has been between them; but no one really cares. Mr. Wemyss himself, as Flossie thought, did the best thing possible under the circumstances; he went to Europe on the Parthia, and has stayed there ever since. Let us dismiss him from our thoughts; he is surely not a hero of romance, nor yet even a man in a French play, as he fondly fancied; nor yet even a real man at all. Perhaps there will even be no Décadence.

Of his life he made a poor play; yet could not even play it to the end.

# CHAPTER XL.

## THE FLOWERS IN THE HARVEST.

O sheriff's warrant was ever served on Mr. Townley. Lionel Derwent took care of that, and stayed with him (for he was childless) for some few weeks, until the old man died, of softening of the brain. Then Derwent went away again; to Asia, I believe, or to Africa, or Australia. Before he left, Gracie had a very curious call from him. He said a word or two to her of Mamie, and then a word or two of Arthur, and then a word or two of John Haviland; and then he took his leave, shaking hands with her in his awkward English way, and she never saw him more. For he never met another woman whom he loved.

He did not ask to take farewell of Mamie, and she was very glad when she heard that he was gone. She had no love for him; and she had had none even for Charlie Townley. But for this young man she did now feel a vast pity; he was a fugitive from justice, and yet all the world admitted he had been innocent of purposed wrong. Mamie herself could, perhaps, have brought the heaviest indictment against him; but it had never occurred to her that so great a personage as he could have sought her out for any worldly reasons. Now, perhaps, she measures excellence with different eyes; but she was very sorry for him, and I know not what might have happened had Charlie, in his poorest days, asked her to be his wife. But he never did, and the suits against him were soon withdrawn, and now he is again in business in a small way.

And soon the glass roof, and the tempered light, and the parent trees about which Mamie's pretty flower had thrived so pleasantly, were gone, and her poor vanities were rudely stripped away; for Mr. Livingstone did not survive his loss of fortune and his oldest friend's disgrace, and his wife soon followed him; and Mamie was left—no, not alone; with Gracie. It is only Gracie who was lonely then. Gracie had little money, and Mamie was left almost poor; but she grew up to be a very lovely woman, and I know two or three good fellows who are now in love with her.

And Arthur, our hero—did I say he was our hero? All the world will still tell you, Arthur Holyoke is a successful young man. His practicable ambitions have all been realized. And, after all, which one of us has realized our youthful dreams? Arthur has written no poem, to be sure, but he is making money; enough to pay all his club bills, and his salmon fishing, and his trip to Europe once a year. And nobody blames him for not having written any poem; on the contrary, they praise him for his clever head, and his handsome face, young looking for his age, and admire his faultless style. He is a butterfly, but a butterfly with a bee's brains; he has a head for business; of such is the republic of America, not of wan, unpractical poets. Will he ever marry? Oh, yes, perhaps he will, at forty; perhaps he will not. But what does it matter to the reader?

On that snowless winter's day, Gracie, sitting alone in her one own room, had bidden him in her heart farewell. She was glad to hear that he was doing well, and she will be the kinder to his sons and daughters, when he has them; they will not know why, but they will be fond of her. His friendship with Mrs. Gower continued; but he saw Gracie less and less.

When the old people died, Gracie and Mamie lived together, as I have said; and I wish that I could tell how our friend Haviland went on, and worked, and watched for her, and dreamed of her, and won her at the last. But that would be writing another novel, would it not?

It is now three years since the great fire. James Starbuck has not been heard of since; not yet, at least. John Haviland and Gracie have been married, and Mamie still lives with them. They live in a smaller house than Mrs. Gower's, to be sure, but they manage to be happy; and their sons will be strong-souled, large-hearted, to meet the Jem Starbucks that are to come; and Gracie's daughters will be like to her, and bear from her the vestal fire, each one to her own household; not advertised, perhaps, to thousands, but yet a kindly warmth to the few that stand within its circle of light.

For on gentle people such as these shall the future of our land depend.

www.ingramcontent.com/pod-product-compliance
Lightning Source LLC
Chambersburg PA
CBHW031814270326
41932CB00008B/422
* 9 7 8 3 7 4 4 6 7 5 6 9 7 *